POLITICALLY,

FASHIONABLY, AND

AERODYNAMICALLY

INCORRECT

BOOKS BY BERKELEY BREATHED

Loose Tails

'Toons for Our Times

Penguin Dreams and Stranger Things

Bloom County Babylon: Five Years of Basic Naughtiness

Billy and the Boingers Bootleg

Tales Too Ticklish to Tell

The Night of the Mary Kay Commandos

Happy Trails

Classics of Western Literature: *Bloom County* 1986–1989

A Wish for Wings That Work

The Last Basselope

Politically, Fashionably, and Aerodynamically Incorrect: The First *Outland* Collection

# POLITICALLY, FASHIONABLY, and AERODYNAMICALLY INCORRECT

THE FIRST *OUTLAND* COLLECTION

Berkeley Breathed

LITTLE, BROWN AND COMPANY  Boston Toronto London

FIRST EDITION

*Outland* is syndicated by the Washington Post Writers Group.

LIBRARY OF CONGRESS CATALOGING-IN-PUBLICATION DATA
Breathed, Berke.
    (Outland. Selections)
    Politically, fashionably, and aerodynamically incorrect: the first
Outland collection / Berkeley Breathed. — 1st ed.
        p.    cm.
    "An Outland book."

    1. Comic books, strips, etc. — United States. I. Title
II. Title: Outland.
PN6728.B57094   1992
741.5'973 — dc20                                      92-12632

10  9  8  7  6  5  4  3  2  1

RRD-OH

Designed by Barbara Werden

Published simultaneously in Canada by Little, Brown & Company (Canada) Limited

Printed in the United States of America

I'm proud of the 'toons in this book. I had more fun drawing many of these than usual. As in *Bloom County* usual. Look at the earlier *Outlands* reproduced here. You can see me playing, experimenting, even doodling, looking for unexplored nooks and creative crannies. But when I look at these myself, I smile because I know that like the wild caribou, I was doomed to return to familiar territory. *Outland* is, of course, *Bloom County* without the continuing narrative that a daily appearance allows. But *Bloom County* was never about children or cats or penguins. It was about a loopy perspective — my dubious legacy to this world, and in plentiful evidence within this volume.

Enjoy. I have.

But no more than finally getting to compare myself to a wild caribou.

Berkeley Breathed
*March 1992*

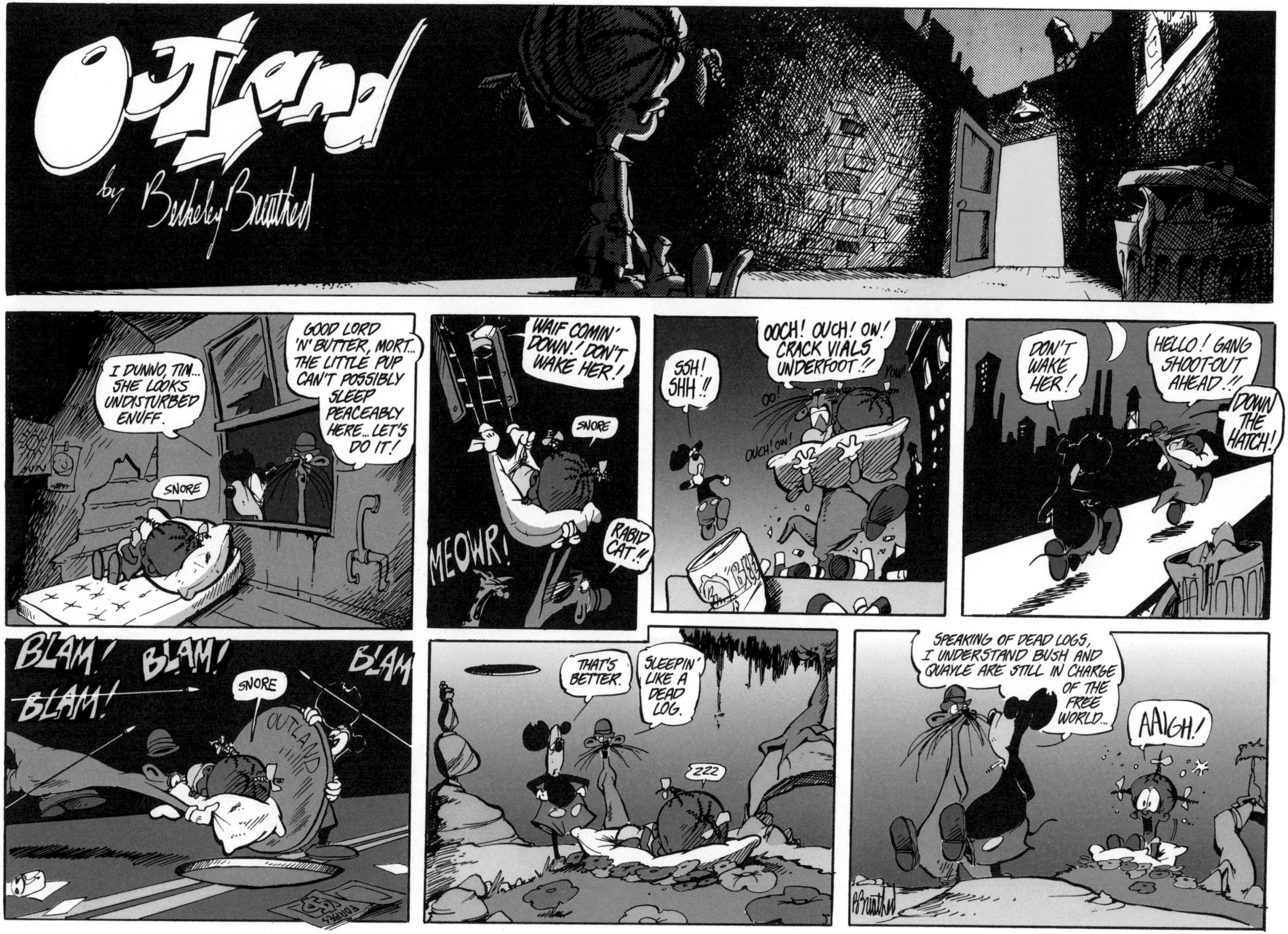
OUTLAND
by Berkeley Breathed
I DUNNO, TIM... SHE LOOKS UNDISTURBED ENUFF.
GOOD LORD 'N' BUTTER, MORT... THE LITTLE PUP CAN'T POSSIBLY SLEEP PEACEABLY HERE... LET'S DO IT!
SNORE
WAIF COMIN' DOWN! DON'T WAKE HER!
SNORE
MEOWR!
RABID CAT!!
SSH! SHH!!
OOCH! OUCH! OW! CRACK VIALS UNDERFOOT!!
YOW!
OUCH! OW!
DON'T WAKE HER!
HELLO! GANG SHOOT-OUT AHEAD!!
DOWN THE HATCH!
BLAM! BLAM! BLAM BLAM!
SNORE
OUTLAND
THAT'S BETTER.
SLEEPIN' LIKE A DEAD LOG.
ZZZ
SPEAKING OF DEAD LOGS, I UNDERSTAND BUSH AND QUAYLE ARE STILL IN CHARGE OF THE FREE WORLD...
AAIGH!
B Breathed

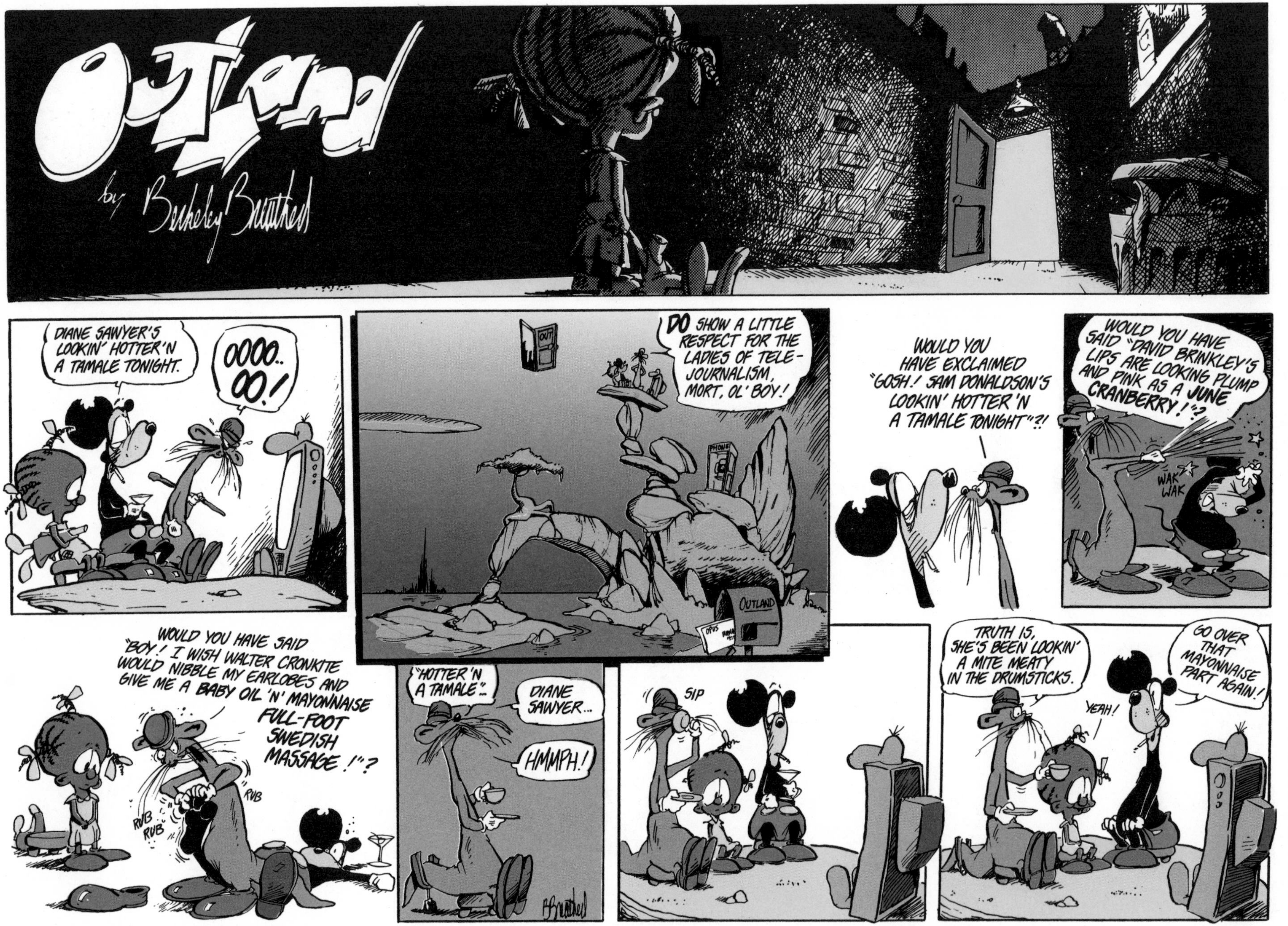
Outland
by Berkeley Breathed
DIANE SAWYER'S LOOKIN' HOTTER 'N A TAMALE TONIGHT.
OOOO.. OO.!
OUT
DO SHOW A LITTLE RESPECT FOR THE LADIES OF TELE-JOURNALISM, MORT, OL' BOY!
PHONE
OUTLAND
OPUS
WOULD YOU HAVE EXCLAIMED "GOSH! SAM DONALDSON'S LOOKIN' HOTTER 'N A TAMALE TONIGHT"?!
WOULD YOU HAVE SAID "DAVID BRINKLEY'S LIPS ARE LOOKING PLUMP AND PINK AS A JUNE CRANBERRY!"?
WAK WAK
WOULD YOU HAVE SAID "BOY! I WISH WALTER CRONKITE WOULD NIBBLE MY EARLOBES AND GIVE ME A BABY OIL 'N' MAYONNAISE FULL-FOOT SWEDISH MASSAGE!"?
RUB RUB RUB
"HOTTER 'N A TAMALE"...
DIANE SAWYER...
HMMPH!
SIP
TRUTH IS, SHE'S BEEN LOOKIN' A MITE MEATY IN THE DRUMSTICKS.
YEAH!
GO OVER THAT MAYONNAISE PART AGAIN!

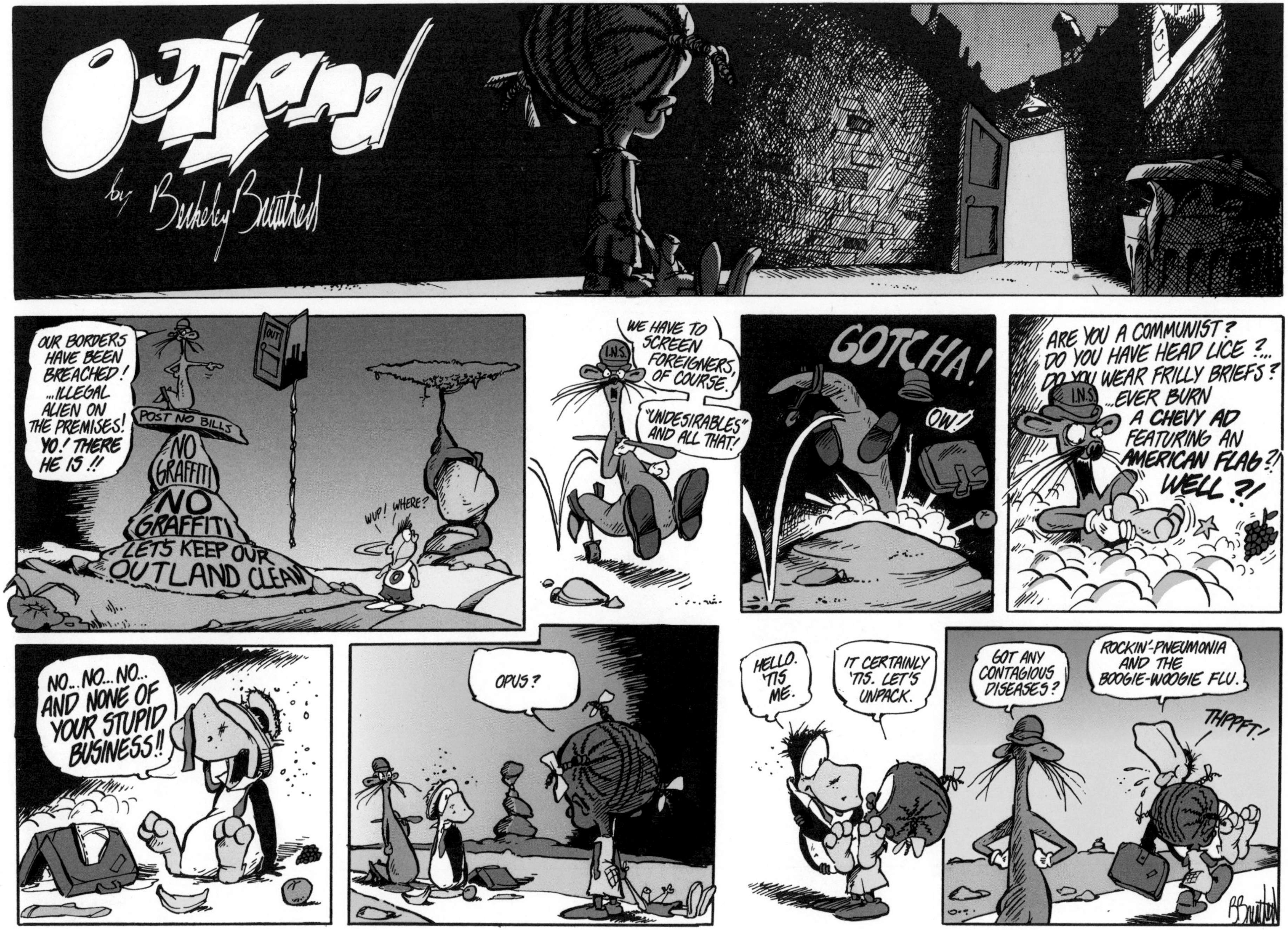

OUTLAND
by Berkeley Breathed
OUR BORDERS HAVE BEEN BREACHED! ...ILLEGAL ALIEN ON THE PREMISES! YO! THERE HE IS!!
OUT
POST NO BILLS
NO GRAFFITI
NO GRAFFITI
LET'S KEEP OUR OUTLAND CLEAN
WUP! WHERE?
WE HAVE TO SCREEN FOREIGNERS, OF COURSE.
I.N.S.
"UNDESIRABLES" AND ALL THAT!
GOTCHA!
OW!
ARE YOU A COMMUNIST? DO YOU HAVE HEAD LICE?... DO YOU WEAR FRILLY BRIEFS? ...EVER BURN A CHEVY AD FEATURING AN AMERICAN FLAG?!
I.N.S.
WELL?!
NO...NO...NO... AND NONE OF YOUR STUPID BUSINESS!!
OPUS?
HELLO. 'TIS ME.
IT CERTAINLY 'TIS. LET'S UNPACK.
GOT ANY CONTAGIOUS DISEASES?
ROCKIN'-PNEUMONIA AND THE BOOGIE-WOOGIE FLU.
THPPFT!
B Breathed

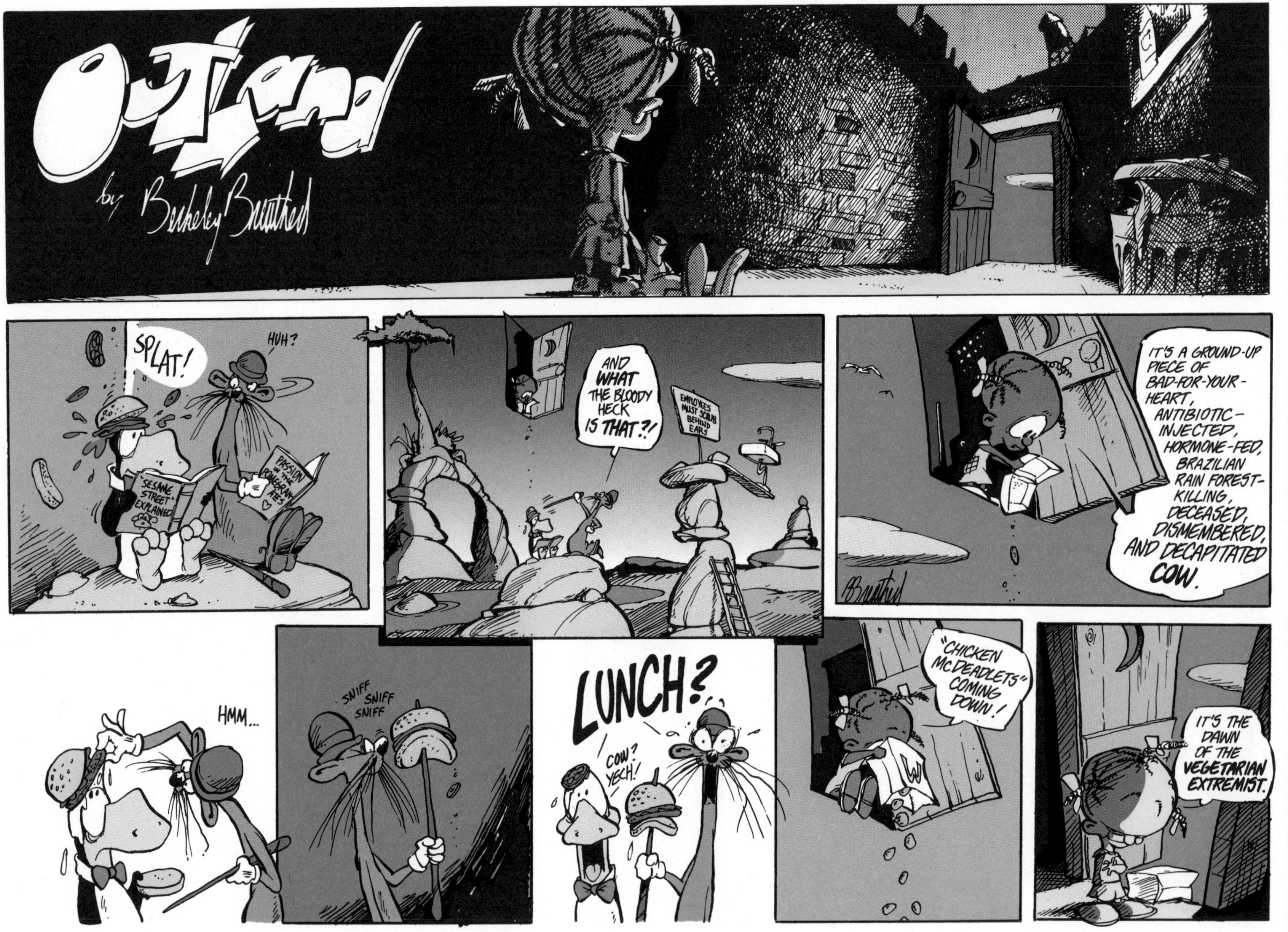

Outland
by Berkeley Breathed
SPLAT!
HUH?
SESAME STREET EXPLAINED
PASSION IN THE POMEGRANATES
AND WHAT THE BLOODY HECK IS THAT?!
EMPLOYEES MUST SCRUB BEHIND EARS
IT'S A GROUND-UP PIECE OF BAD-FOR-YOUR-HEART, ANTIBIOTIC-INJECTED, HORMONE-FED, BRAZILIAN RAIN FOREST-KILLING, DECEASED, DISMEMBERED, AND DECAPITATED COW.
HMM...
SNIFF SNIFF SNIFF
LUNCH?
COW? YECH!
"CHICKEN McDEADLETS" COMING DOWN!
IT'S THE DAWN OF THE VEGETARIAN EXTREMIST.

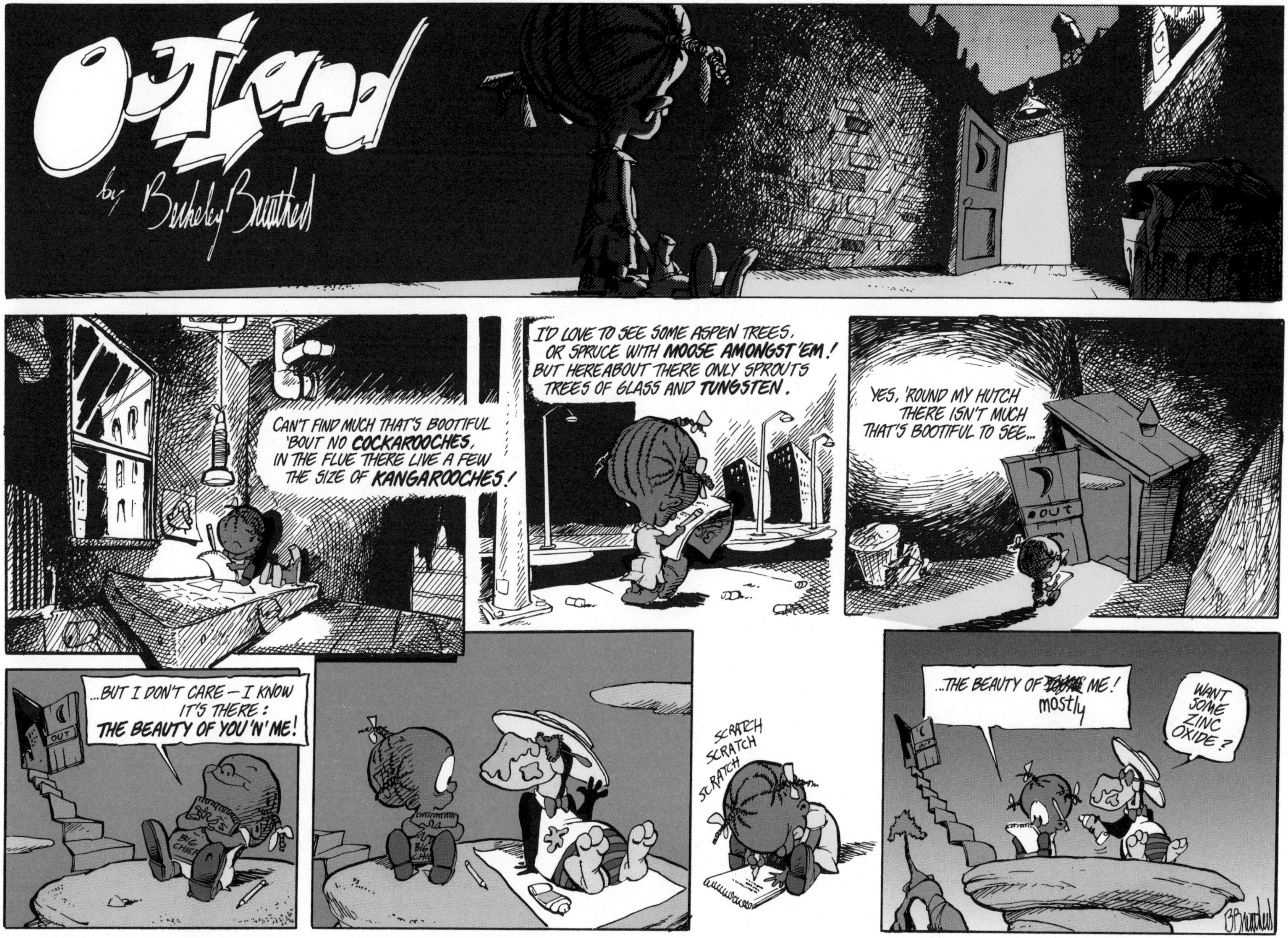
Outland
by Berkeley Breathed
CAN'T FIND MUCH THAT'S BOOTIFUL 'BOUT NO COCKAROOCHES, IN THE FLUE THERE LIVE A FEW THE SIZE OF KANGAROOCHES!
I'D LOVE TO SEE SOME ASPEN TREES, OR SPRUCE WITH MOOSE AMONGST 'EM! BUT HEREABOUT THERE ONLY SPROUTS TREES OF GLASS AND TUNGSTEN.
YES, 'ROUND MY HUTCH THERE ISN'T MUCH THAT'S BOOTIFUL TO SEE...
OUT
...BUT I DON'T CARE — I KNOW IT'S THERE: THE BEAUTY OF YOU'N'ME!
OUT
BIG CHIEF
SCRATCH
SCRATCH
SCRATCH
...THE BEAUTY OF mostly ME!
WANT SOME ZINC OXIDE?
B Breathed

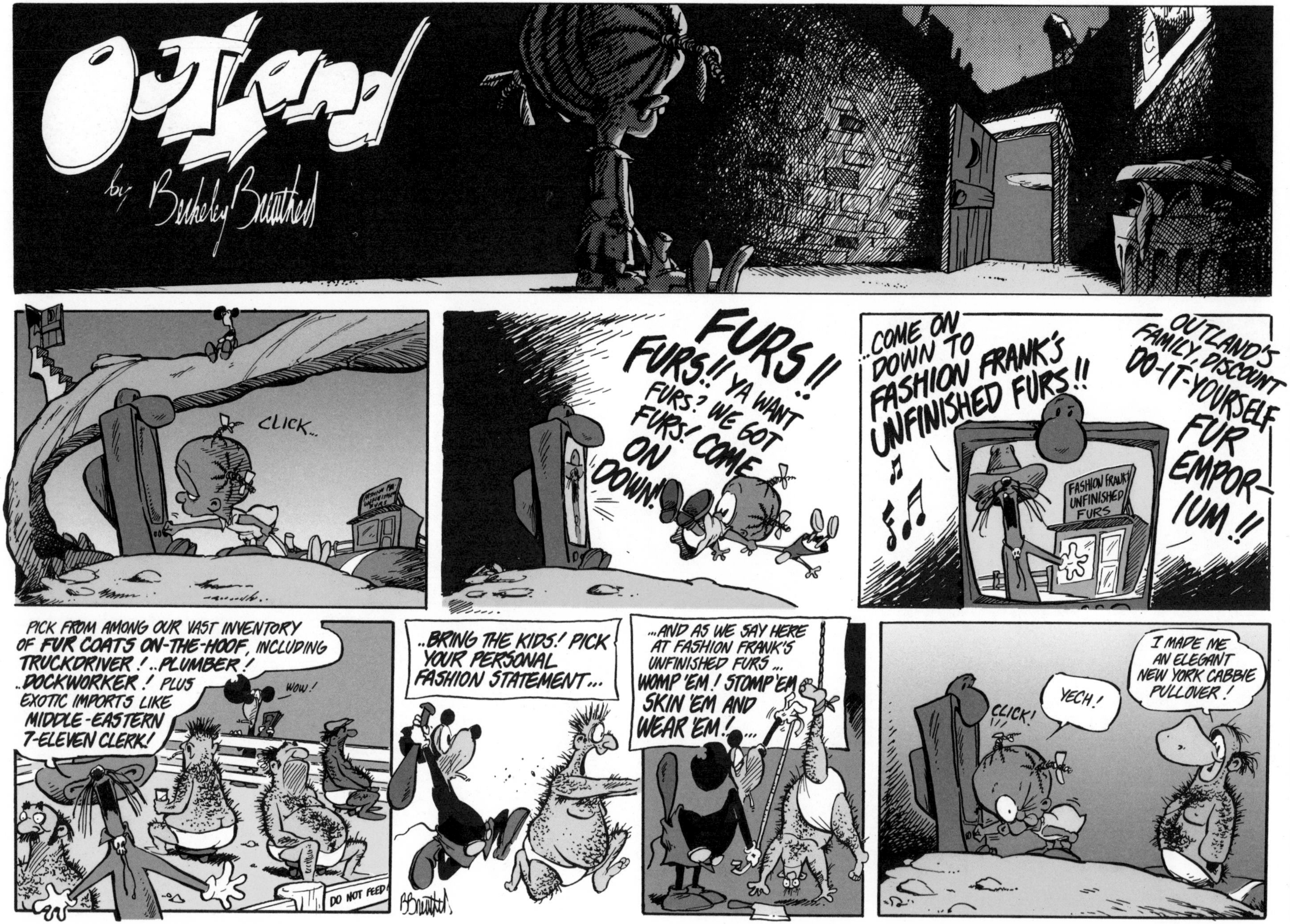
Outland
by Berkeley Breathed
CLICK...
FURS!!
FURS!! YA WANT FURS? WE GOT FURS! COME ON DOWN!
...COME ON DOWN TO FASHION FRANK'S UNFINISHED FURS!!
OUTLAND'S FAMILY, DISCOUNT DO-IT-YOURSELF FUR EMPORIUM!!
FASHION FRANK'S UNFINISHED FURS
PICK FROM AMONG OUR VAST INVENTORY OF FUR COATS ON-THE-HOOF, INCLUDING TRUCKDRIVER! ..PLUMBER! ..DOCKWORKER! PLUS EXOTIC IMPORTS LIKE MIDDLE-EASTERN 7-ELEVEN CLERK!
WOW!
DO NOT FEED
..BRING THE KIDS! PICK YOUR PERSONAL FASHION STATEMENT...
B.Breathed
...AND AS WE SAY HERE AT FASHION FRANK'S UNFINISHED FURS... WOMP 'EM! STOMP 'EM SKIN 'EM AND WEAR 'EM!...
CLICK!
YECH!
I MADE ME AN ELEGANT NEW YORK CABBIE PULLOVER!

OUTLAND
by Berkeley Breathed
OUT
MORTIMER, I HAVEN'T THE FOGGIEST IDEA WHERE WE ARE.
AWW, PIGEON POOP. MUST'VE VEERED WHEN I SHOULDA VAMOOSED.
THERE'S SOMEONE. ASK HER.
LEAVE BEFORE IT'S TOO LATE
GOOD DAY, MADAM! I...ER...
UH-OH.
GOD LOVES YOU! AND SO DO JIM AND I! ..JIM WOULD BE HERE TODAY, BUT HE'S UNDER A CHAIR GURGLING IN A FETAL POSITION! I THINK I'LL SING!
OOOH, I'VE WALKED WITH THE LAMBS...BUT I'VE BEEN GOOSED BY THE DEVIL!!
LOVELY! EXCUSE ME, TAMMY!
YIKES! ZSA ZSA!!
I VON'T GO TO JAIL VITH LESBIANS, YOU TERRIBLE, AWFUL MAN!...
I VON'T!...I VON'T! I VON'T!
OW! OW! OW!
OPUS! GET IN THE CAR!
GO! GO! GO!
LEONA HELMSLEY'S BLOCKING THE ROAD!
SCREECH!
GOOD LORD 'N' BUTTER! WHERE WERE WE?
Valley of The Dames You Wouldn't Want to Lock Dental Braces With
NEXT LEFT

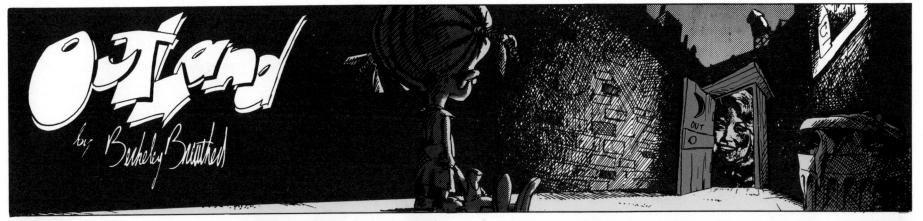

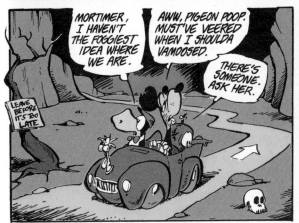

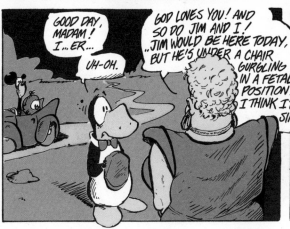

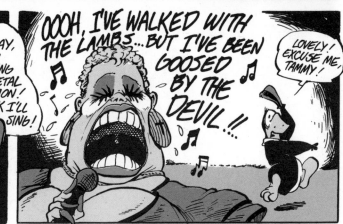

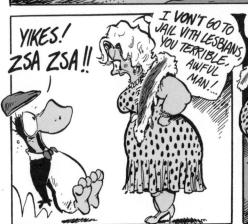

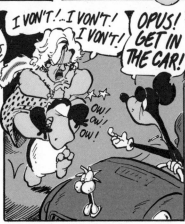

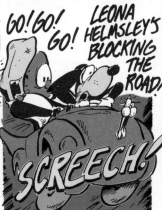

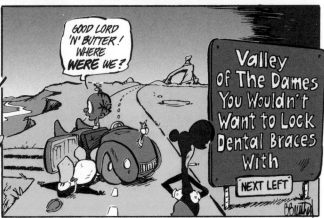

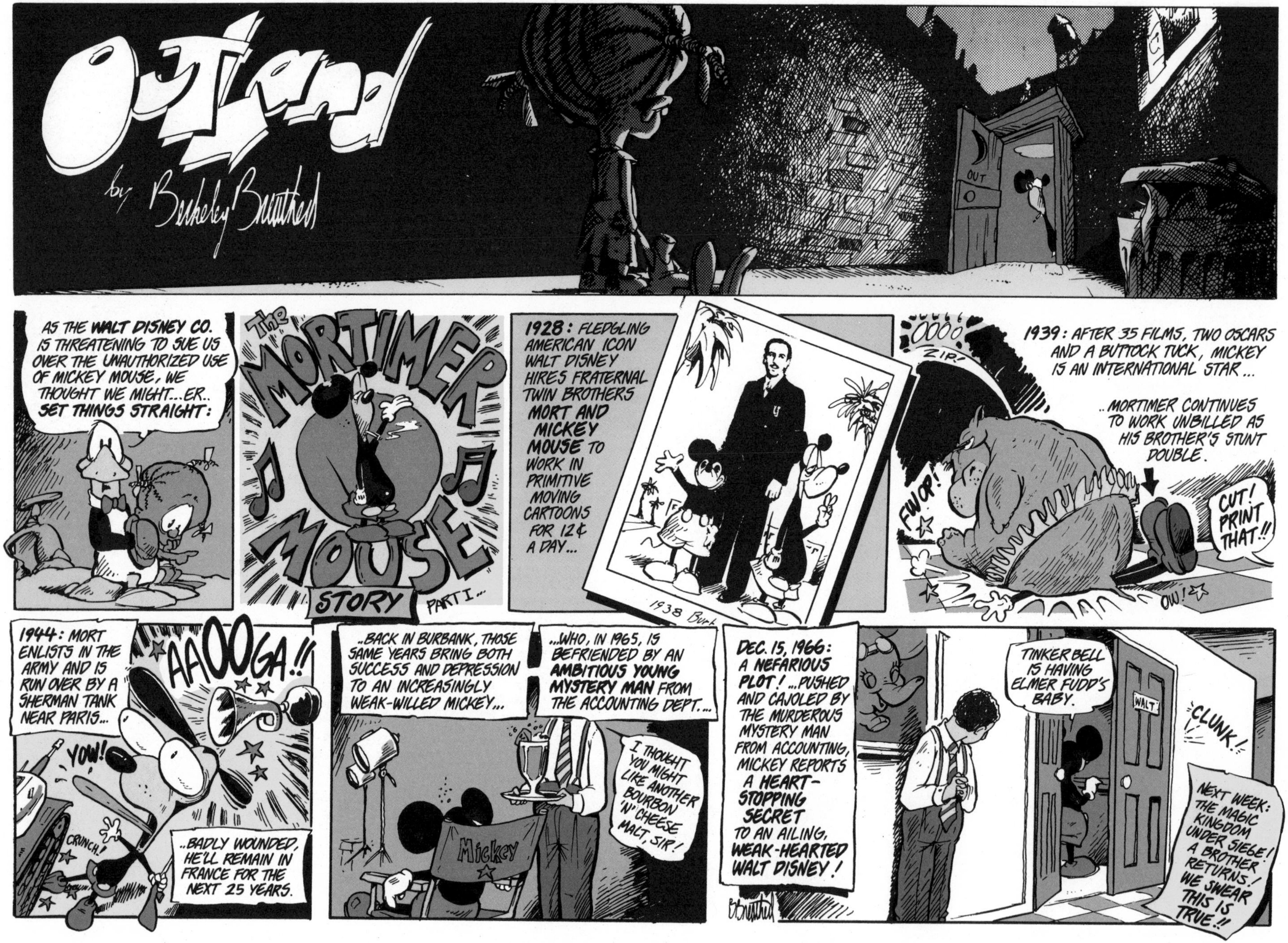
Outland
by Berkeley Breathed
OUT
AS THE WALT DISNEY CO. IS THREATENING TO SUE US OVER THE UNAUTHORIZED USE OF MICKEY MOUSE, WE THOUGHT WE MIGHT...ER.. SET THINGS STRAIGHT:
The MORTIMER MOUSE STORY PART I...
1928: FLEDGLING AMERICAN ICON WALT DISNEY HIRES FRATERNAL TWIN BROTHERS MORT AND MICKEY MOUSE TO WORK IN PRIMITIVE MOVING CARTOONS FOR 12¢ A DAY...
1938 Burb
OOOO
ZIP!
1939: AFTER 35 FILMS, TWO OSCARS AND A BUTTOCK TUCK, MICKEY IS AN INTERNATIONAL STAR...
..MORTIMER CONTINUES TO WORK UNBILLED AS HIS BROTHER'S STUNT DOUBLE.
FWOP!
CUT! PRINT THAT!!
OW!
1944: MORT ENLISTS IN THE ARMY AND IS RUN OVER BY A SHERMAN TANK NEAR PARIS...
AAOOGA!!
YOW!
CRUNCH!
..BADLY WOUNDED, HE'LL REMAIN IN FRANCE FOR THE NEXT 25 YEARS.
..BACK IN BURBANK, THOSE SAME YEARS BRING BOTH SUCCESS AND DEPRESSION TO AN INCREASINGLY WEAK-WILLED MICKEY...
...WHO, IN 1965, IS BEFRIENDED BY AN AMBITIOUS YOUNG MYSTERY MAN FROM THE ACCOUNTING DEPT....
I THOUGHT YOU MIGHT LIKE ANOTHER BOURBON 'N' CHEESE MALT, SIR!
Mickey
DEC. 15, 1966: A NEFARIOUS PLOT! ...PUSHED AND CAJOLED BY THE MURDEROUS MYSTERY MAN FROM ACCOUNTING, MICKEY REPORTS A HEART-STOPPING SECRET TO AN AILING, WEAK-HEARTED WALT DISNEY!
TINKER BELL IS HAVING ELMER FUDD'S BABY.
WALT
CLUNK!
NEXT WEEK: THE MAGIC KINGDOM UNDER SIEGE! A BROTHER RETURNS! WE SWEAR THIS IS TRUE!!
BBreathed

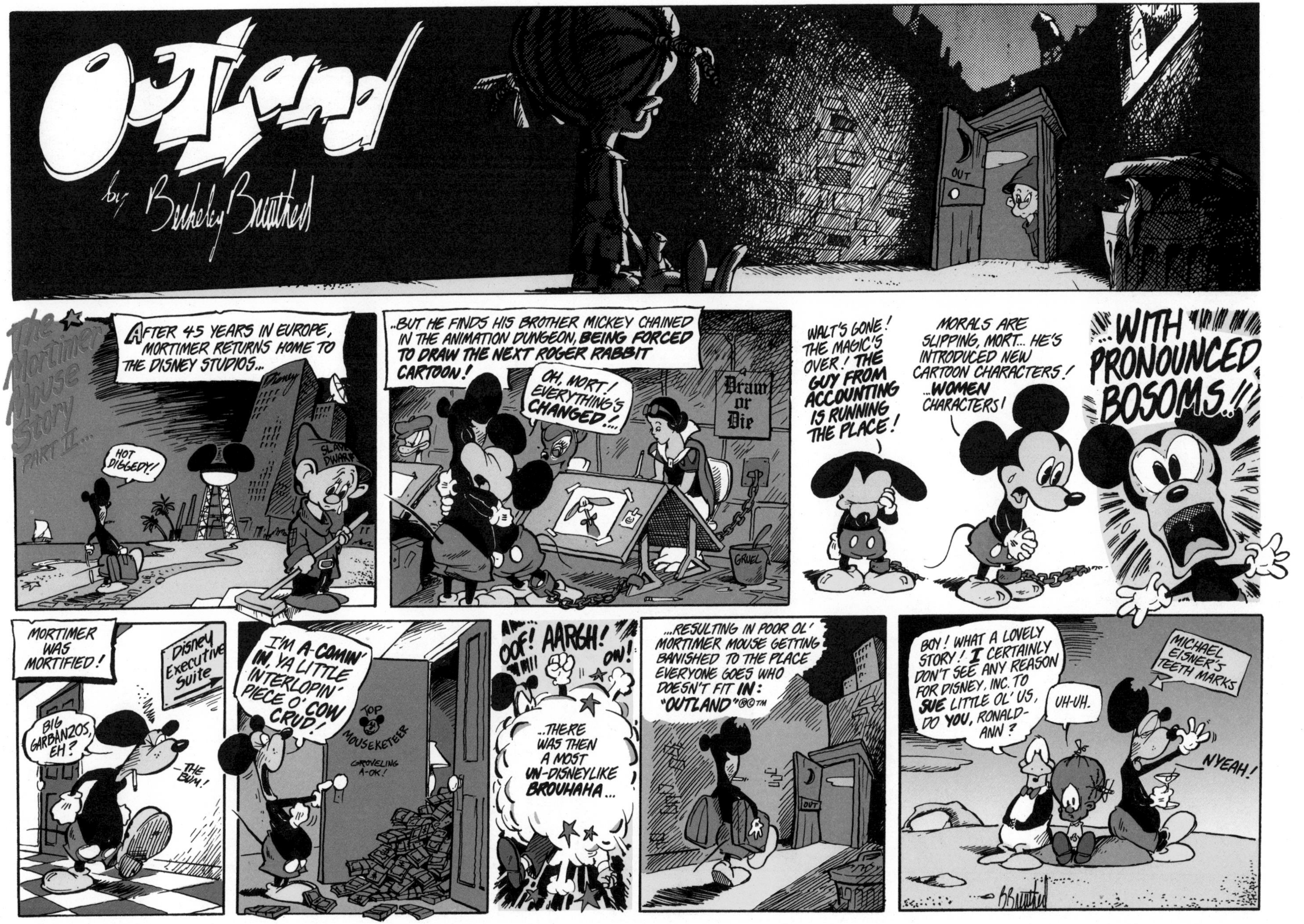

OUTLAND
by Berkeley Breathed
OUT
The Mortimer Mouse Story Part II...
AFTER 45 YEARS IN EUROPE, MORTIMER RETURNS HOME TO THE DISNEY STUDIOS...
Disney
HOT DIGGEDY!
SLAVE DWARF
..BUT HE FINDS HIS BROTHER MICKEY CHAINED IN THE ANIMATION DUNGEON, BEING FORCED TO DRAW THE NEXT ROGER RABBIT CARTOON!
OH, MORT! EVERYTHING'S CHANGED!...
Draw or Die
GRUEL
WALT'S GONE! THE MAGIC'S OVER! THE GUY FROM ACCOUNTING IS RUNNING THE PLACE!
MORALS ARE SLIPPING, MORT... HE'S INTRODUCED NEW CARTOON CHARACTERS! ...WOMEN CHARACTERS!
...WITH PRONOUNCED BOSOMS..!!
MORTIMER WAS MORTIFIED!
Disney Executive Suite
BIG GARBANZOS, EH?
—THE BUM!
I'M A-COMIN' IN, YA LITTLE INTERLOPIN' PIECE O' COW CRUD!
TOP MOUSEKETEER
GROVELING A-OK!
OOF! AARGH! OW!
..THERE WAS THEN A MOST UN-DISNEYLIKE BROUHAHA...
...RESULTING IN POOR OL' MORTIMER MOUSE GETTING BANISHED TO THE PLACE EVERYONE GOES WHO DOESN'T FIT IN: "OUTLAND"®©™
OUT
BOY! WHAT A LOVELY STORY! I CERTAINLY DON'T SEE ANY REASON FOR DISNEY, INC. TO SUE LITTLE OL' US, DO YOU, RONALD-ANN?
UH-UH.
MICHAEL EISNER'S TEETH MARKS
NYEAH!
B Breathed

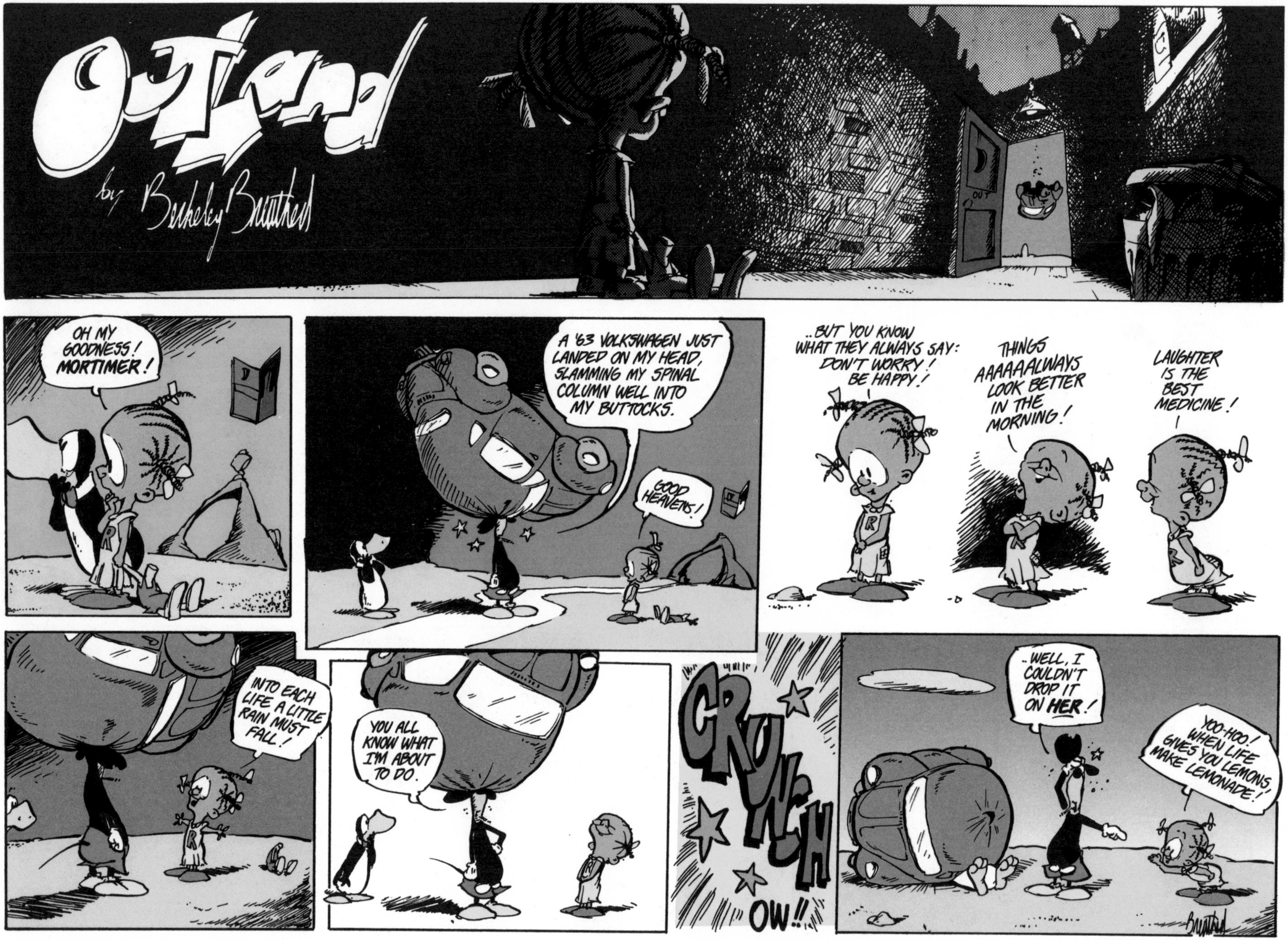
Outland
by Berkeley Breathed
OUT
OH MY GOODNESS! MORTIMER!
A '63 VOLKSWAGEN JUST LANDED ON MY HEAD, SLAMMING MY SPINAL COLUMN WELL INTO MY BUTTOCKS.
GOOD HEAVENS!
..BUT YOU KNOW WHAT THEY ALWAYS SAY: DON'T WORRY! BE HAPPY!
THINGS AAAAAALWAYS LOOK BETTER IN THE MORNING!
LAUGHTER IS THE BEST MEDICINE!
INTO EACH LIFE A LITTLE RAIN MUST FALL!
YOU ALL KNOW WHAT I'M ABOUT TO DO.
CRUNCH
OW!!
..WELL, I COULDN'T DROP IT ON HER!
YOO-HOO! WHEN LIFE GIVES YOU LEMONS, MAKE LEMONADE!
Breathed

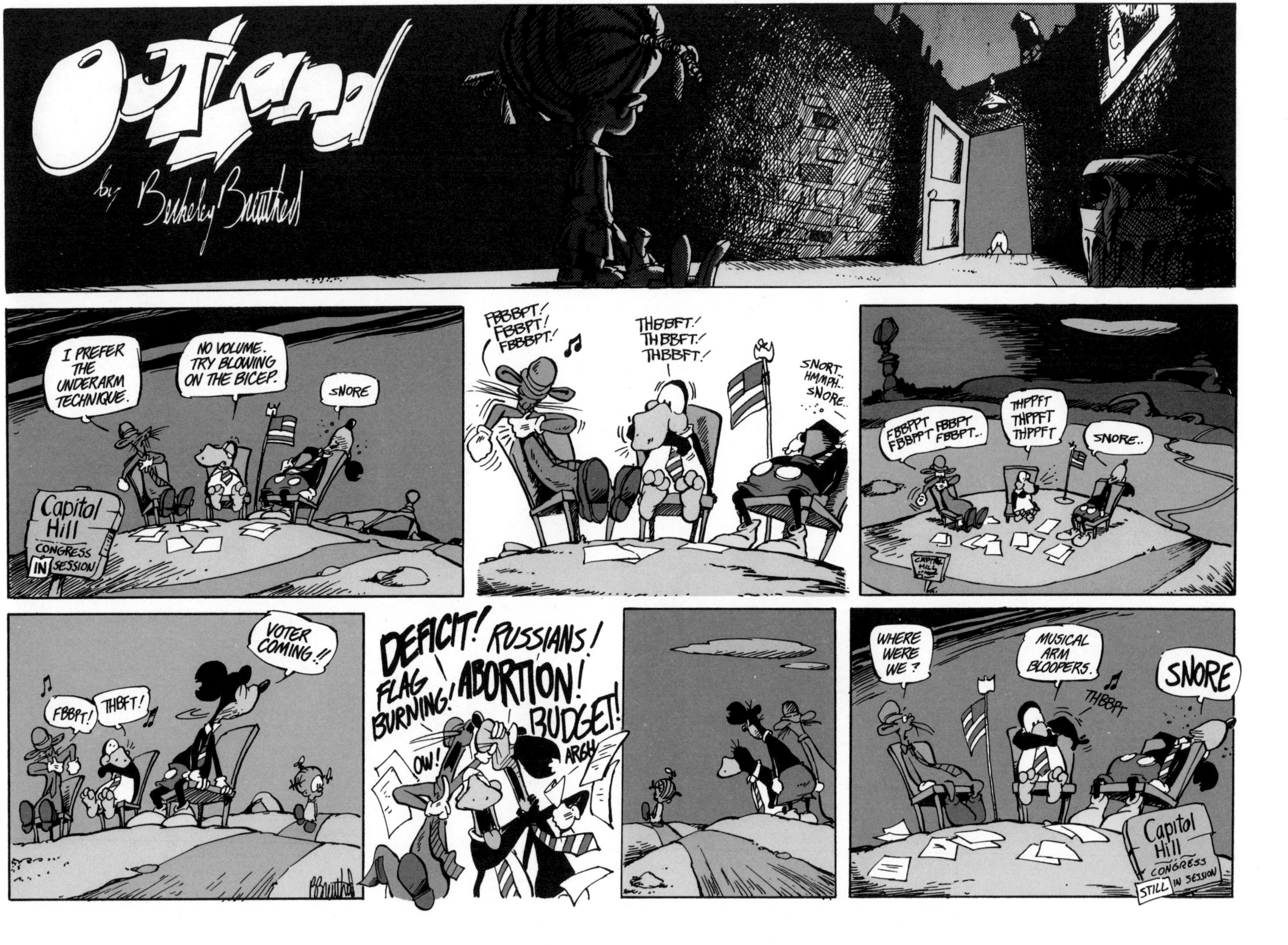

Outland
by Berkeley Breathed
I PREFER THE UNDERARM TECHNIQUE.
NO VOLUME. TRY BLOWING ON THE BICEP.
SNORE
Capital Hill
CONGRESS IN SESSION
FBBBPT! FBBPT! FBBBPT!
THBBFT! THBBFT! THBBFT!
SNORT.. HMMPH.. SNORE..
FBBPPT FBBPPT FBBPT FBBPT..
THPPFT THPPFT THPPFT
SNORE..
FBBPT!
THBFT!
VOTER COMING!!
DEFICIT!
RUSSIANS!
FLAG BURNING!
ABORTION!
BUDGET!
OW!
ARGH
WHERE WERE WE?
MUSICAL ARM BLOOPERS.
THBBPT
SNORE
Capital Hill
CONGRESS
STILL IN SESSION

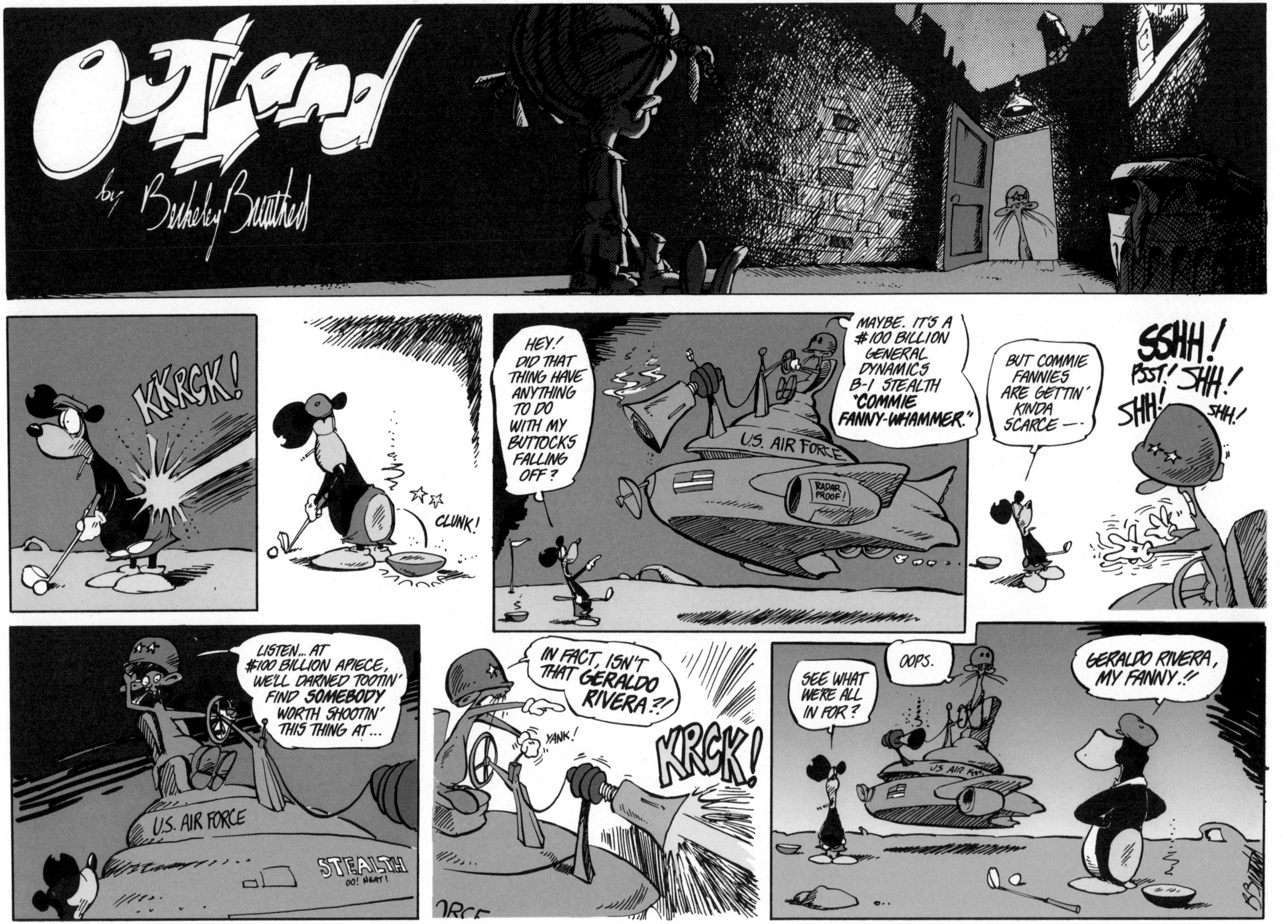
Outland
by Berkeley Breathed
KKRCK!
CLUNK!
HEY! DID THAT THING HAVE ANYTHING TO DO WITH MY BUTTOCKS FALLING OFF?
MAYBE. IT'S A $100 BILLION GENERAL DYNAMICS B-1 STEALTH "COMMIE FANNY-WHAMMER."
U.S. AIR FORCE
RADAR PROOF!
BUT COMMIE FANNIES ARE GETTIN' KINDA SCARCE —
SSHH! PSST! SHH! SHH! SHH!
LISTEN... AT $100 BILLION APIECE, WE'LL DARNED TOOTIN' FIND SOMEBODY WORTH SHOOTIN' THIS THING AT...
U.S. AIR FORCE
STEALTH
OO! NEAT!
IN FACT, ISN'T THAT GERALDO RIVERA?!
YANK!
KRCK!
SEE WHAT WE'RE ALL IN FOR?
OOPS.
GERALDO RIVERA, MY FANNY.!!

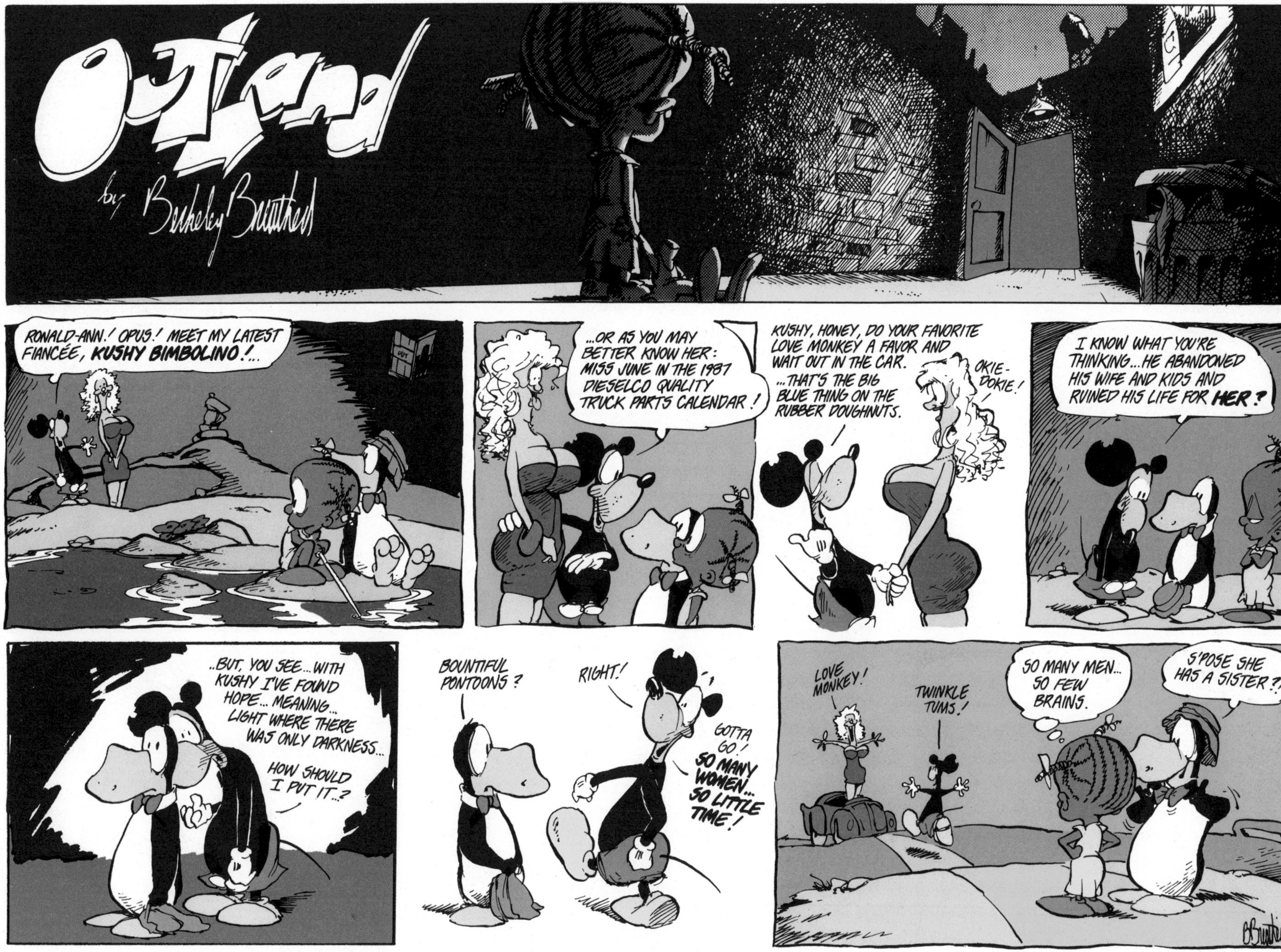

Outland
by Berkeley Breathed
RONALD-ANN! OPUS! MEET MY LATEST FIANCÉE, **KUSHY BIMBOLINO!**...
...OR AS YOU MAY BETTER KNOW HER: MISS JUNE IN THE 1987 DIESELCO QUALITY TRUCK PARTS CALENDAR!
KUSHY, HONEY, DO YOUR FAVORITE LOVE MONKEY A FAVOR AND WAIT OUT IN THE CAR. ...THAT'S THE BIG BLUE THING ON THE RUBBER DOUGHNUTS.
OKIE-DOKIE!
I KNOW WHAT YOU'RE THINKING... HE ABANDONED HIS WIFE AND KIDS AND RUINED HIS LIFE FOR **HER?**
..BUT, YOU SEE... WITH KUSHY I'VE FOUND HOPE... MEANING... LIGHT WHERE THERE WAS ONLY DARKNESS...
HOW SHOULD I PUT IT..?
BOUNTIFUL PONTOONS?
RIGHT!
GOTTA GO! **SO MANY WOMEN... SO LITTLE TIME!**
LOVE MONKEY!
TWINKLE TUMS!
SO MANY MEN... SO FEW BRAINS.
S'POSE SHE HAS A SISTER?!

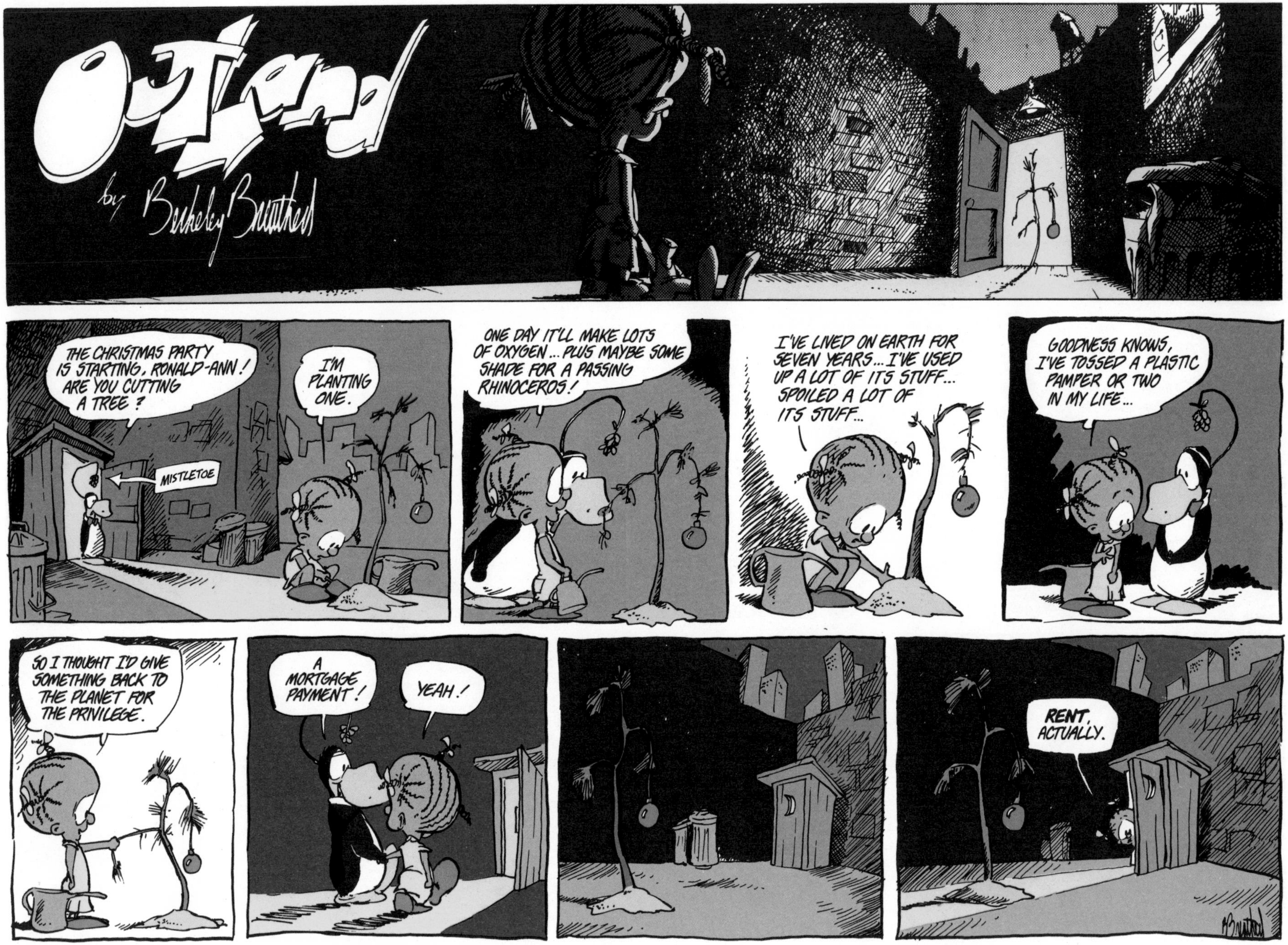

Outland
by Berkeley Breathed
THE CHRISTMAS PARTY IS STARTING, RONALD-ANN! ARE YOU CUTTING A TREE?
MISTLETOE
I'M PLANTING ONE.
ONE DAY IT'LL MAKE LOTS OF OXYGEN... PLUS MAYBE SOME SHADE FOR A PASSING RHINOCEROS!
I'VE LIVED ON EARTH FOR SEVEN YEARS... I'VE USED UP A LOT OF ITS STUFF... SPOILED A LOT OF ITS STUFF...
GOODNESS KNOWS, I'VE TOSSED A PLASTIC PAMPER OR TWO IN MY LIFE...
SO I THOUGHT I'D GIVE SOMETHING BACK TO THE PLANET FOR THE PRIVILEGE.
A MORTGAGE PAYMENT!
YEAH!
RENT, ACTUALLY.

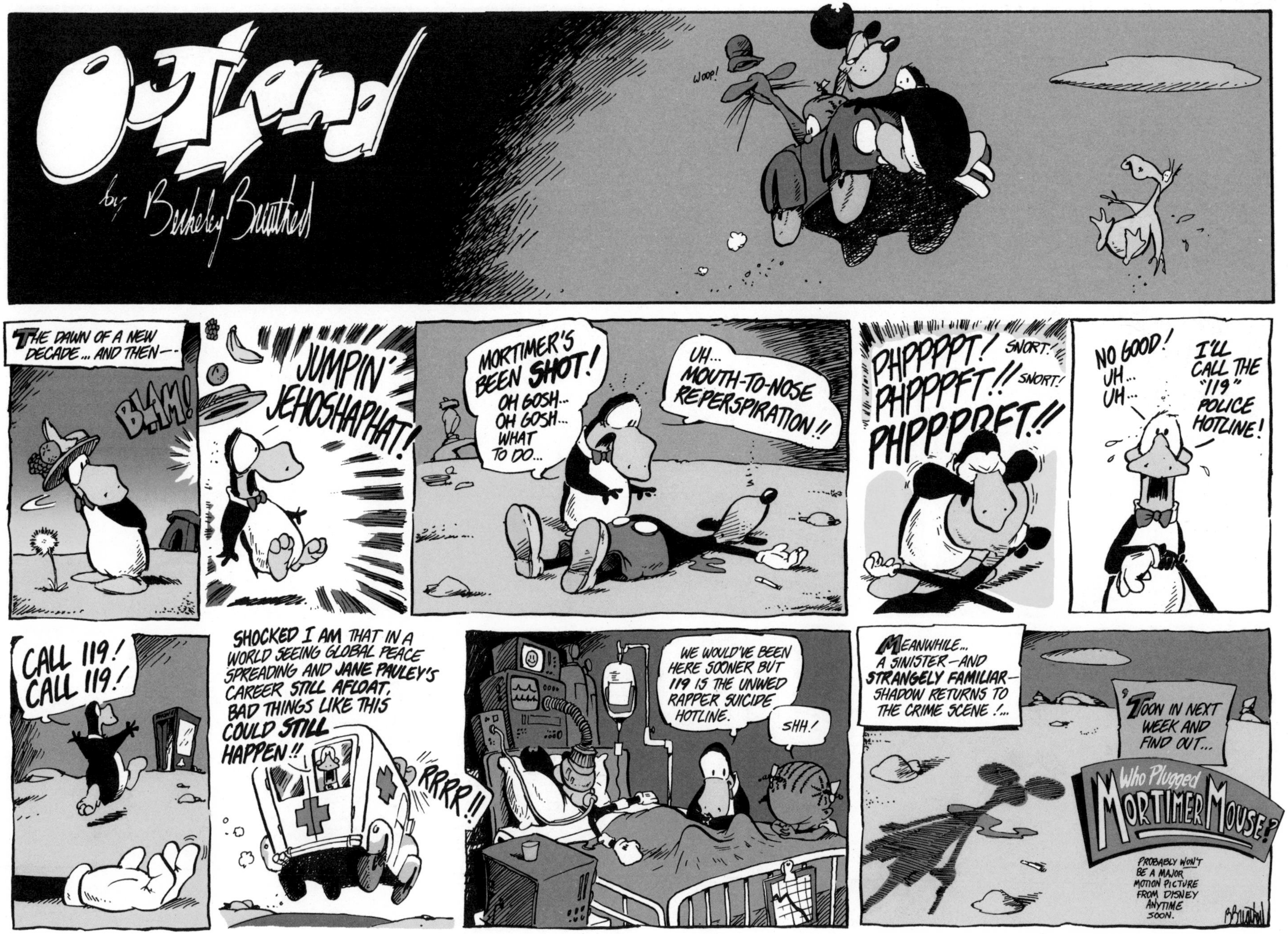

Outland
by Berkeley Breathed
WOOP!
THE DAWN OF A NEW DECADE... AND THEN---
BLAM!
JUMPIN' JEHOSHAPHAT!
MORTIMER'S BEEN SHOT!
OH GOSH... OH GOSH... WHAT TO DO...
UH... MOUTH-TO-NOSE REPERSPIRATION!!
PHPPPPT! PHPPPFT!! PHPPPPFT!!
SNORT! SNORT!
NO GOOD! UH... UH...
I'LL CALL THE "119" POLICE HOTLINE!
CALL 119! CALL 119!
SHOCKED I AM THAT IN A WORLD SEEING GLOBAL PEACE SPREADING AND JANE PAULEY'S CAREER STILL AFLOAT, BAD THINGS LIKE THIS COULD STILL HAPPEN!!
RRRR!!
WE WOULD'VE BEEN HERE SOONER BUT 119 IS THE UNWED RAPPER SUICIDE HOTLINE.
SHH!
MEANWHILE... A SINISTER—AND STRANGELY FAMILIAR—SHADOW RETURNS TO THE CRIME SCENE!...
TOON IN NEXT WEEK AND FIND OUT...
Who Plugged MORTIMER MOUSE?
PROBABLY WON'T BE A MAJOR MOTION PICTURE FROM DISNEY ANYTIME SOON.
B. Breathed

**Outland** by Berkeley Breathed

**Who Plugged MORTIMER MOUSE**

Our Story: MORTIMER HOVERS NEAR DEATH... **FELLED** BY A COWARDLY MYSTERY ASSASSIN'S BULLET...

I'VE NARROWED THE SUSPECTS DOWN TO **FOUR**:

**JEANE J. KIRKPATRICK**
FORMER UNITED NATIONS PARTY ANIMAL
• MOTIVE: ONE OF THOSE "FATAL ATTRACTION" THINGS.

**BILLY RODNICK, 15**
PRESIDENT OF THE BOISE "BRING BACK BLOOM COUNTY" CLUB
• MOTIVE: TERRORISM

**WILLIE HORTON**
REPUBLICAN FUND-RAISER
• MOTIVE: WOKE UP IN POOPY MOOD.

**MICKEY MOUSE**
MORT'S WELL-HEELED BROTHER.
• MOTIVE: DERANGED IMPULSE RESULTING FROM 61 YEARS OF CELIBACY WITH MINNIE.

LATER...AT THE HOSPITAL...

AM...AM I IN RODENT HEAVEN?

MORT! WHO PLUGGED YA, MORT? WHAT'D HE LOOK LIKE?

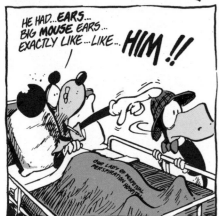

HE HAD...EARS... BIG MOUSE EARS... EXACTLY LIKE...LIKE... **HIM!!**

OUR LADY OF PERPETUAL PERSPIRATION HOSPITAL

B-BILL THE CAT?

WAAAAAAAA!!

ACK! KILL! ACK

OBVIOUSLY BRAIN-WASHED

KILL! ACK! KILL!!

**WAAAAA!!**

↑ CLEARLY NOT HIMSELF AT ALL

JEEZ! WHO'S BEHIND THIS?! NEXT WEEK: THE WHOLE TERRIBLE SHOCKING GOOSE-BUMPLY Republic-Crumbling **CONCLUSION!**

HURRY! THANK YOU.

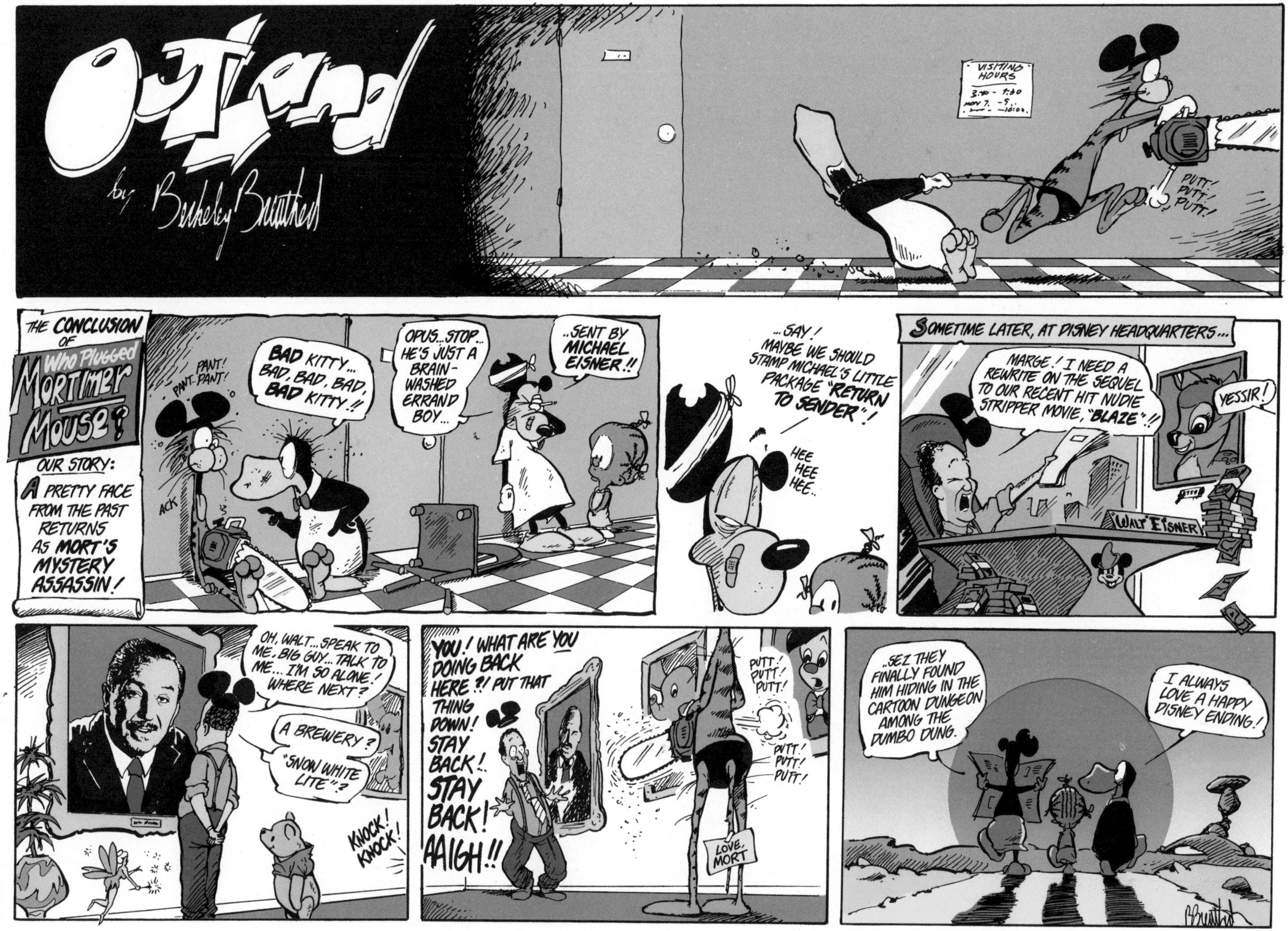
Outland
by Berkeley Breathed
VISITING HOURS
PUTT! PUTT! PUTT!
THE CONCLUSION OF Who Plugged Mortimer Mouse?
OUR STORY: A PRETTY FACE FROM THE PAST RETURNS AS MORT'S MYSTERY ASSASSIN!
PANT! PANT! PANT!
BAD KITTY... BAD, BAD, BAD, BAD KITTY!!
ACK
OPUS...STOP... HE'S JUST A BRAIN-WASHED ERRAND BOY...
..SENT BY MICHAEL EISNER!!
...SAY! MAYBE WE SHOULD STAMP MICHAEL'S LITTLE PACKAGE "RETURN TO SENDER"!
HEE HEE HEE..
SOMETIME LATER, AT DISNEY HEADQUARTERS...
MARGE! I NEED A REWRITE ON THE SEQUEL TO OUR RECENT HIT NUDIE STRIPPER MOVIE, "BLAZE"!!
YESSIR!
WALT EISNER
OH, WALT... SPEAK TO ME.. BIG GUY... TALK TO ME... I'M SO ALONE! WHERE NEXT?
A BREWERY?
"SNOW WHITE LITE"?
KNOCK! KNOCK!
YOU! WHAT ARE YOU DOING BACK HERE?! PUT THAT THING DOWN! STAY BACK! STAY BACK! AAIGH!!
PUTT! PUTT! PUTT!
PUTT! PUTT! PUTT!
LOVE, MORT
..SEZ THEY FINALLY FOUND HIM HIDING IN THE CARTOON DUNGEON AMONG THE DUMBO DUNG.
I ALWAYS LOVE A HAPPY DISNEY ENDING!
BBreathed

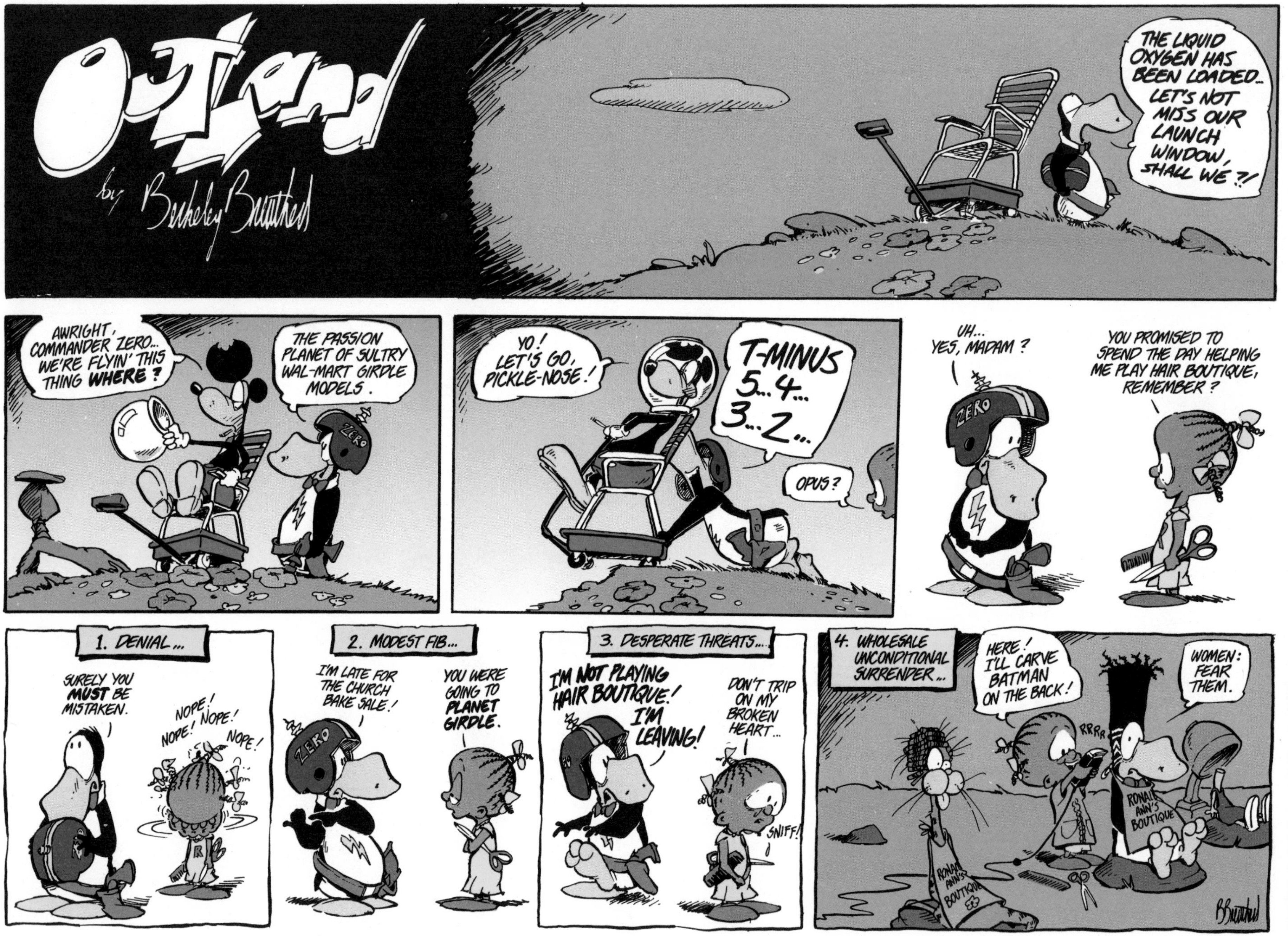
Outland
by Berkeley Breathed
THE LIQUID OXYGEN HAS BEEN LOADED... LET'S NOT MISS OUR LAUNCH WINDOW, SHALL WE ?!
AWRIGHT, COMMANDER ZERO... WE'RE FLYIN' THIS THING WHERE ?
THE PASSION PLANET OF SULTRY WAL-MART GIRDLE MODELS.
ZERO
YO! LET'S GO, PICKLE-NOSE!
T-MINUS 5...4... 3...2...
OPUS?
UH... YES, MADAM?
YOU PROMISED TO SPEND THE DAY HELPING ME PLAY HAIR BOUTIQUE, REMEMBER?
ZERO
1. DENIAL...
SURELY YOU MUST BE MISTAKEN.
NOPE! NOPE! NOPE! NOPE!
2. MODEST FIB...
I'M LATE FOR THE CHURCH BAKE SALE!
ZERO
YOU WERE GOING TO PLANET GIRDLE.
3. DESPERATE THREATS...
I'M NOT PLAYING HAIR BOUTIQUE! I'M LEAVING!
DON'T TRIP ON MY BROKEN HEART...
SNIFF!
4. WHOLESALE UNCONDITIONAL SURRENDER...
HERE! I'LL CARVE BATMAN ON THE BACK!
RRRR
WOMEN: FEAR THEM.
RONALD-ANN'S BOUTIQUE
RONALD-ANN'S BOUTIQUE
BBreathed

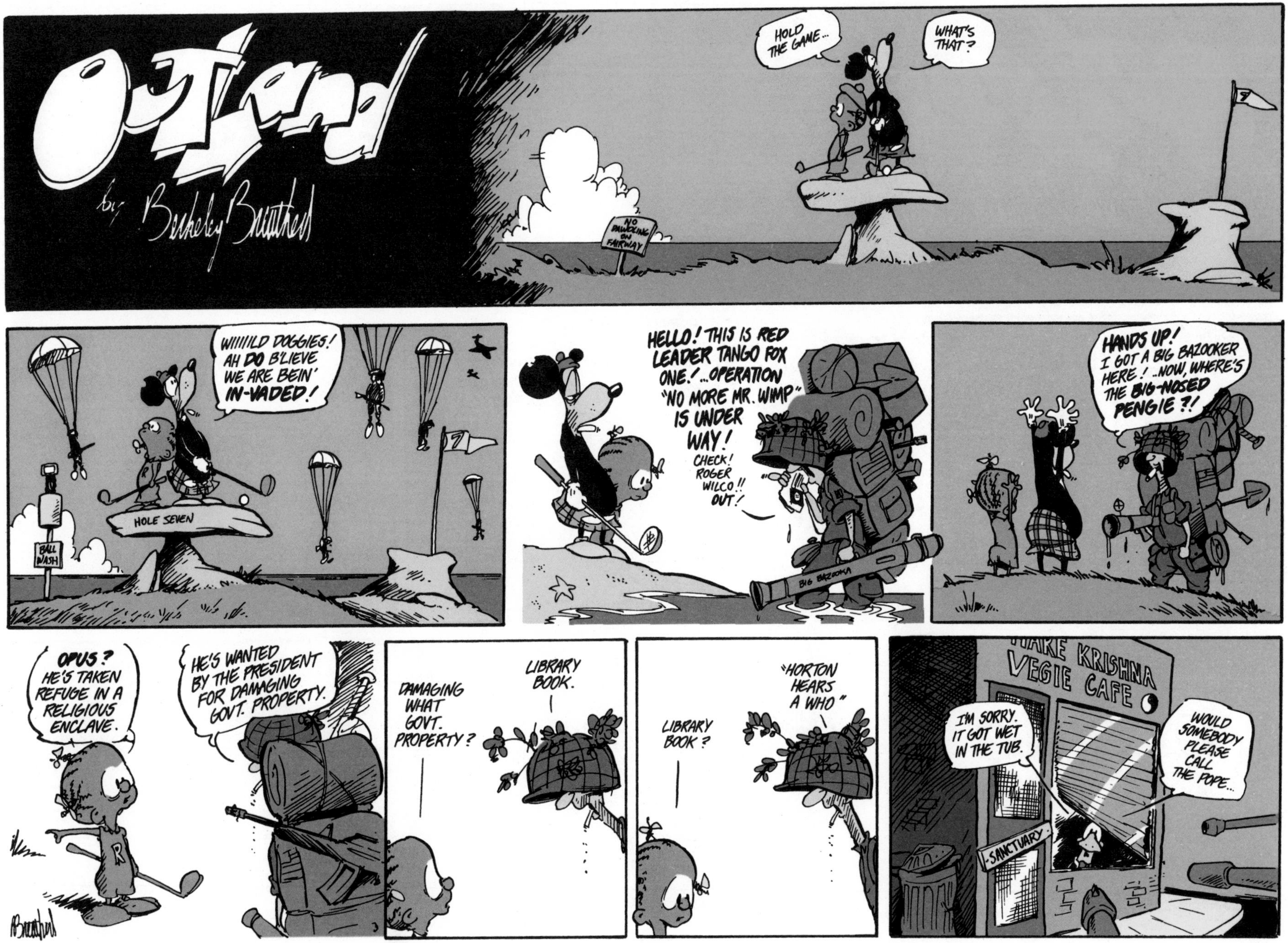

Outland
by Berkeley Breathed
HOLD THE GAME...
WHAT'S THAT?
NO DAWDLING ON FAIRWAY
WIIIIILD DOGGIES! AH DO B'LIEVE WE ARE BEIN' IN-VADED!
HOLE SEVEN
BALL WASH
HELLO! THIS IS RED LEADER TANGO FOX ONE! ...OPERATION "NO MORE MR. WIMP" IS UNDER WAY!
CHECK! ROGER WILCO!! OUT!
BIG BAZOOKA
HANDS UP! I GOT A BIG BAZOOKER HERE! ..NOW, WHERE'S THE BIG-NOSED PENGIE?!
OPUS? HE'S TAKEN REFUGE IN A RELIGIOUS ENCLAVE.
HE'S WANTED BY THE PRESIDENT FOR DAMAGING GOVT. PROPERTY.
DAMAGING WHAT GOVT. PROPERTY?
LIBRARY BOOK.
LIBRARY BOOK?
"HORTON HEARS A WHO"
VEGIE CAFE
SANCTUARY
I'M SORRY. IT GOT WET IN THE TUB.
WOULD SOMEBODY PLEASE CALL THE POPE...

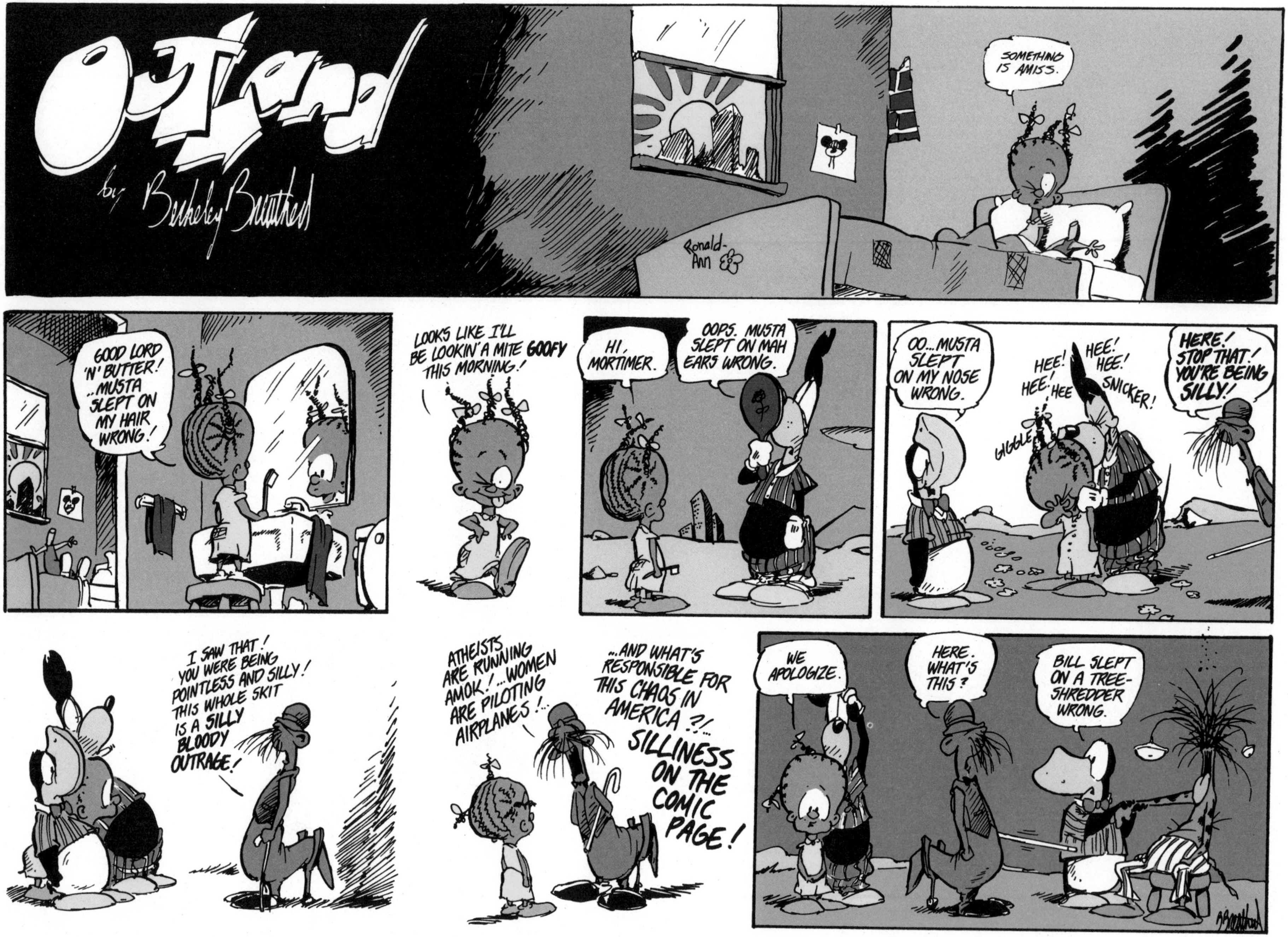

Outland
by Berkeley Breathed
SOMETHING IS AMISS.
Ronald-Ann
GOOD LORD 'N' BUTTER! ...MUSTA SLEPT ON MY HAIR WRONG!
LOOKS LIKE I'LL BE LOOKIN' A MITE GOOFY THIS MORNING!
HI, MORTIMER.
OOPS. MUSTA SLEPT ON MAH EARS WRONG.
OO... MUSTA SLEPT ON MY NOSE WRONG.
HEE! HEE! HEE
HEE! HEE!
SNICKER!
GIGGLE
HERE! STOP THAT! YOU'RE BEING SILLY!
I SAW THAT! YOU WERE BEING POINTLESS AND SILLY! THIS WHOLE SKIT IS A SILLY BLOODY OUTRAGE!
ATHEISTS ARE RUNNING AMOK! ...WOMEN ARE PILOTING AIRPLANES!..
...AND WHAT'S RESPONSIBLE FOR THIS CHAOS IN AMERICA?!
SILLINESS ON THE COMIC PAGE!
WE APOLOGIZE.
HERE. WHAT'S THIS?
BILL SLEPT ON A TREE-SHREDDER WRONG.

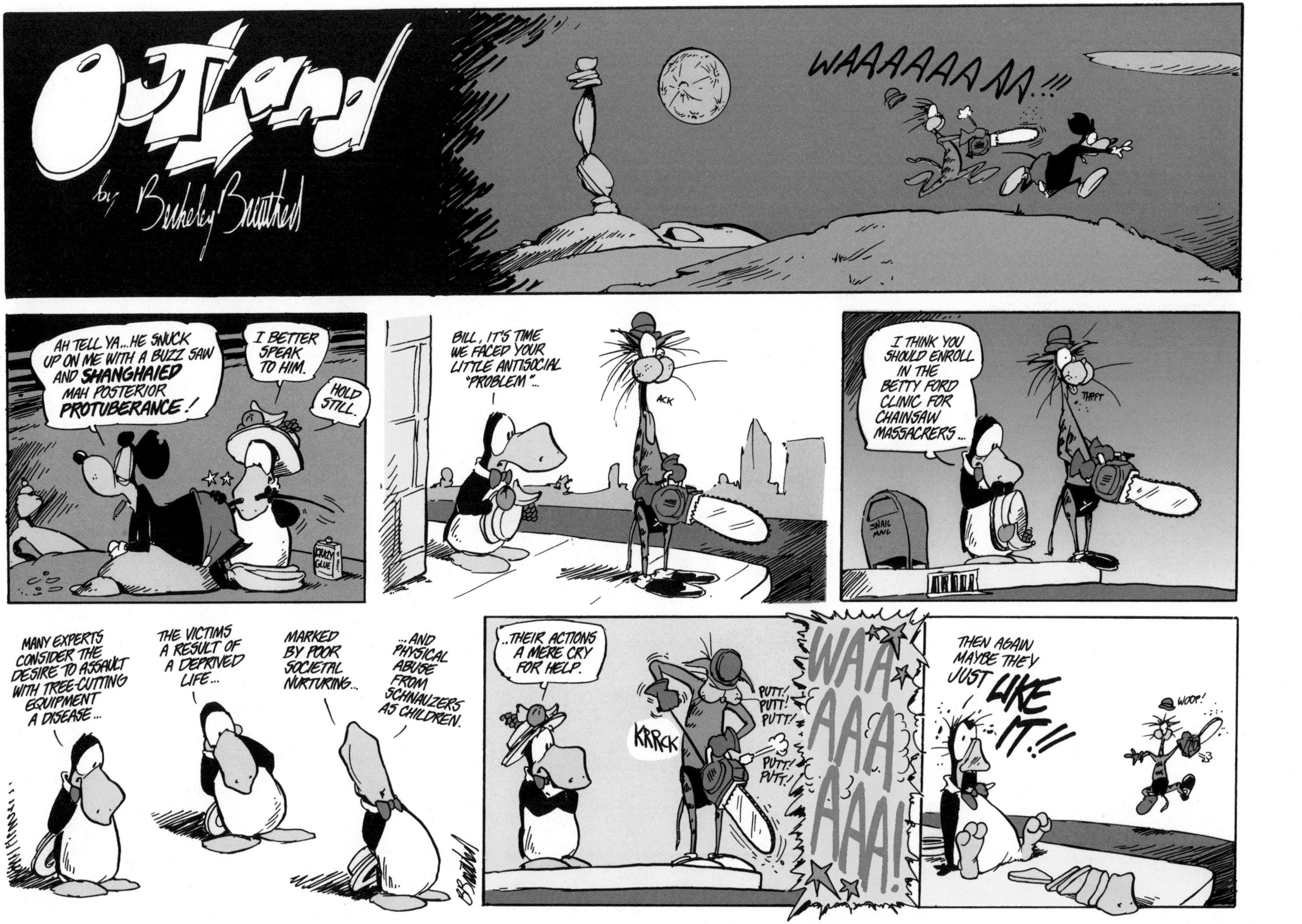
Outland
by Berkeley Breathed
WAAAAAAAA..!!!
AH TELL YA...HE SNUCK UP ON ME WITH A BUZZ SAW AND SHANGHAIED MAH POSTERIOR PROTUBERANCE!
I BETTER SPEAK TO HIM.
HOLD STILL.
CRAZY GLUE
BILL, IT'S TIME WE FACED YOUR LITTLE ANTISOCIAL "PROBLEM"...
ACK
I THINK YOU SHOULD ENROLL IN THE BETTY FORD CLINIC FOR CHAINSAW MASSACRERS...
THPFT
SNAIL MAIL
MANY EXPERTS CONSIDER THE DESIRE TO ASSAULT WITH TREE-CUTTING EQUIPMENT A DISEASE...
THE VICTIMS A RESULT OF A DEPRIVED LIFE...
MARKED BY POOR SOCIETAL NURTURING...
...AND PHYSICAL ABUSE FROM SCHNAUZERS AS CHILDREN.
..THEIR ACTIONS A MERE CRY FOR HELP.
KRRCK
PUTT! PUTT! PUTT!
PUTT! PUTT!
WAAAAAAAAA!
THEN AGAIN MAYBE THEY JUST LIKE IT!!!
WOOP!

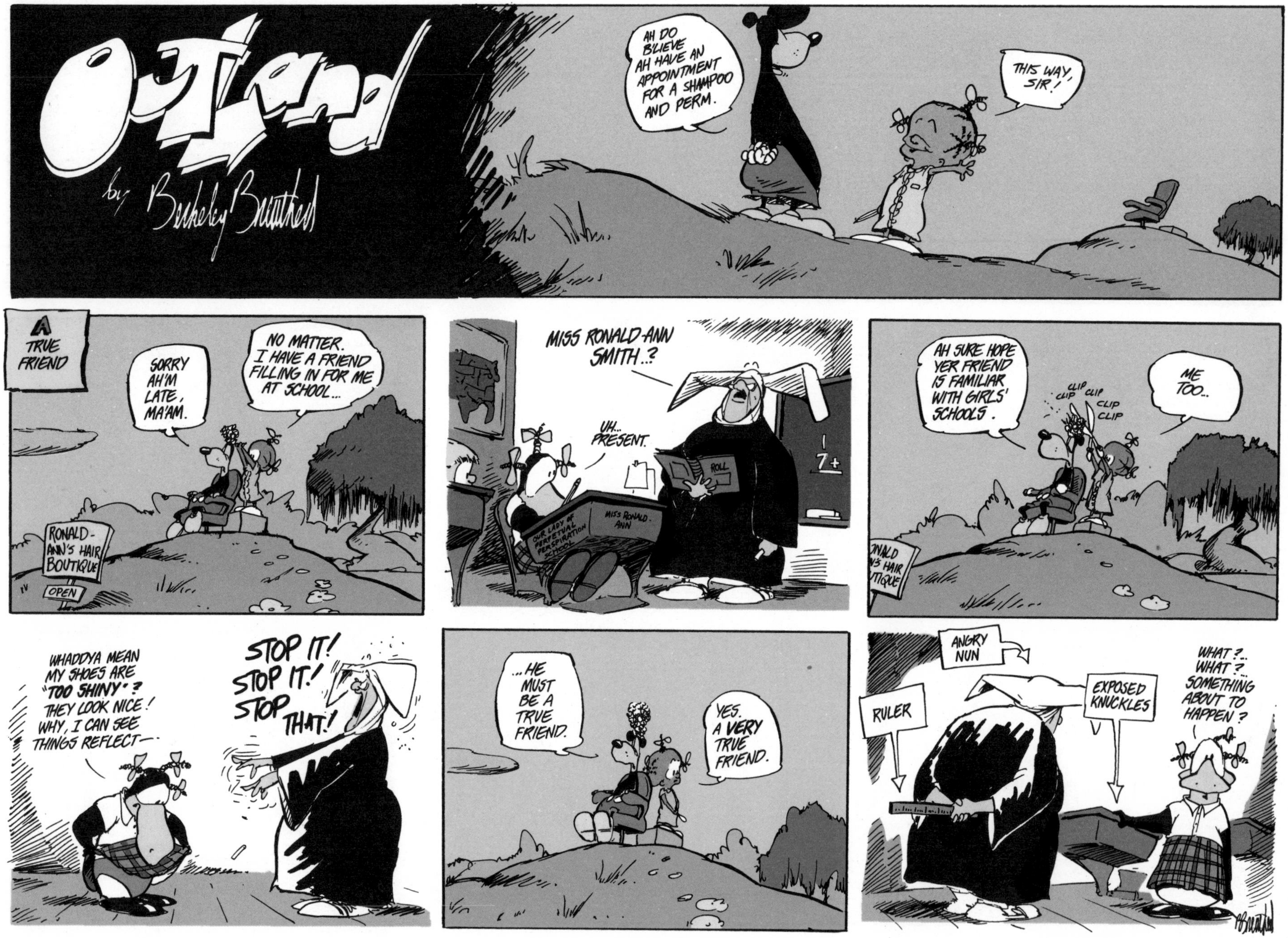

Outland
by Berkeley Breathed
AH DO B'LIEVE AH HAVE AN APPOINTMENT FOR A SHAMPOO AND PERM.
THIS WAY, SIR!
A TRUE FRIEND
SORRY AH'M LATE, MA'AM.
NO MATTER. I HAVE A FRIEND FILLING IN FOR ME AT SCHOOL...
RONALD-ANN'S HAIR BOUTIQUE
OPEN
MISS RONALD-ANN SMITH..?
UH... PRESENT.
OUR LADY OF PERPETUAL PERSPIRATION SCHOOL
MISS RONALD-ANN
ROLL
AH SURE HOPE YER FRIEND IS FAMILIAR WITH GIRLS' SCHOOLS.
CLIP CLIP CLIP CLIP CLIP
ME TOO...
WHADDYA MEAN MY SHOES ARE "TOO SHINY"? THEY LOOK NICE! WHY, I CAN SEE THINGS REFLECT—
STOP IT! STOP IT! STOP THAT!
...HE MUST BE A TRUE FRIEND.
YES. A VERY TRUE FRIEND.
ANGRY NUN
RULER
EXPOSED KNUCKLES
WHAT?.. WHAT?.. SOMETHING ABOUT TO HAPPEN?

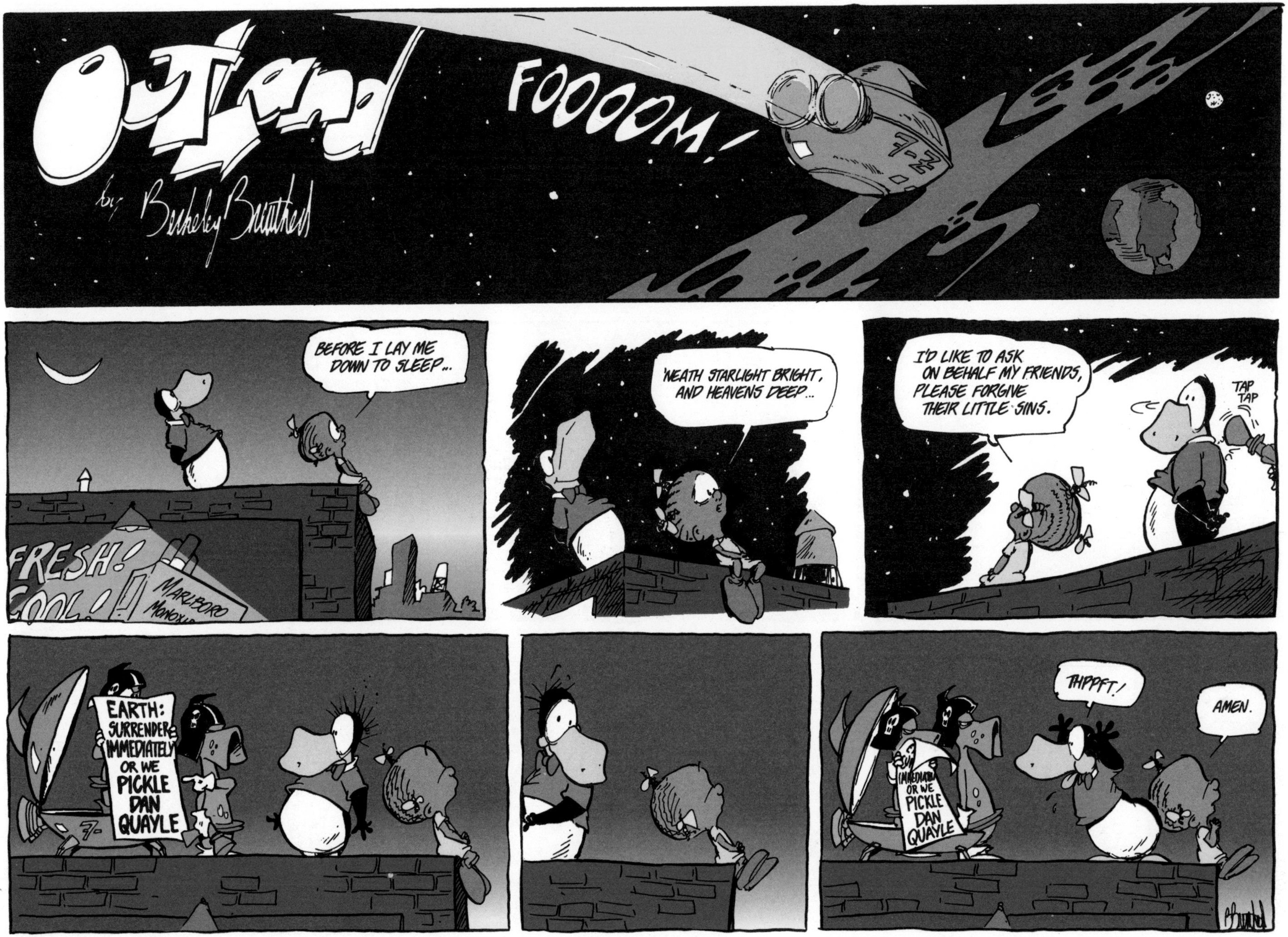
Outland
by Berkeley Breathed
FOOOOM!
7-Z
BEFORE I LAY ME DOWN TO SLEEP...
FRESH! COOL!
MARLBORO
'NEATH STARLIGHT BRIGHT, AND HEAVENS DEEP...
I'D LIKE TO ASK ON BEHALF MY FRIENDS, PLEASE FORGIVE THEIR LITTLE SINS.
TAP TAP
EARTH: SURRENDER IMMEDIATELY OR WE PICKLE DAN QUAYLE
THPPFT!
AMEN.
BBreathed

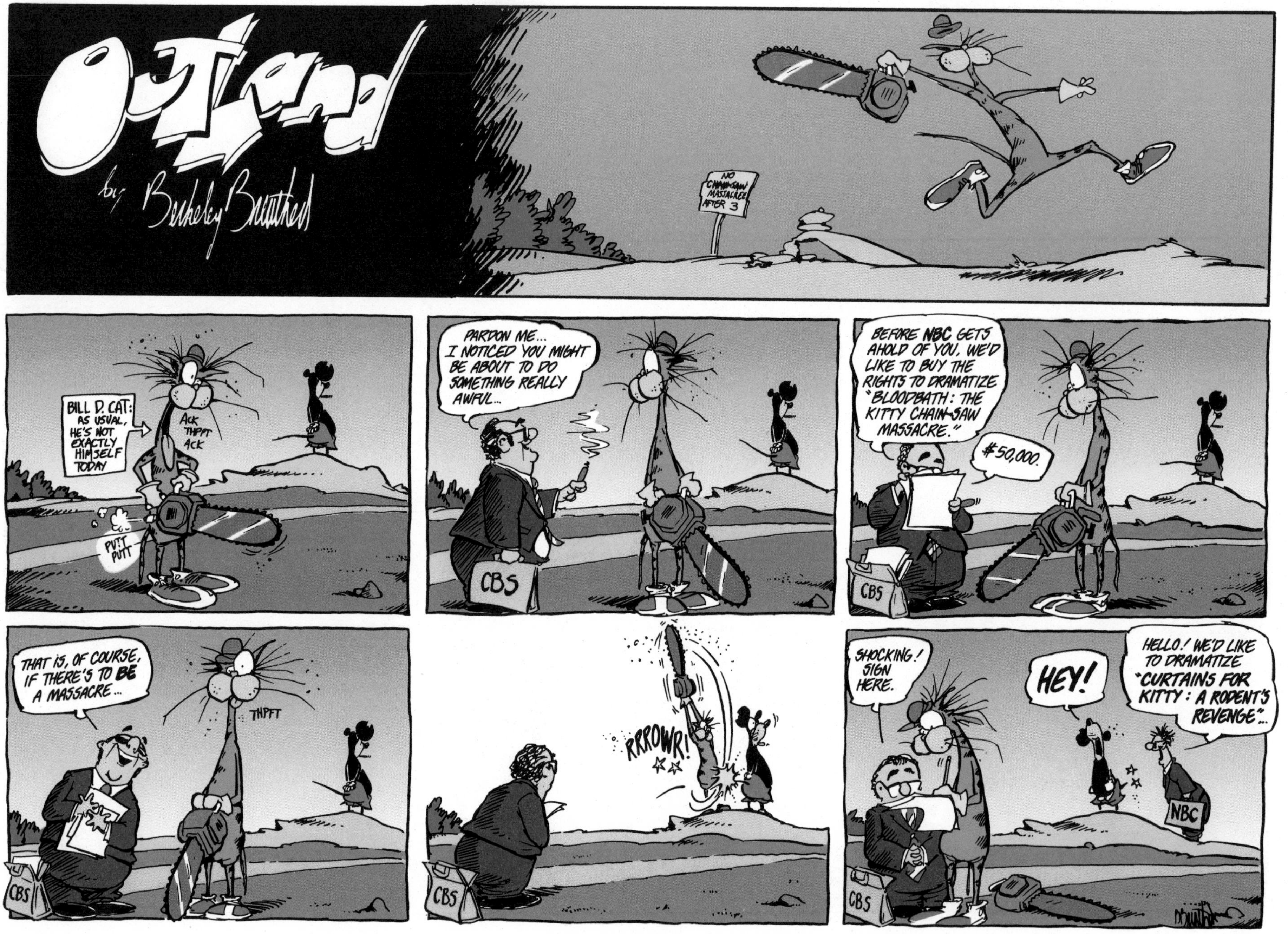

Outland
by Berkeley Breathed
NO CHAIN-SAW MASSACREE AFTER 3
BILL D. CAT: AS USUAL, HE'S NOT EXACTLY HIMSELF TODAY
ACK THPPT ACK
PUTT PUTT
PARDON ME... I NOTICED YOU MIGHT BE ABOUT TO DO SOMETHING REALLY AWFUL...
CBS
BEFORE NBC GETS AHOLD OF YOU, WE'D LIKE TO BUY THE RIGHTS TO DRAMATIZE "BLOODBATH: THE KITTY CHAIN-SAW MASSACRE."
$50,000.
CBS
THAT IS, OF COURSE, IF THERE'S TO BE A MASSACRE...
THPFT
CBS
RRROWR!
CBS
SHOCKING! SIGN HERE.
HEY!
HELLO! WE'D LIKE TO DRAMATIZE "CURTAINS FOR KITTY: A RODENT'S REVENGE"...
CBS
NBC

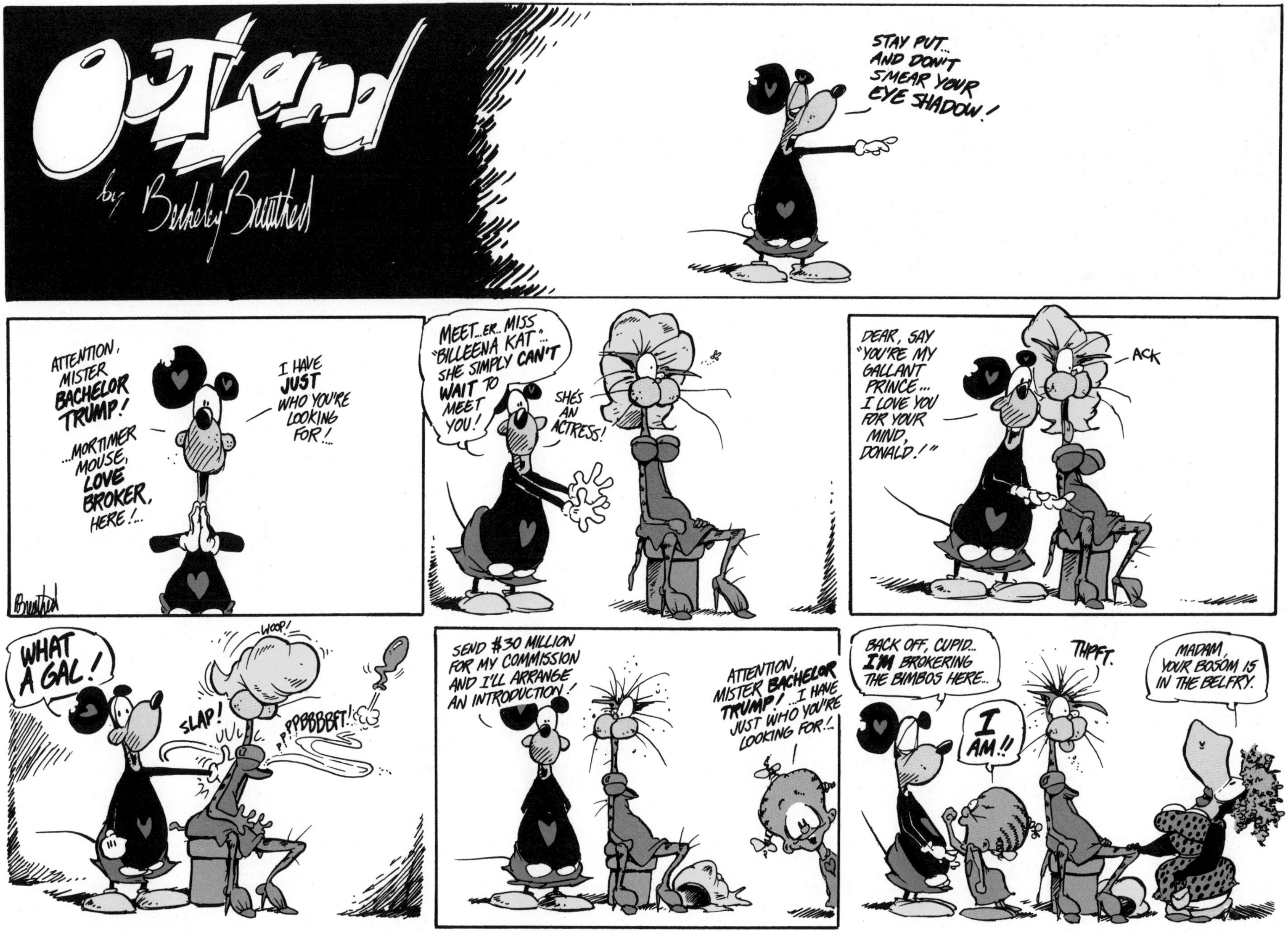

Outland
by Berkeley Breathed
STAY PUT... AND DON'T SMEAR YOUR EYE SHADOW!
ATTENTION, MISTER BACHELOR TRUMP!
...MORTIMER MOUSE, LOVE BROKER, HERE!...
I HAVE JUST WHO YOU'RE LOOKING FOR!...
MEET...ER.. MISS "BILLEENA KAT"... SHE SIMPLY CAN'T WAIT TO MEET YOU!
SHE'S AN ACTRESS!
DEAR, SAY "YOU'RE MY GALLANT PRINCE... I LOVE YOU FOR YOUR MIND, DONALD!"
ACK
WHAT A GAL!
WOOP!
SLAP!
PPPBBBBFT!
SEND $30 MILLION FOR MY COMMISSION AND I'LL ARRANGE AN INTRODUCTION!
ATTENTION, MISTER BACHELOR TRUMP! ...I HAVE JUST WHO YOU'RE LOOKING FOR!...
BACK OFF, CUPID... I'M BROKERING THE BIMBOS HERE..
I AM!!
THPFT.
MADAM, YOUR BOSOM IS IN THE BELFRY.

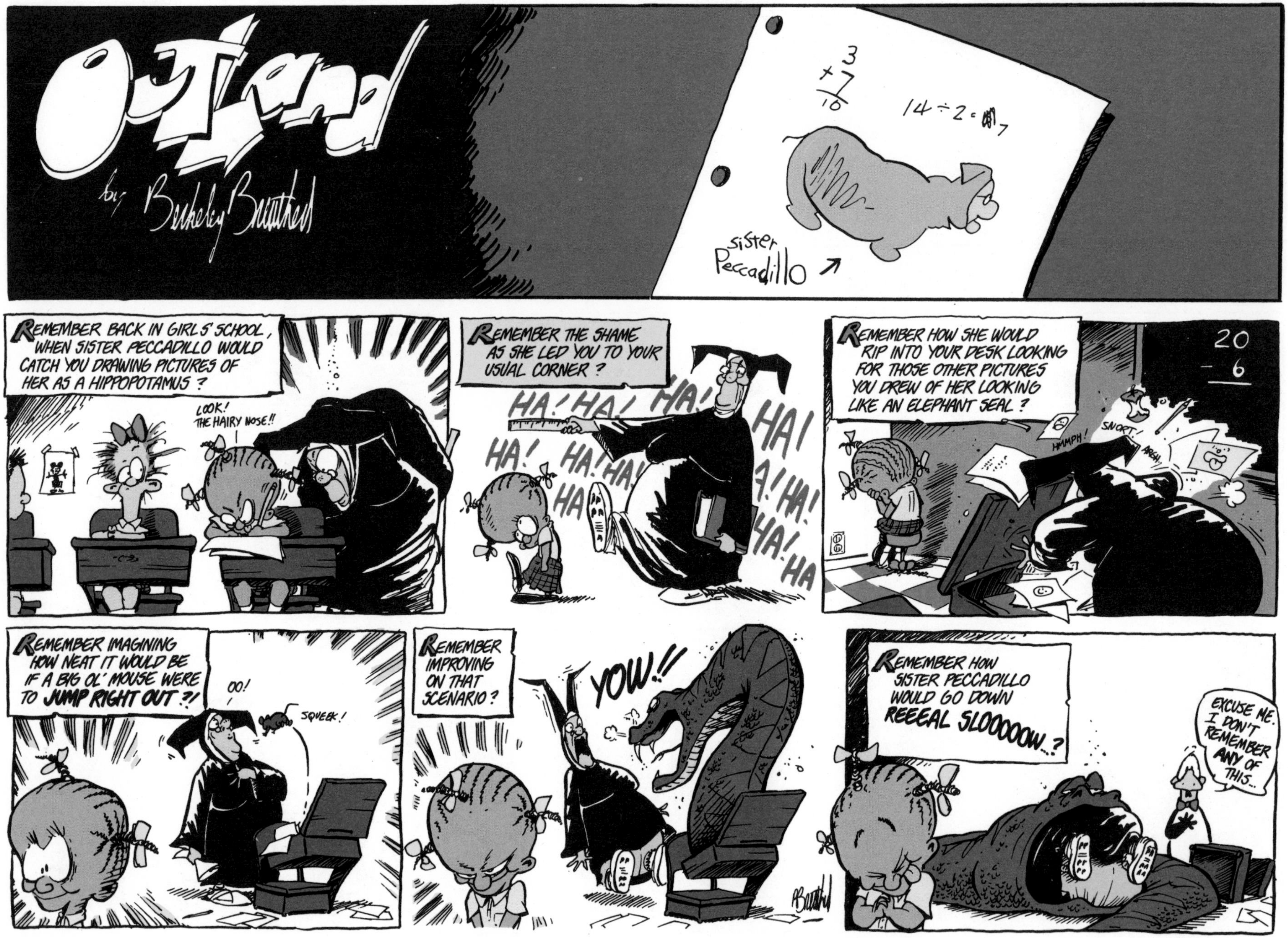
Outland
by Berkeley Breathed
3
+7
10
14 ÷ 2 =
7
sister Peccadillo
REMEMBER BACK IN GIRLS' SCHOOL, WHEN SISTER PECCADILLO WOULD CATCH YOU DRAWING PICTURES OF HER AS A HIPPOPOTAMUS ?
LOOK! THE HAIRY NOSE!!
REMEMBER THE SHAME AS SHE LED YOU TO YOUR USUAL CORNER ?
HA! HA! HA! HA! HA! HA! HA! HA! HA! HA! HA! HA! HA!
REMEMBER HOW SHE WOULD RIP INTO YOUR DESK LOOKING FOR THOSE OTHER PICTURES YOU DREW OF HER LOOKING LIKE AN ELEPHANT SEAL ?
20
- 6
HMMPH!
SNORT!
REMEMBER IMAGINING HOW NEAT IT WOULD BE IF A BIG OL' MOUSE WERE TO **JUMP RIGHT OUT** ?!
OO!
SQUEEK!
REMEMBER IMPROVING ON THAT SCENARIO ?
YOW!!
REMEMBER HOW SISTER PECCADILLO WOULD GO DOWN **REEEAL SLOOOOOW..**?
EXCUSE ME. I DON'T REMEMBER **ANY** OF THIS..

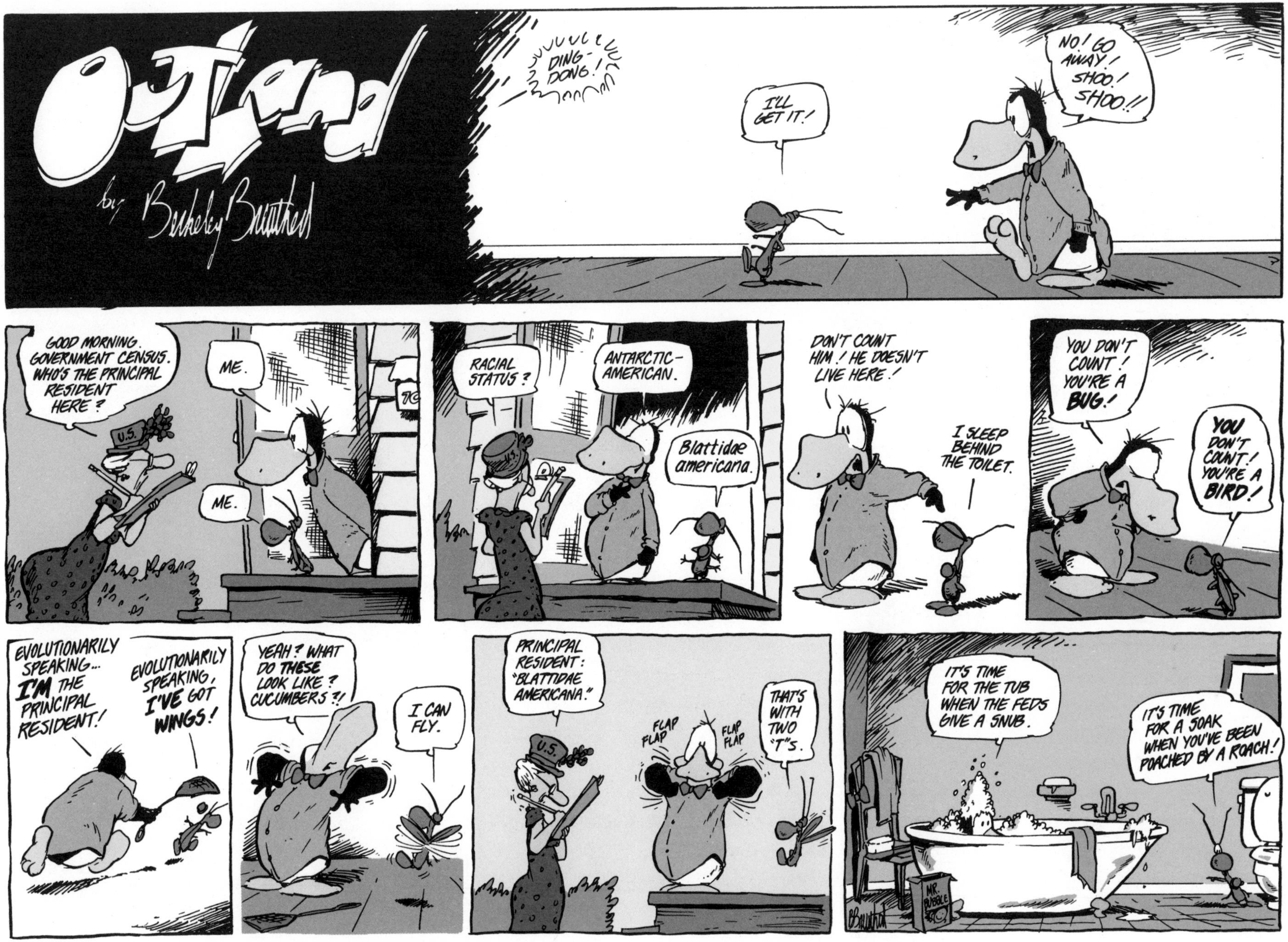
Outland
by Berkeley Breathed
DING-DONG!
I'LL GET IT!
NO! GO AWAY! SHOO! SHOO!!
GOOD MORNING. GOVERNMENT CENSUS. WHO'S THE PRINCIPAL RESIDENT HERE?
ME.
ME.
U.S.
RACIAL STATUS?
ANTARCTIC-AMERICAN.
Blattidae americana.
DON'T COUNT HIM! HE DOESN'T LIVE HERE!
I SLEEP BEHIND THE TOILET.
YOU DON'T COUNT! YOU'RE A **BUG**!
**YOU** DON'T COUNT! YOU'RE A **BIRD**!
EVOLUTIONARILY SPEAKING... **I'M** THE PRINCIPAL RESIDENT!
EVOLUTIONARILY SPEAKING, **I'VE** GOT **WINGS**!
YEAH? WHAT DO **THESE** LOOK LIKE? CUCUMBERS?!
I CAN FLY.
PRINCIPAL RESIDENT: "BLATTIDAE AMERICANA."
FLAP FLAP
FLAP FLAP
THAT'S WITH TWO "T"S.
IT'S TIME FOR THE TUB WHEN THE FEDS GIVE A SNUB.
IT'S TIME FOR A SOAK WHEN YOU'VE BEEN POACHED BY A ROACH!
MR. BUBBLE

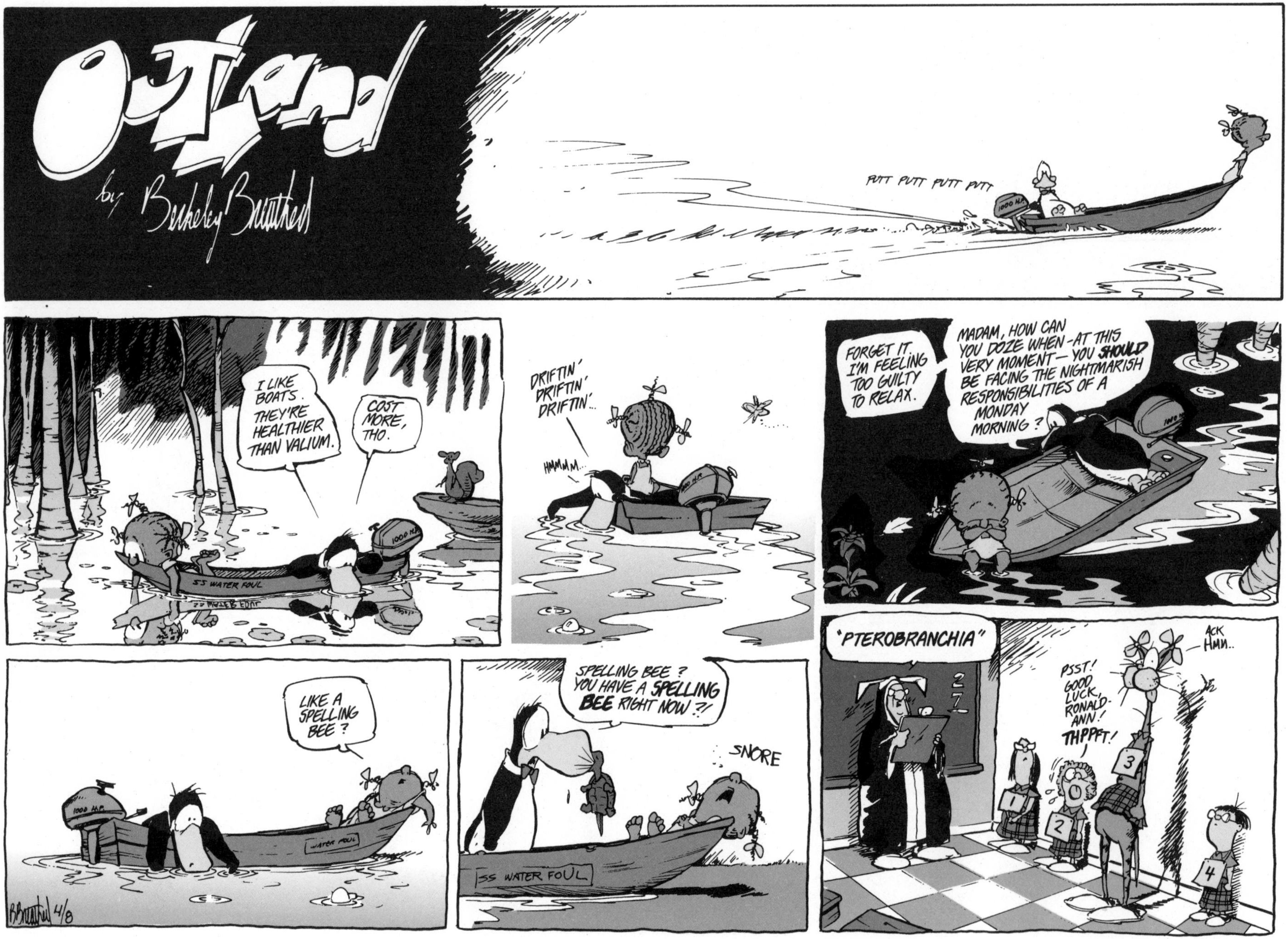
Outland
by Berkeley Breathed
PUTT PUTT PUTT PUTT
1000 H.P.
I LIKE BOATS. THEY'RE HEALTHIER THAN VALIUM.
COST MORE, THO.
SS WATER FOUL
DRIFTIN' DRIFTIN' DRIFTIN'...
HMMM...
FORGET IT. I'M FEELING TOO GUILTY TO RELAX.
MADAM, HOW CAN YOU DOZE WHEN—AT THIS VERY MOMENT— YOU SHOULD BE FACING THE NIGHTMARISH RESPONSIBILITIES OF A MONDAY MORNING?
LIKE A SPELLING BEE?
SPELLING BEE? YOU HAVE A SPELLING BEE RIGHT NOW?!
SNORE
"PTEROBRANCHIA"
ACK HMM..
PSST! GOOD LUCK, RONALD-ANN! THPPFT!
BBreathed 4/8

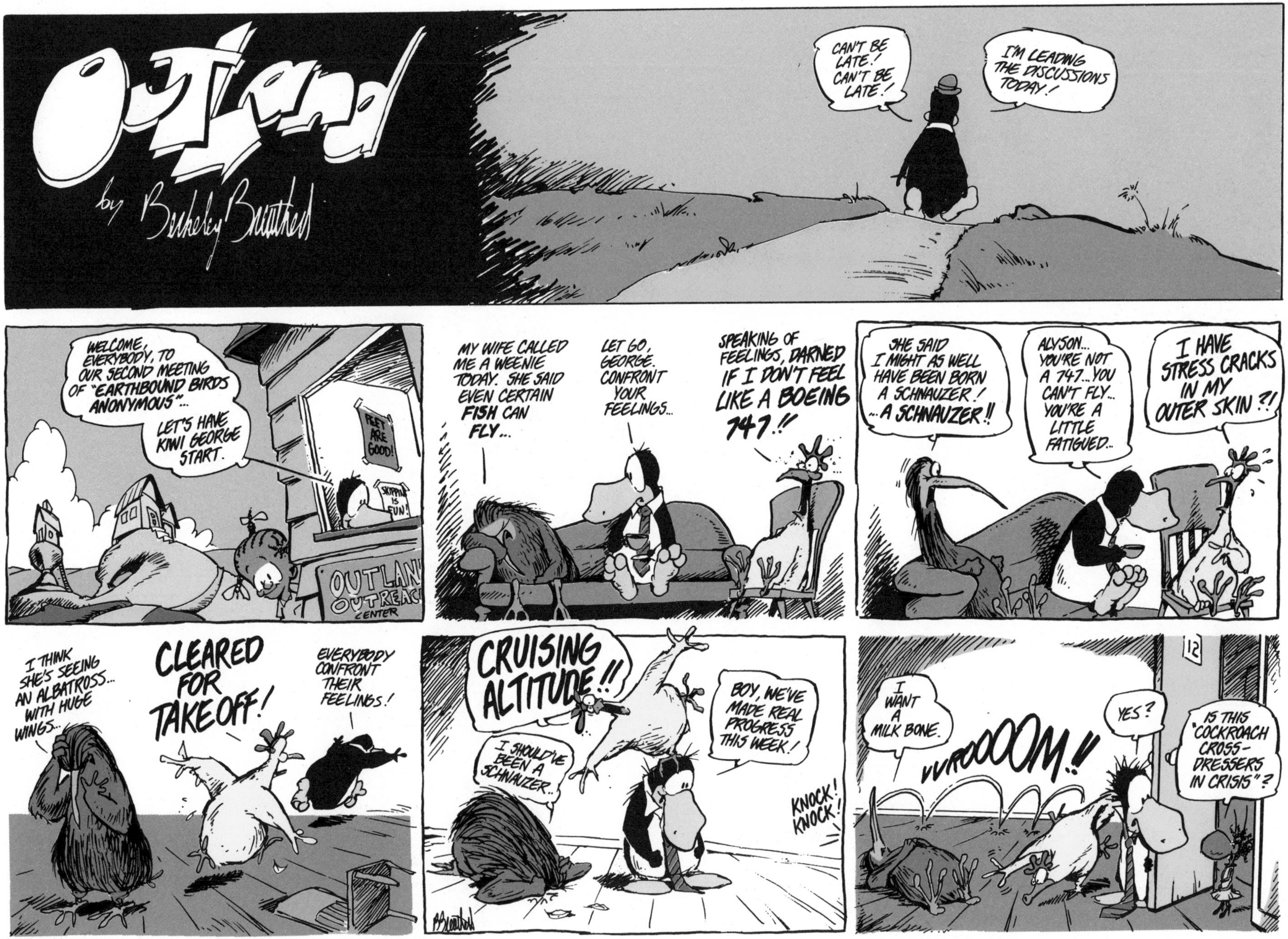

Outland
by Berkeley Breathed
CAN'T BE LATE! CAN'T BE LATE!
I'M LEADING THE DISCUSSIONS TODAY!
WELCOME, EVERYBODY, TO OUR SECOND MEETING OF "EARTHBOUND BIRDS ANONYMOUS"...
LET'S HAVE KIWI GEORGE START.
FEET ARE GOOD!
SKIPPING IS FUN!
OUTLAND OUTREACH CENTER
MY WIFE CALLED ME A WEENIE TODAY. SHE SAID EVEN CERTAIN FISH CAN FLY...
LET GO, GEORGE. CONFRONT YOUR FEELINGS...
SPEAKING OF FEELINGS, DARNED IF I DON'T FEEL LIKE A BOEING 747!!
SHE SAID I MIGHT AS WELL HAVE BEEN BORN A SCHNAUZER! ...A SCHNAUZER!!
ALYSON... YOU'RE NOT A 747... YOU CAN'T FLY... YOU'RE A LITTLE FATIGUED...
I HAVE STRESS CRACKS IN MY OUTER SKIN?!
I THINK SHE'S SEEING AN ALBATROSS... WITH HUGE WINGS...
CLEARED FOR TAKEOFF!
EVERYBODY CONFRONT THEIR FEELINGS!
CRUISING ALTITUDE!!
I SHOULD'VE BEEN A SCHNAUZER...
BOY, WE'VE MADE REAL PROGRESS THIS WEEK!
KNOCK! KNOCK!
I WANT A MILK BONE.
VVROOOOOM!!
YES?
IS THIS "COCKROACH CROSS-DRESSERS IN CRISIS"?
12

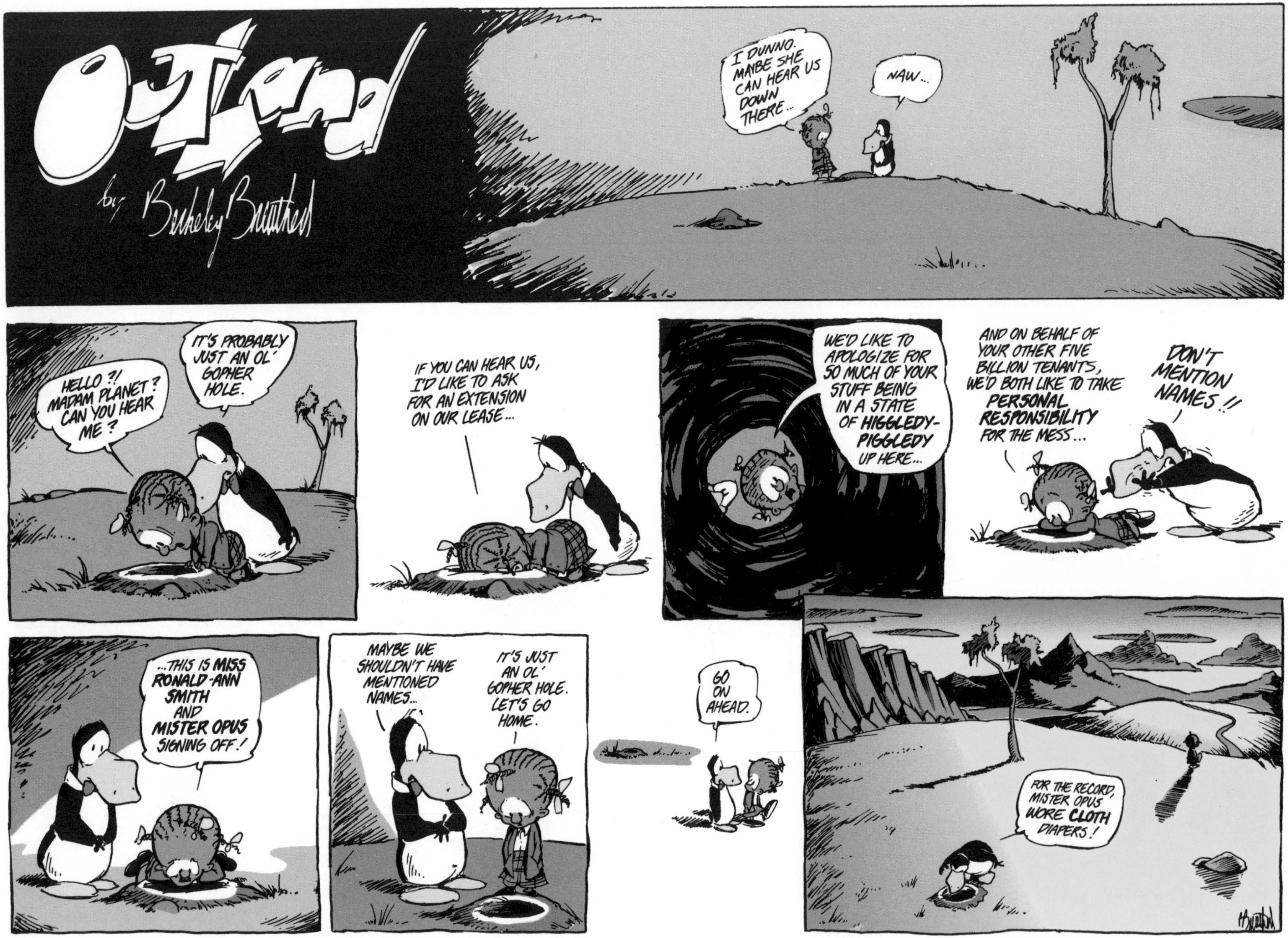

Outland
by Berkeley Breathed
I DUNNO. MAYBE SHE CAN HEAR US DOWN THERE...
NAW...
HELLO ?! MADAM PLANET? CAN YOU HEAR ME ?
IT'S PROBABLY JUST AN OL' GOPHER HOLE.
IF YOU CAN HEAR US, I'D LIKE TO ASK FOR AN EXTENSION ON OUR LEASE...
WE'D LIKE TO APOLOGIZE FOR SO MUCH OF YOUR STUFF BEING IN A STATE OF HIGGLEDY-PIGGLEDY UP HERE...
AND ON BEHALF OF YOUR OTHER FIVE BILLION TENANTS, WE'D BOTH LIKE TO TAKE PERSONAL RESPONSIBILITY FOR THE MESS...
DON'T MENTION NAMES !!
...THIS IS MISS RONALD-ANN SMITH AND MISTER OPUS SIGNING OFF !
MAYBE WE SHOULDN'T HAVE MENTIONED NAMES...
IT'S JUST AN OL' GOPHER HOLE. LET'S GO HOME.
GO ON AHEAD.
FOR THE RECORD, MISTER OPUS WORE CLOTH DIAPERS !

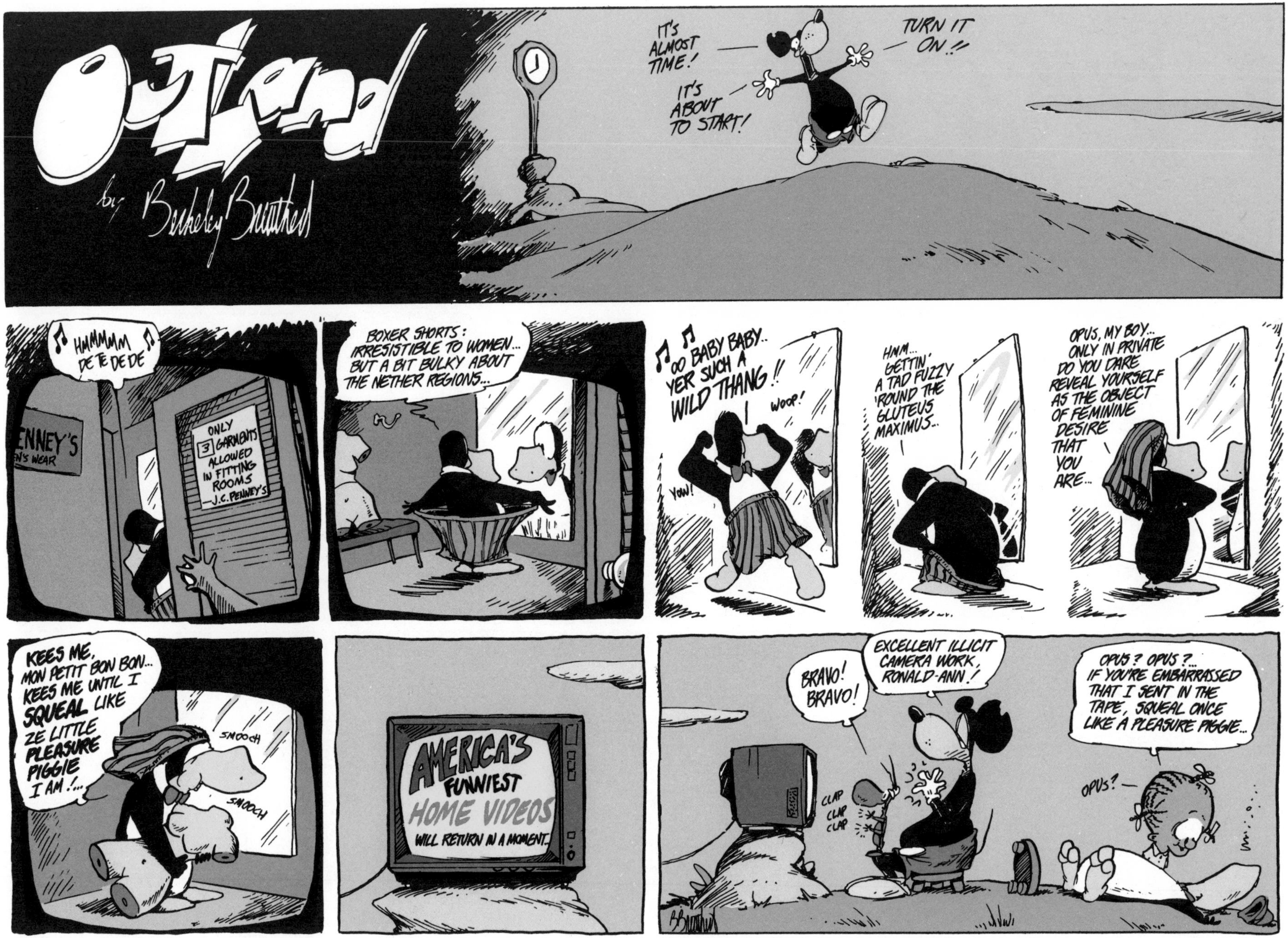

Outland
by Berkeley Breathed
IT'S ALMOST TIME!
IT'S ABOUT TO START!
TURN IT ON!!
♫ HMMMMM DE TE DE DE ♫
ENNEY'S
N'S WEAR
ONLY 3 GARMENTS ALLOWED IN FITTING ROOMS —J.C. PENNEY'S
BOXER SHORTS: IRRESISTIBLE TO WOMEN... BUT A BIT BULKY ABOUT THE NETHER REGIONS...
♫ ♫ OO BABY BABY.. YER SUCH A WILD THANG!!
WOOP!
YOW!
HMM... GETTIN' A TAD FUZZY 'ROUND THE GLUTEUS MAXIMUS..
OPUS, MY BOY... ONLY IN PRIVATE DO YOU DARE REVEAL YOURSELF AS THE OBJECT OF FEMININE DESIRE THAT YOU ARE...
KEES ME, MON PETIT BON BON... KEES ME UNTIL I SQUEAL LIKE ZE LITTLE PLEASURE PIGGIE I AM!...
SMOOCH
SMOOCH
AMERICA'S FUNNIEST HOME VIDEOS WILL RETURN IN A MOMENT.
BRAVO! BRAVO!
EXCELLENT ILLICIT CAMERA WORK, RONALD-ANN!
CLAP CLAP CLAP
OPUS? OPUS?... IF YOU'RE EMBARRASSED THAT I SENT IN THE TAPE, SQUEAL ONCE LIKE A PLEASURE PIGGIE...
OPUS?

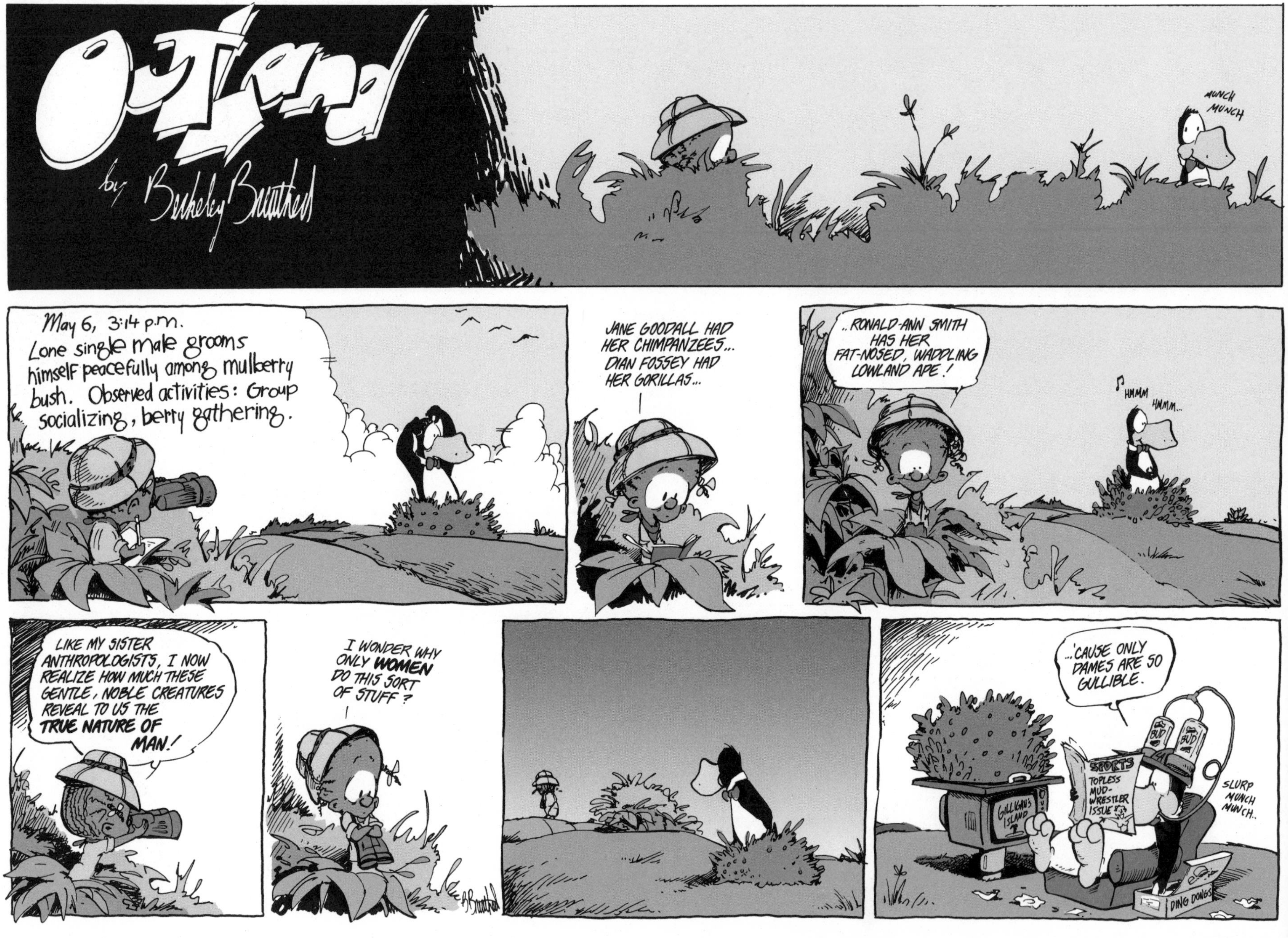

Outland
by Berkeley Breathed
MUNCH MUNCH
May 6, 3:14 p.m. Lone single male grooms himself peacefully among mulberry bush. Observed activities: Group socializing, berry gathering.
JANE GOODALL HAD HER CHIMPANZEES... DIAN FOSSEY HAD HER GORILLAS...
..RONALD-ANN SMITH HAS HER FAT-NOSED, WADDLING LOWLAND APE!
HMMM HMMM...
LIKE MY SISTER ANTHROPOLOGISTS, I NOW REALIZE HOW MUCH THESE GENTLE, NOBLE CREATURES REVEAL TO US THE TRUE NATURE OF MAN!
I WONDER WHY ONLY WOMEN DO THIS SORT OF STUFF?
..'CAUSE ONLY DAMES ARE SO GULLIBLE.
SPORTS
TOPLESS MUD-WRESTLER ISSUE
GILLIGAN'S ISLAND
BUD
BUD
DING DONGS
SLURP MUNCH MUNCH..

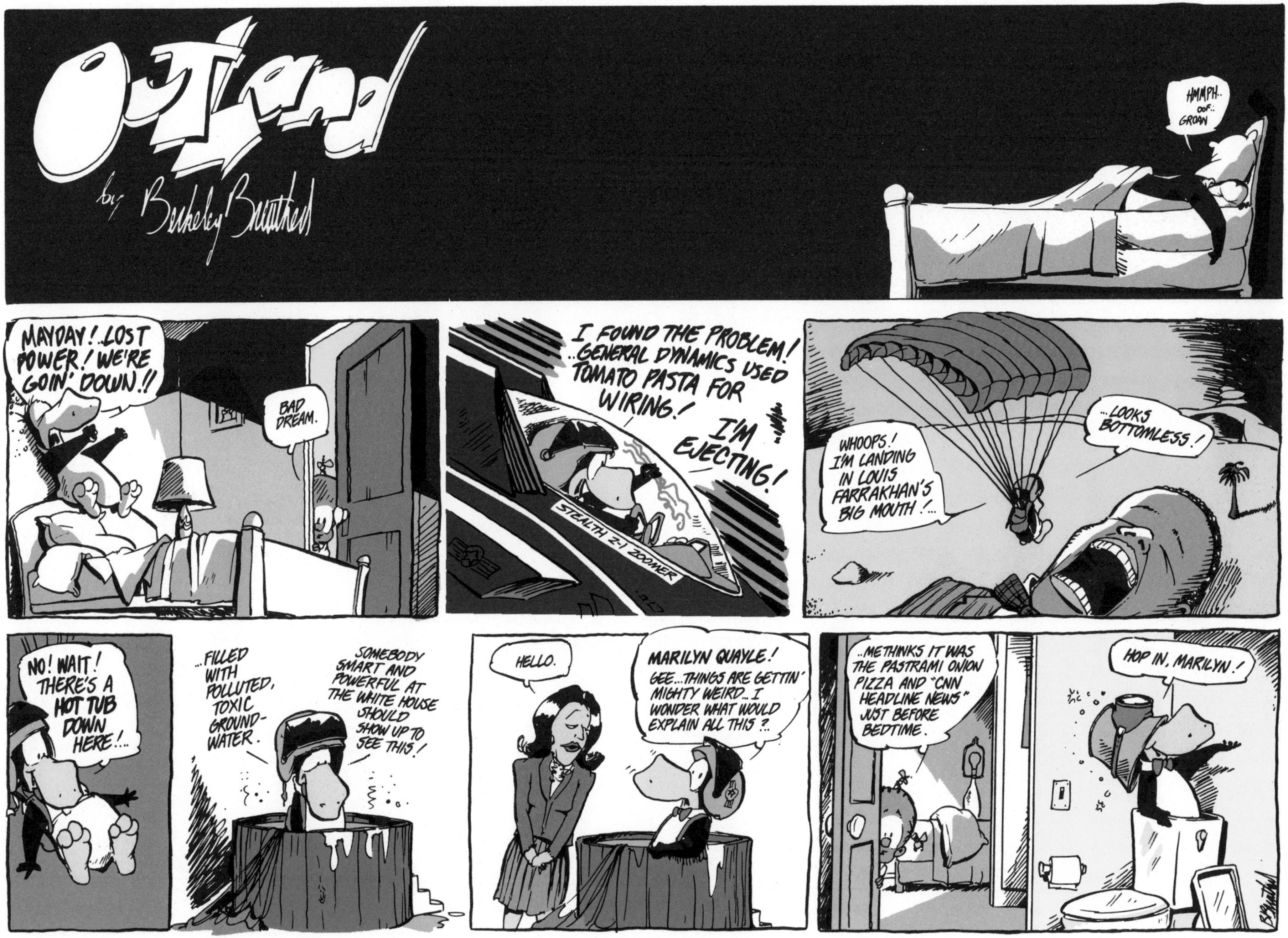
Outland
by Berkeley Breathed
HMMPH.. OOF.. GROAN
MAYDAY! ..LOST POWER! WE'RE GOIN' DOWN!!
BAD DREAM.
I FOUND THE PROBLEM! ..GENERAL DYNAMICS USED TOMATO PASTA FOR WIRING!
I'M EJECTING!
STEALTH Z-1 ZOOMER
WHOOPS! I'M LANDING IN LOUIS FARRAKHAN'S BIG MOUTH!...
...LOOKS BOTTOMLESS!
NO! WAIT! THERE'S A HOT TUB DOWN HERE!...
...FILLED WITH POLLUTED, TOXIC GROUND-WATER.
SOMEBODY SMART AND POWERFUL AT THE WHITE HOUSE SHOULD SHOW UP TO SEE THIS!
HELLO.
MARILYN QUAYLE!
GEE...THINGS ARE GETTIN' MIGHTY WEIRD... I WONDER WHAT WOULD EXPLAIN ALL THIS?
..METHINKS IT WAS THE PASTRAMI ONION PIZZA AND "CNN HEADLINE NEWS" JUST BEFORE BEDTIME.
HOP IN, MARILYN!
BBreathed

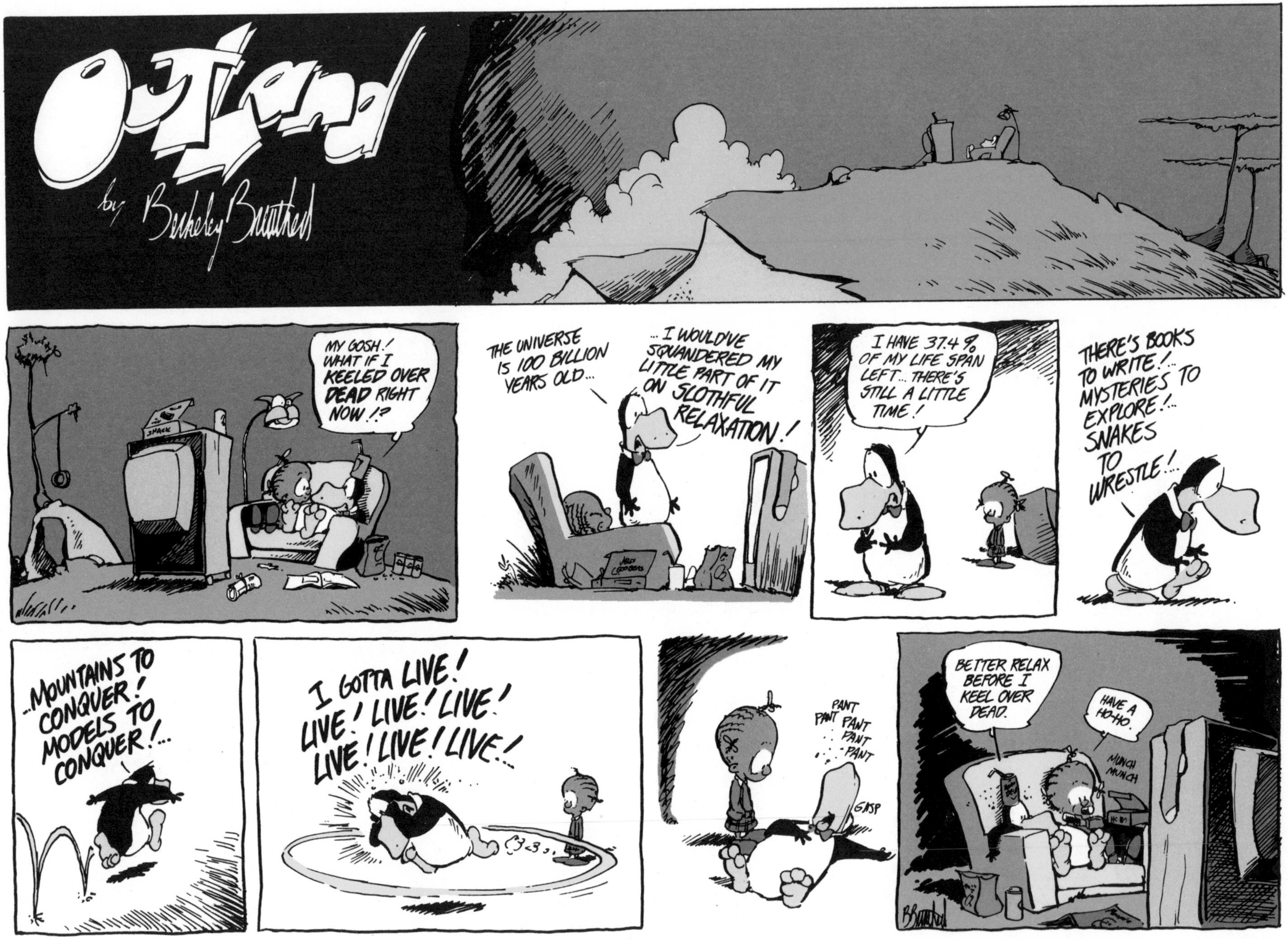

Outland
by Berkeley Breathed
MY GOSH! WHAT IF I KEELED OVER DEAD RIGHT NOW!?
THE UNIVERSE IS 100 BILLION YEARS OLD...
...I WOULD'VE SQUANDERED MY LITTLE PART OF IT ON SLOTHFUL RELAXATION!
I HAVE 37.4% OF MY LIFE SPAN LEFT... THERE'S STILL A LITTLE TIME!
THERE'S BOOKS TO WRITE!... MYSTERIES TO EXPLORE!... SNAKES TO WRESTLE!...
...MOUNTAINS TO CONQUER! MODELS TO CONQUER!...
I GOTTA LIVE! LIVE! LIVE! LIVE! LIVE! LIVE! LIVE!
PANT PANT PANT PANT PANT
GASP
BETTER RELAX BEFORE I KEEL OVER DEAD.
HAVE A HO-HO.
MUNCH MUNCH

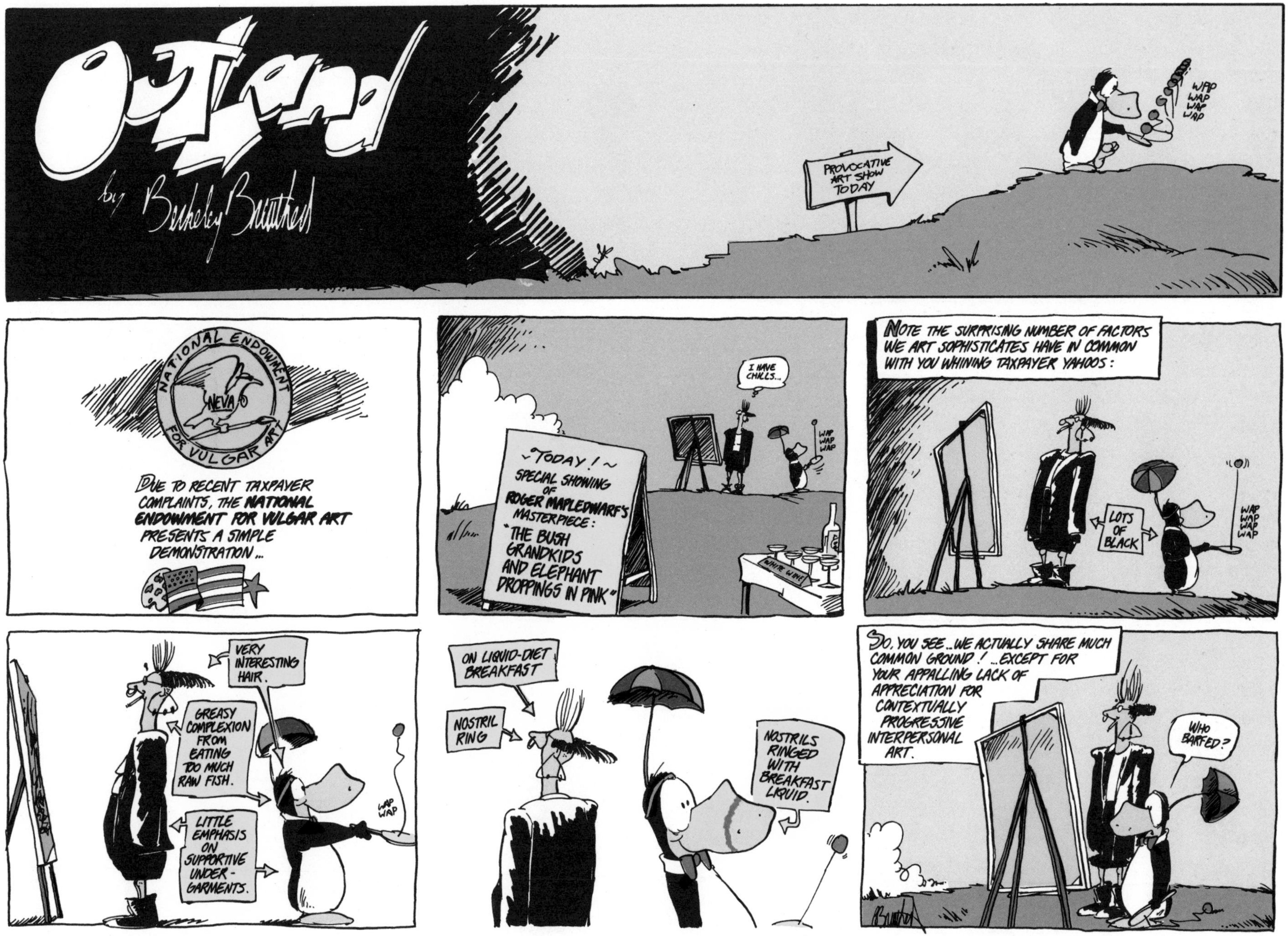

Outland
by Berkeley Breathed
PROVOCATIVE ART SHOW TODAY
WAP WAP WAP WAP
NATIONAL ENDOWMENT FOR VULGAR ART
NEVA
DUE TO RECENT TAXPAYER COMPLAINTS, THE NATIONAL ENDOWMENT FOR VULGAR ART PRESENTS A SIMPLE DEMONSTRATION...
I HAVE CHILLS...
WAP WAP WAP
~TODAY!~ SPECIAL SHOWING OF ROGER MAPLEDWARF'S MASTERPIECE: "THE BUSH GRANDKIDS AND ELEPHANT DROPPINGS IN PINK"
WHITE WINE
NOTE THE SURPRISING NUMBER OF FACTORS WE ART SOPHISTICATES HAVE IN COMMON WITH YOU WHINING TAXPAYER YAHOOS:
LOTS OF BLACK
WAP WAP WAP WAP
VERY INTERESTING HAIR.
GREASY COMPLEXION FROM EATING TOO MUCH RAW FISH.
LITTLE EMPHASIS ON SUPPORTIVE UNDER-GARMENTS.
WAP WAP
ON LIQUID-DIET BREAKFAST
NOSTRIL RING
NOSTRILS RINGED WITH BREAKFAST LIQUID.
SO, YOU SEE...WE ACTUALLY SHARE MUCH COMMON GROUND! ...EXCEPT FOR YOUR APPALLING LACK OF APPRECIATION FOR CONTEXTUALLY PROGRESSIVE INTERPERSONAL ART.
WHO BARFED?

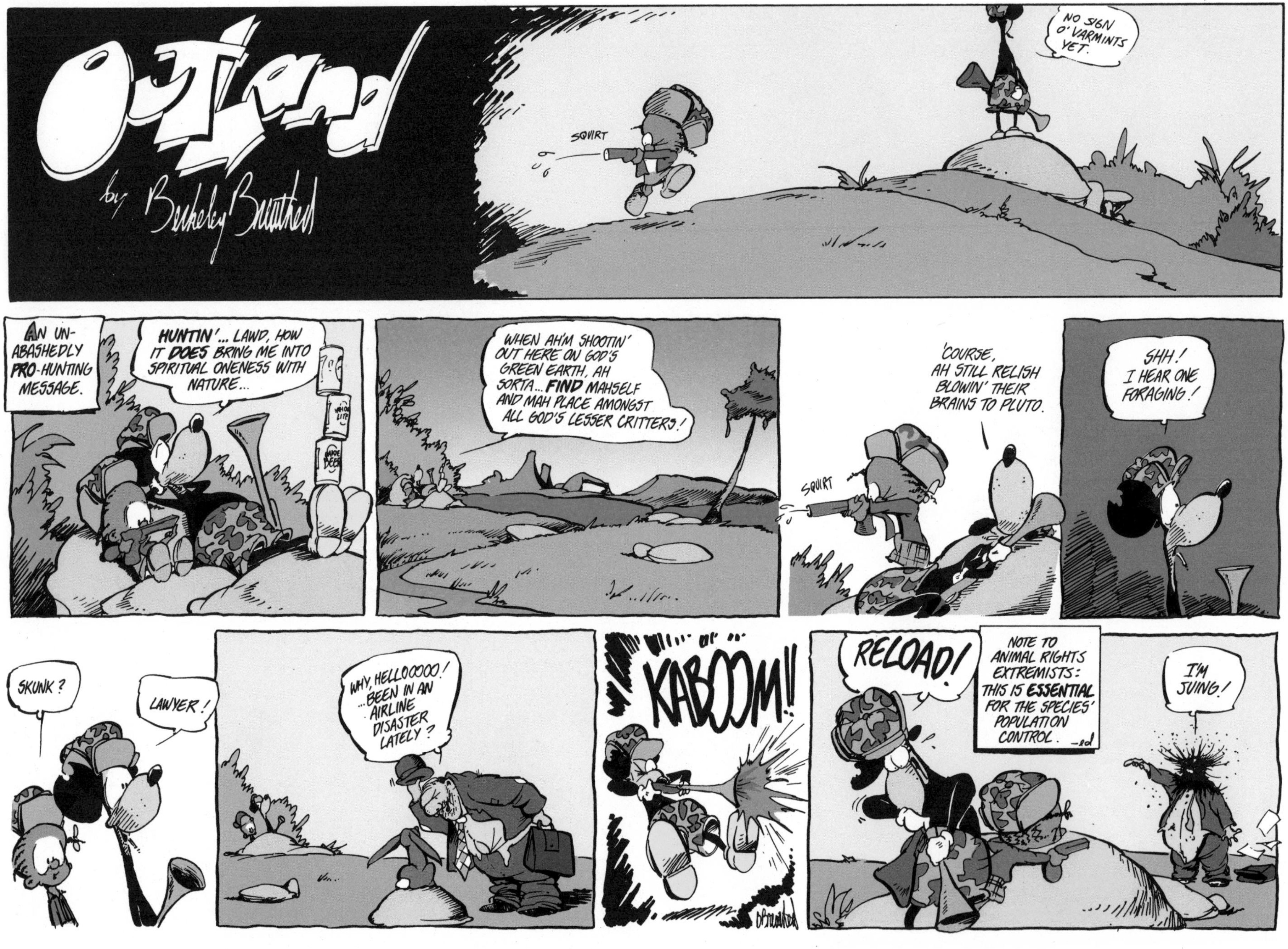
Outland
by Berkeley Breathed
SQUIRT
NO SIGN O' VARMINTS YET.
AN UN-ABASHEDLY PRO-HUNTING MESSAGE.
HUNTIN'... LAWD, HOW IT DOES BRING ME INTO SPIRITUAL ONENESS WITH NATURE...
WHEN AH'M SHOOTIN' OUT HERE ON GOD'S GREEN EARTH, AH SORTA... FIND MAHSELF AND MAH PLACE AMONGST ALL GOD'S LESSER CRITTERS!
SQUIRT
'COURSE, AH STILL RELISH BLOWIN' THEIR BRAINS TO PLUTO.
SHH! I HEAR ONE FORAGING!
SKUNK?
LAWYER!
WHY, HELLOOOOO! ...BEEN IN AN AIRLINE DISASTER LATELY?
KABOOM!!
RELOAD!
NOTE TO ANIMAL RIGHTS EXTREMISTS: THIS IS ESSENTIAL FOR THE SPECIES' POPULATION CONTROL. —ed
I'M JUING!

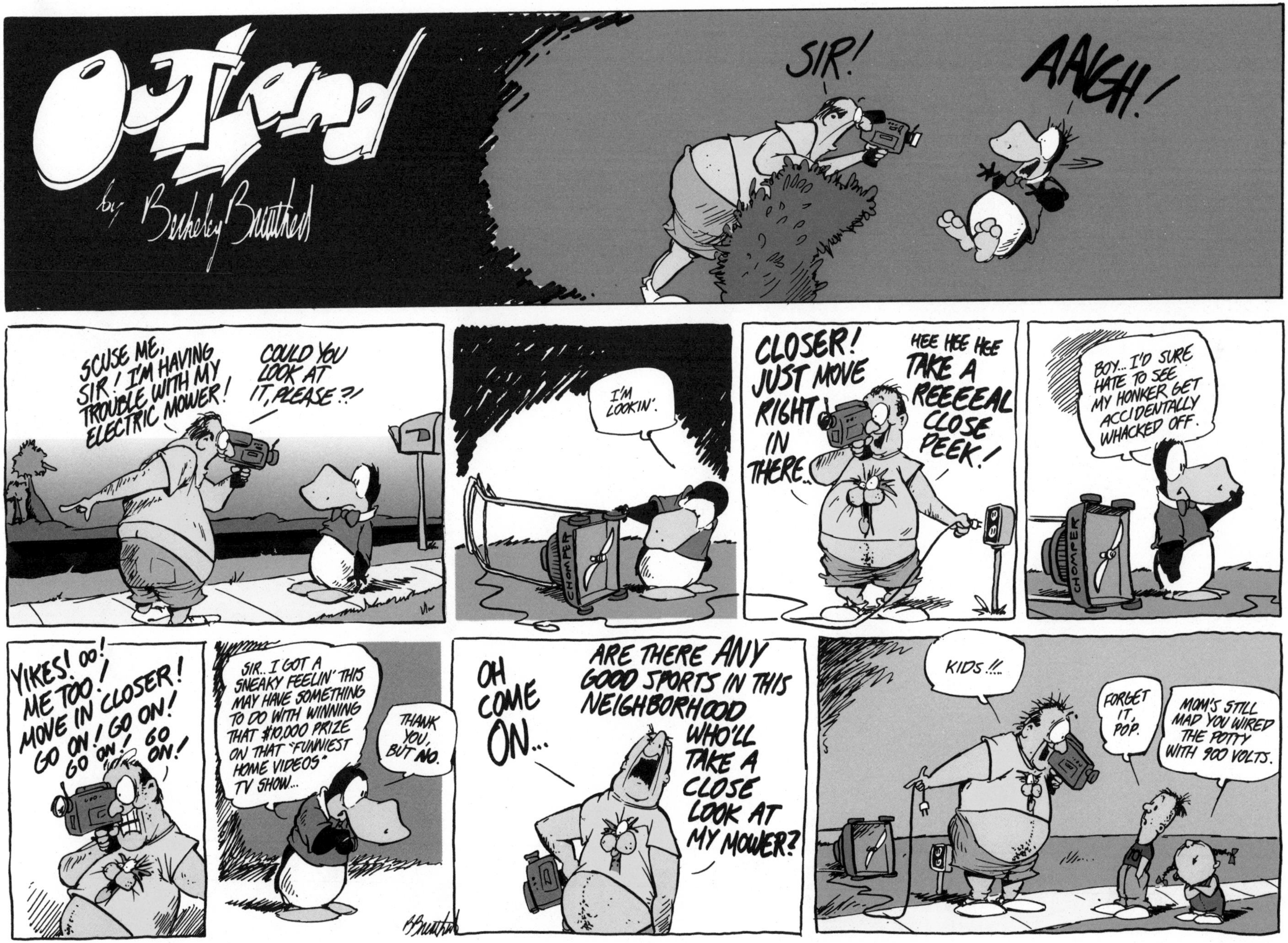
Outland
by Berkeley Breathed
SIR!
AAGH!
SCUSE ME, SIR! I'M HAVING TROUBLE WITH MY ELECTRIC MOWER!
COULD YOU LOOK AT IT, PLEASE ?!
I'M LOOKIN'.
CHOMPER
CLOSER! JUST MOVE RIGHT IN THERE..
HEE HEE HEE
TAKE A REEEEAL CLOSE PEEK!
BOY... I'D SURE HATE TO SEE MY HONKER GET ACCIDENTALLY WHACKED OFF.
CHOMPER
YIKES! OO! ME TOO! MOVE IN CLOSER! GO ON! GO ON! GO ON! GO ON!
SIR.. I GOT A SNEAKY FEELIN' THIS MAY HAVE SOMETHING TO DO WITH WINNING THAT $10,000 PRIZE ON THAT "FUNNIEST HOME VIDEOS" TV SHOW...
THANK YOU, BUT NO.
OH COME ON...
ARE THERE ANY GOOD SPORTS IN THIS NEIGHBORHOOD WHO'LL TAKE A CLOSE LOOK AT MY MOWER?
KIDS!!!
FORGET IT, POP.
MOM'S STILL MAD YOU WIRED THE POTTY WITH 900 VOLTS.

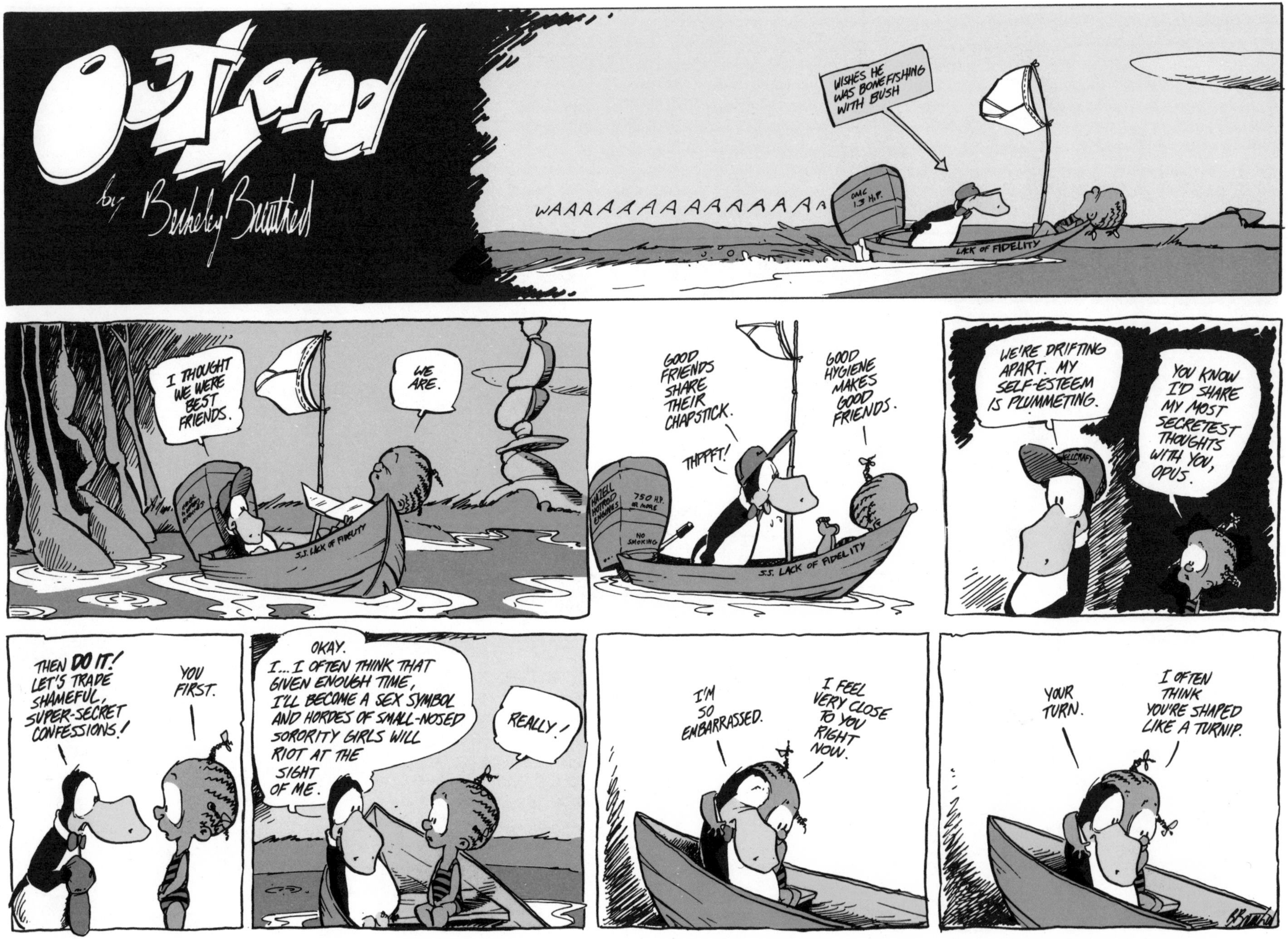
Outland
by Berkeley Breathed
WISHES HE WAS BONEFISHING WITH BUSH
WAAAAAAAAAAAAAAA
OMC 1.3 H.P.
LACK OF FIDELITY
I THOUGHT WE WERE BEST FRIENDS.
WE ARE.
S.S. LACK OF FIDELITY
GOOD FRIENDS SHARE THEIR CHAPSTICK.
GOOD HYGIENE MAKES GOOD FRIENDS.
THPPFT!
HAZELL HOTROD ENGINES
750 H.P. OR MORE
NO SMOKING
S.S. LACK OF FIDELITY
WE'RE DRIFTING APART. MY SELF-ESTEEM IS PLUMMETING.
YOU KNOW I'D SHARE MY MOST SECRETEST THOUGHTS WITH YOU, OPUS.
THEN DO IT! LET'S TRADE SHAMEFUL, SUPER-SECRET CONFESSIONS!
YOU FIRST.
OKAY. I... I OFTEN THINK THAT GIVEN ENOUGH TIME, I'LL BECOME A SEX SYMBOL AND HORDES OF SMALL-NOSED SORORITY GIRLS WILL RIOT AT THE SIGHT OF ME.
REALLY!
I'M SO EMBARRASSED.
I FEEL VERY CLOSE TO YOU RIGHT NOW.
YOUR TURN.
I OFTEN THINK YOU'RE SHAPED LIKE A TURNIP.

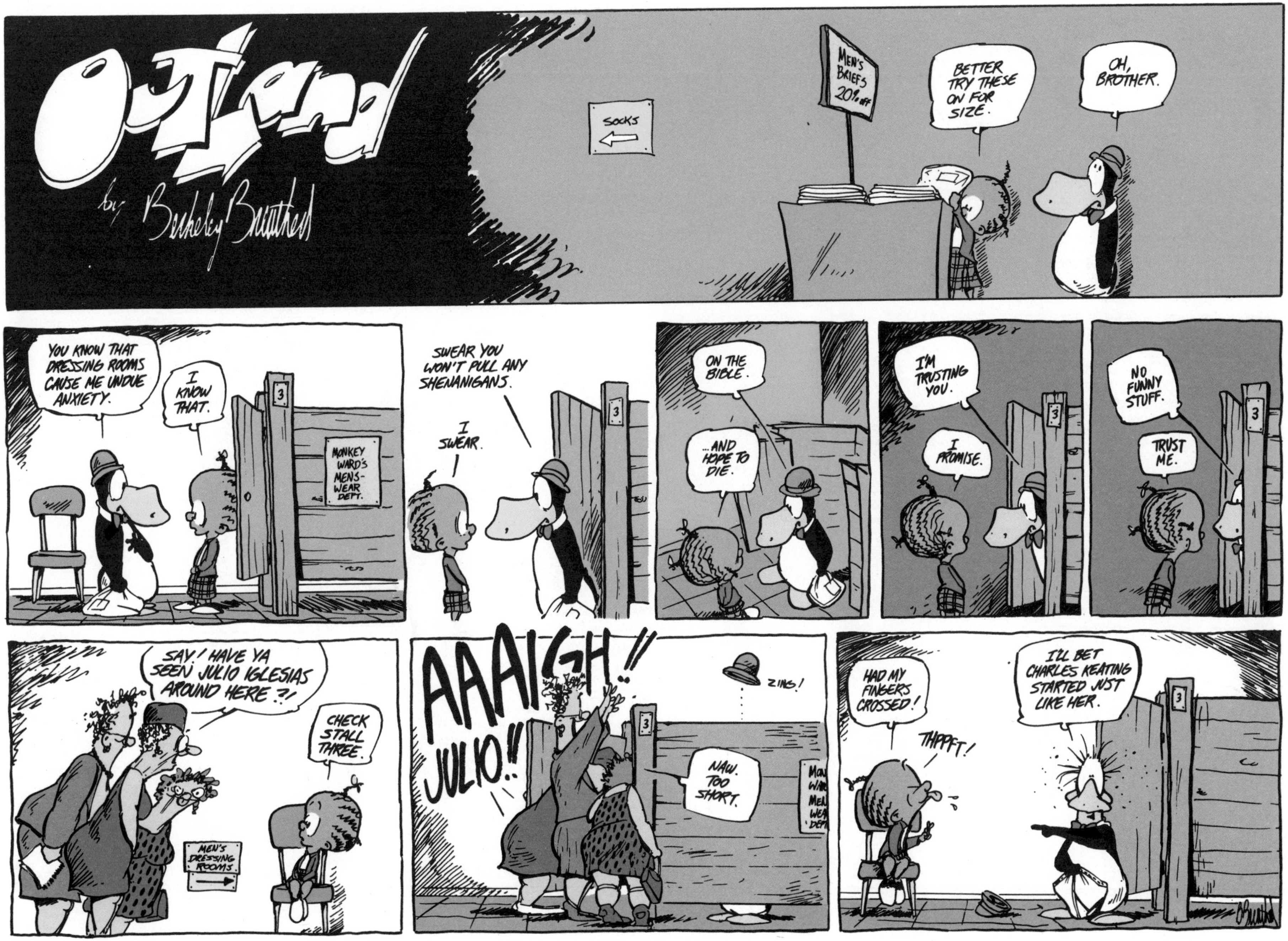

Outland
by Berkeley Breathed
SOCKS
MEN'S BRIEFS 20% OFF
BETTER TRY THESE ON FOR SIZE.
OH, BROTHER.
YOU KNOW THAT DRESSING ROOMS CAUSE ME UNDUE ANXIETY.
I KNOW THAT.
MONKEY WARD'S MENS-WEAR DEPT.
SWEAR YOU WON'T PULL ANY SHENANIGANS.
I SWEAR.
ON THE BIBLE.
...AND HOPE TO DIE.
I'M TRUSTING YOU.
I PROMISE.
NO FUNNY STUFF.
TRUST ME.
SAY! HAVE YA SEEN JULIO IGLESIAS AROUND HERE ?!
CHECK STALL THREE.
MEN'S DRESSING ROOMS
AAAIGH!! JULIO!!
ZING!
NAW. TOO SHORT.
HAD MY FINGERS CROSSED!
THPPFT!
I'LL BET CHARLES KEATING STARTED JUST LIKE HER.

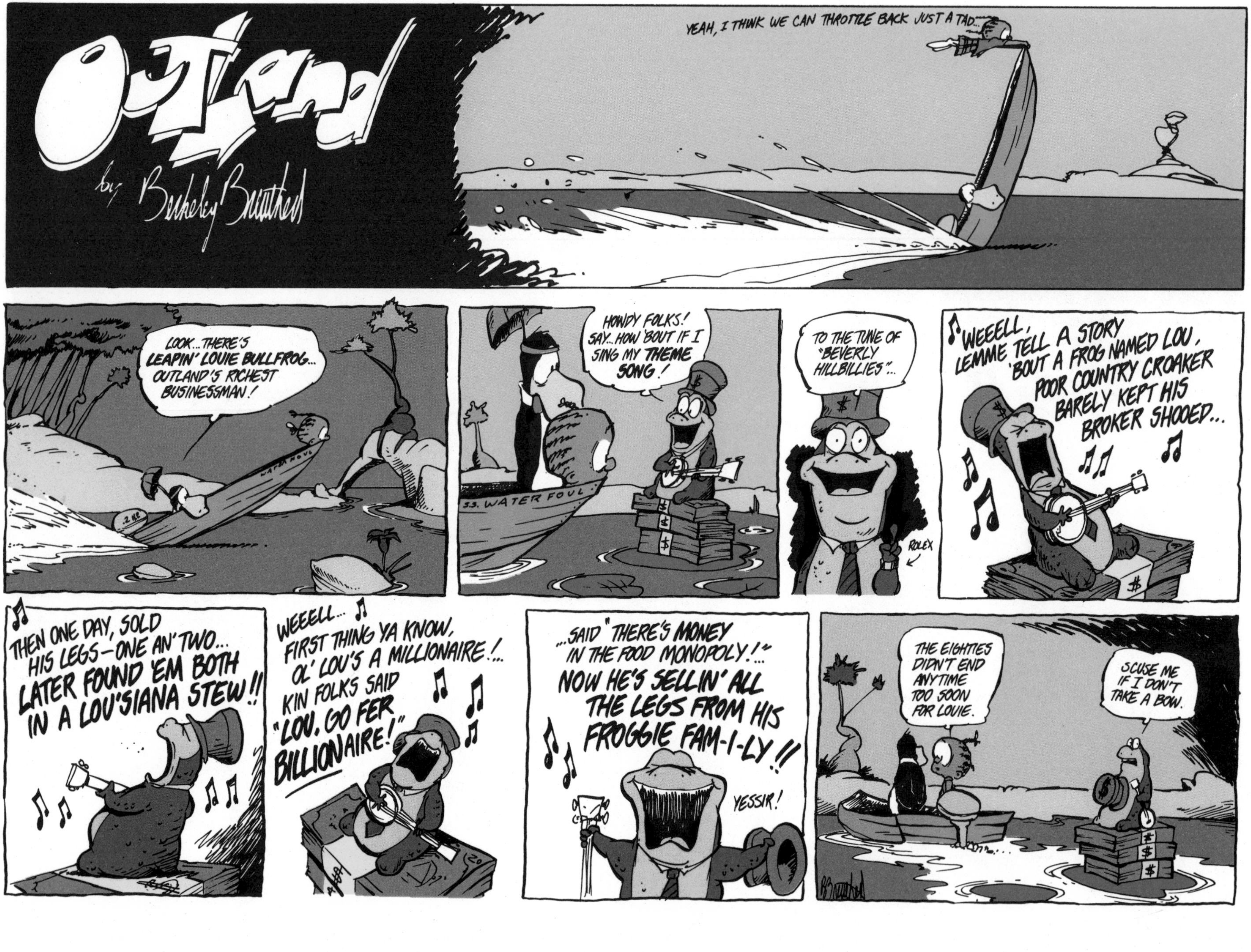
Outland
by Berkeley Breathed
YEAH, I THINK WE CAN THROTTLE BACK JUST A TAD...
LOOK... THERE'S LEAPIN' LOUIE BULLFROG... OUTLAND'S RICHEST BUSINESSMAN!
WATER FOWL
HOWDY FOLKS! SAY... HOW 'BOUT IF I SING MY THEME SONG!
S.S. WATER FOUL
TO THE TUNE OF "BEVERLY HILLBILLIES"...
ROLEX
WEEELL, LEMME TELL A STORY 'BOUT A FROG NAMED LOU, POOR COUNTRY CROAKER BARELY KEPT HIS BROKER SHOOED...
THEN ONE DAY, SOLD HIS LEGS—ONE AN' TWO... LATER FOUND 'EM BOTH IN A LOU'SIANA STEW!!
WEEELL... FIRST THING YA KNOW, OL' LOU'S A MILLIONAIRE!... KIN FOLKS SAID "LOU, GO FER BILLIONAIRE!"
...SAID "THERE'S MONEY IN THE FOOD MONOPOLY!"... NOW HE'S SELLIN' ALL THE LEGS FROM HIS FROGGIE FAM-I-LY!!
YESSIR!
THE EIGHTIES DIDN'T END ANYTIME TOO SOON FOR LOUIE.
SCUSE ME IF I DON'T TAKE A BOW.

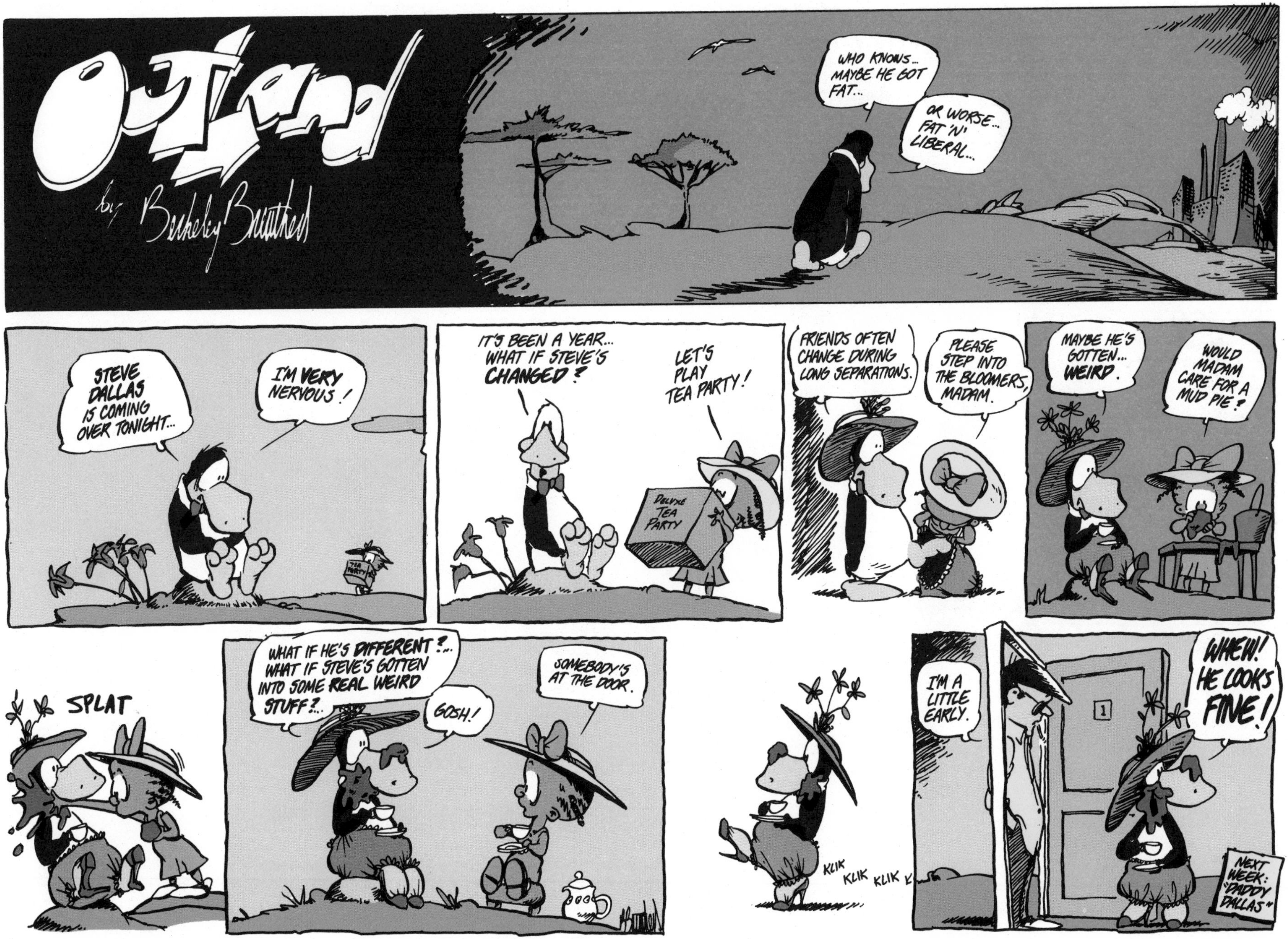

Outland
by Berkeley Breathed
WHO KNOWS... MAYBE HE GOT FAT...
OR WORSE... FAT 'N' LIBERAL...
STEVE DALLAS IS COMING OVER TONIGHT...
I'M VERY NERVOUS!
TEA PARTY
IT'S BEEN A YEAR... WHAT IF STEVE'S CHANGED?
LET'S PLAY TEA PARTY!
DELUXE TEA PARTY
FRIENDS OFTEN CHANGE DURING LONG SEPARATIONS.
PLEASE STEP INTO THE BLOOMERS, MADAM.
MAYBE HE'S GOTTEN... WEIRD.
WOULD MADAM CARE FOR A MUD PIE?
SPLAT
WHAT IF HE'S DIFFERENT?.. WHAT IF STEVE'S GOTTEN INTO SOME REAL WEIRD STUFF?..
GOSH!
SOMEBODY'S AT THE DOOR.
KLIK KLIK KLIK K
I'M A LITTLE EARLY.
1
WHEW! HE LOOKS FINE!
NEXT WEEK: "DADDY DALLAS"

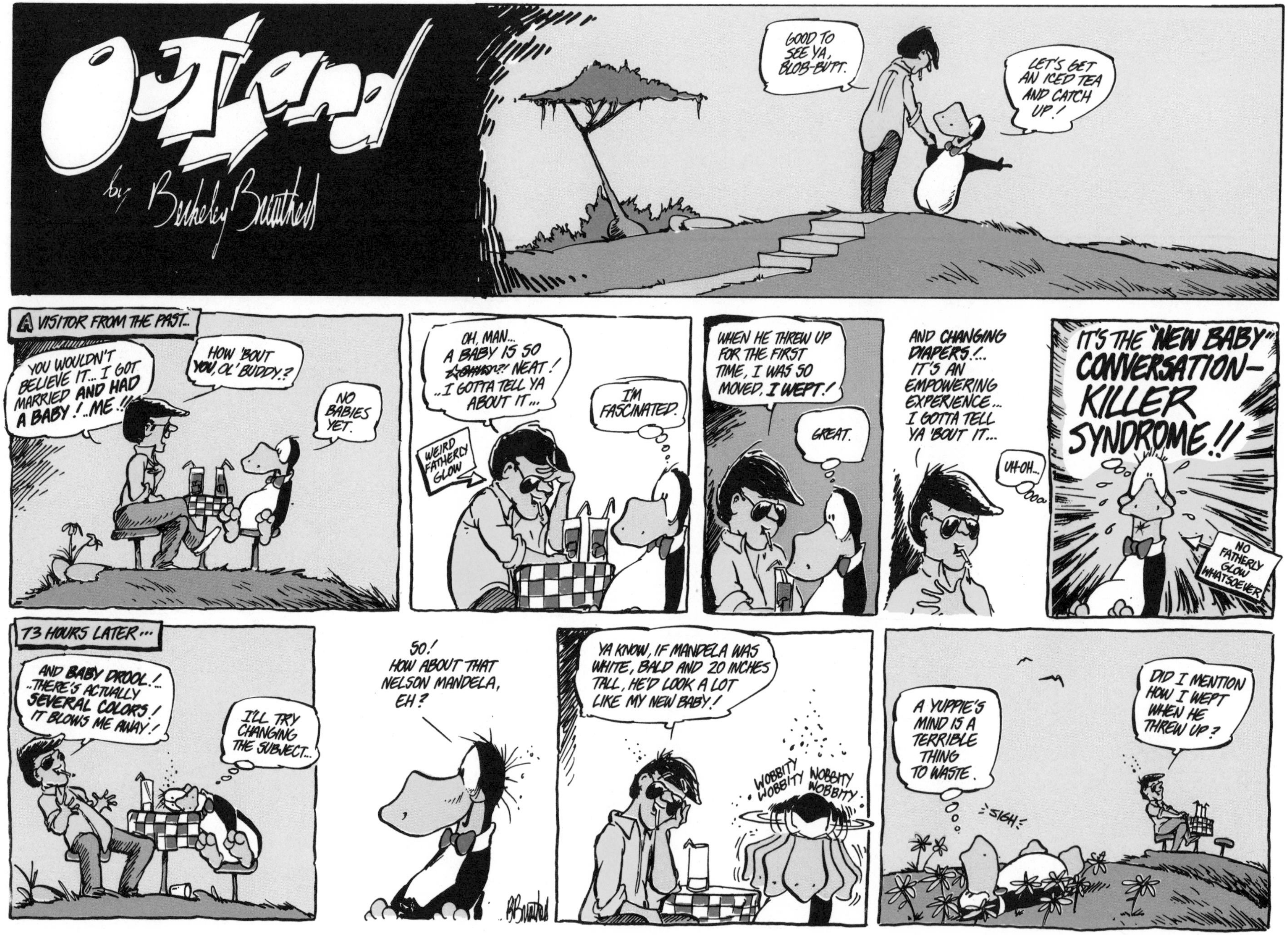
Outland
by Berkeley Breathed
GOOD TO SEE YA, BLOB-BUTT.
LET'S GET AN ICED TEA AND CATCH UP!
A VISITOR FROM THE PAST...
YOU WOULDN'T BELIEVE IT... I GOT MARRIED AND HAD A BABY!..ME!!
HOW 'BOUT YOU, OL' BUDDY..?
NO BABIES YET.
OH, MAN... A BABY IS SO NEAT! ..I GOTTA TELL YA ABOUT IT...
I'M FASCINATED.
WEIRD FATHERLY GLOW
WHEN HE THREW UP FOR THE FIRST TIME, I WAS SO MOVED, I WEPT!
GREAT.
AND CHANGING DIAPERS!... IT'S AN EMPOWERING EXPERIENCE... I GOTTA TELL YA 'BOUT IT...
UH-OH...
IT'S THE "NEW BABY" CONVERSATION-KILLER SYNDROME!!
NO FATHERLY GLOW WHATSOEVER
73 HOURS LATER...
AND BABY DROOL!.. ..THERE'S ACTUALLY SEVERAL COLORS! IT BLOWS ME AWAY!
I'LL TRY CHANGING THE SUBJECT...
SO! HOW ABOUT THAT NELSON MANDELA, EH?
YA KNOW, IF MANDELA WAS WHITE, BALD AND 20 INCHES TALL, HE'D LOOK A LOT LIKE MY NEW BABY!
WOBBITY WOBBITY NOBBITY WOBBITY
A YUPPIE'S MIND IS A TERRIBLE THING TO WASTE.
SIGH
DID I MENTION HOW I WEPT WHEN HE THREW UP?

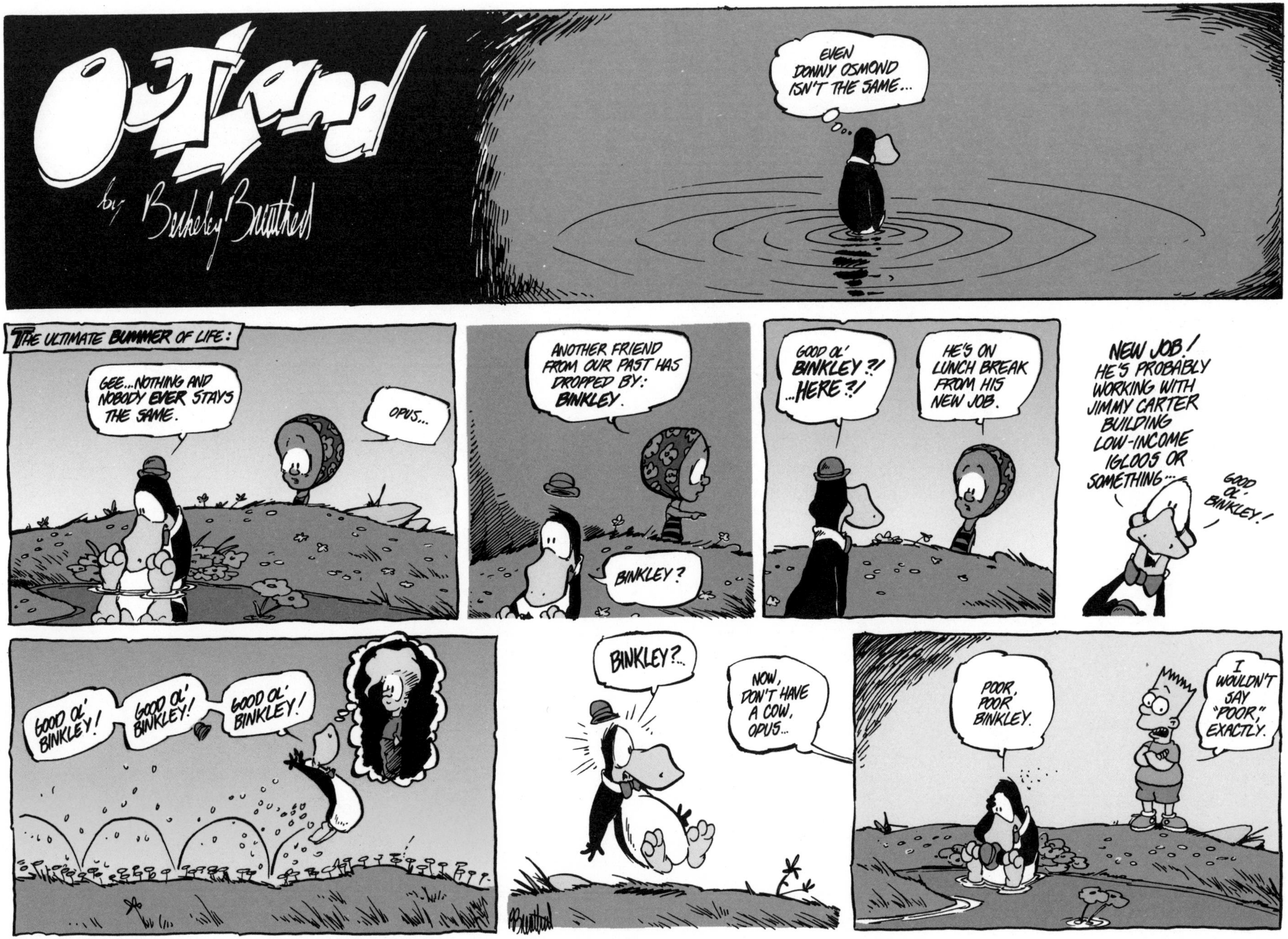

Outland
by Berkeley Breathed
EVEN DONNY OSMOND ISN'T THE SAME...
THE ULTIMATE BUMMER OF LIFE:
GEE...NOTHING AND NOBODY EVER STAYS THE SAME.
OPUS...
ANOTHER FRIEND FROM OUR PAST HAS DROPPED BY: BINKLEY.
BINKLEY?
GOOD OL' BINKLEY?! ...HERE?!
HE'S ON LUNCH BREAK FROM HIS NEW JOB.
NEW JOB! HE'S PROBABLY WORKING WITH JIMMY CARTER BUILDING LOW-INCOME IGLOOS OR SOMETHING...
GOOD OL' BINKLEY!
GOOD OL' BINKLEY!
GOOD OL' BINKLEY!
GOOD OL' BINKLEY!
BINKLEY?...
NOW, DON'T HAVE A COW, OPUS...
POOR, POOR BINKLEY.
I WOULDN'T SAY "POOR," EXACTLY.

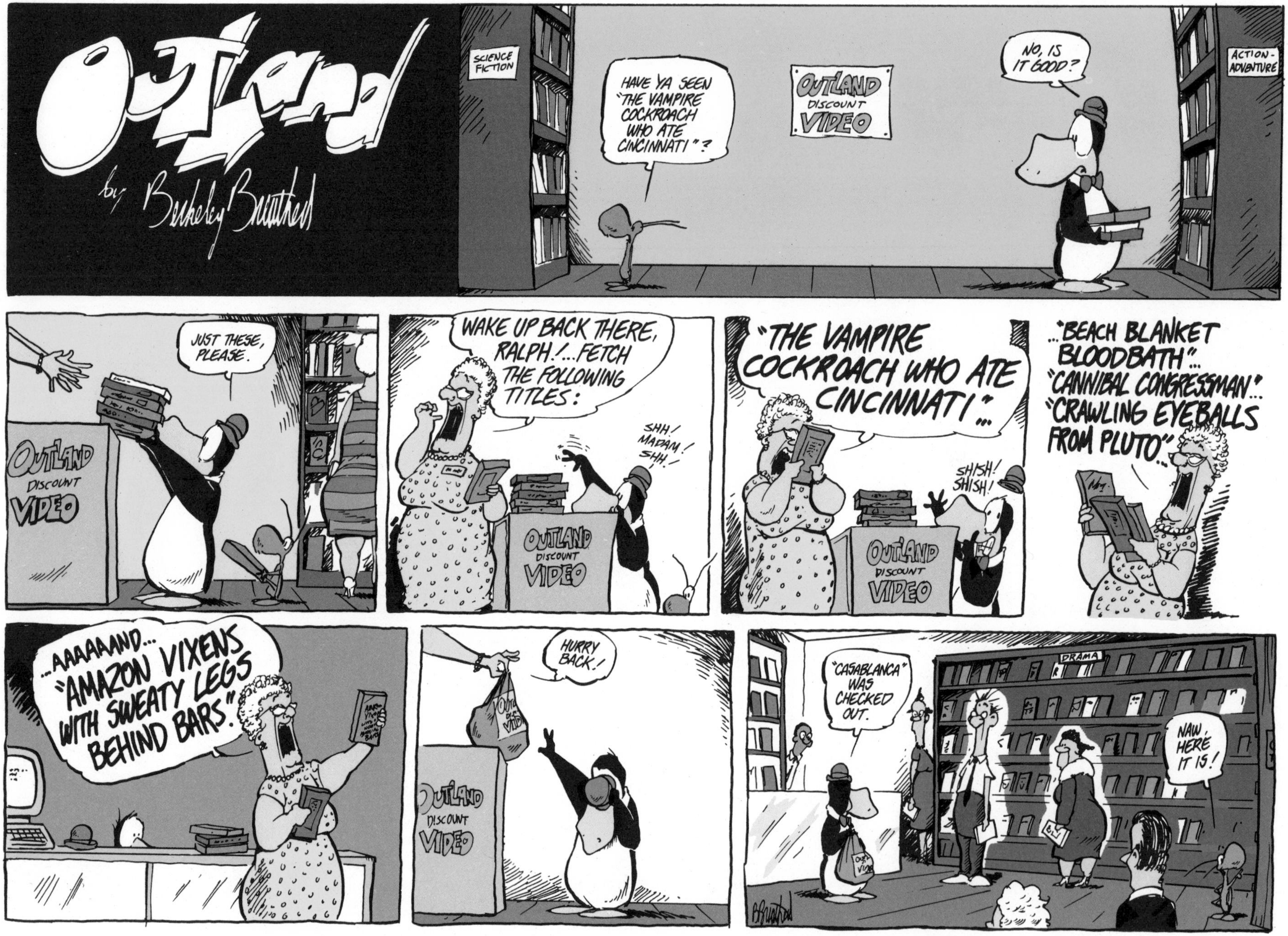

OUTLAND
by Berkeley Breathed
SCIENCE FICTION
HAVE YA SEEN "THE VAMPIRE COCKROACH WHO ATE CINCINNATI"?
OUTLAND DISCOUNT VIDEO
NO, IS IT GOOD?
ACTION-ADVENTURE
JUST THESE, PLEASE.
OUTLAND DISCOUNT VIDEO
WAKE UP BACK THERE, RALPH!...FETCH THE FOLLOWING TITLES:
SHH! MADAM! SHH!
OUTLAND DISCOUNT VIDEO
"THE VAMPIRE COCKROACH WHO ATE CINCINNATI"...
SHISH! SHISH!
OUTLAND DISCOUNT VIDEO
..."BEACH BLANKET BLOODBATH"... "CANNIBAL CONGRESSMAN"... "CRAWLING EYEBALLS FROM PLUTO"...
...AAAAAAND... "AMAZON VIXENS WITH SWEATY LEGS BEHIND BARS."
HURRY BACK!
OUTLAND DISCOUNT VIDEO
DRAMA
"CASABLANCA" WAS CHECKED OUT.
NAW, HERE IT IS!

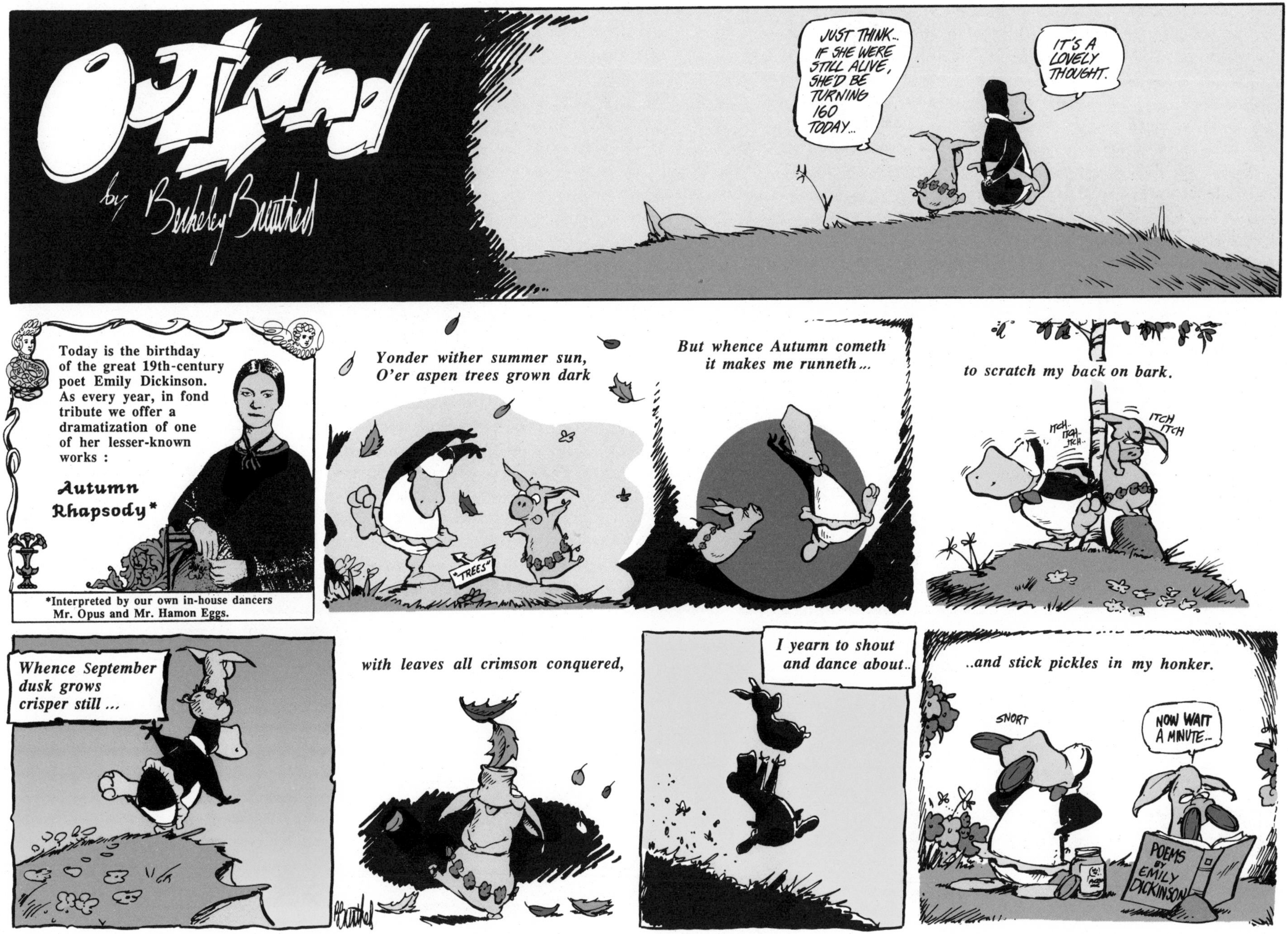
Outland
by Berkeley Breathed
JUST THINK.. IF SHE WERE STILL ALIVE, SHE'D BE TURNING 160 TODAY...
IT'S A LOVELY THOUGHT.
Today is the birthday of the great 19th-century poet Emily Dickinson. As every year, in fond tribute we offer a dramatization of one of her lesser-known works :
Autumn Rhapsody*
*Interpreted by our own in-house dancers Mr. Opus and Mr. Hamon Eggs.
Yonder wither summer sun, O'er aspen trees grown dark
"TREES"
But whence Autumn cometh it makes me runneth...
to scratch my back on bark.
ITCH.. ITCH.. ITCH..
ITCH ITCH
Whence September dusk grows crisper still ...
with leaves all crimson conquered,
I yearn to shout and dance about..
..and stick pickles in my honker.
SNORT
NOW WAIT A MINUTE..
POEMS BY EMILY DICKINSON

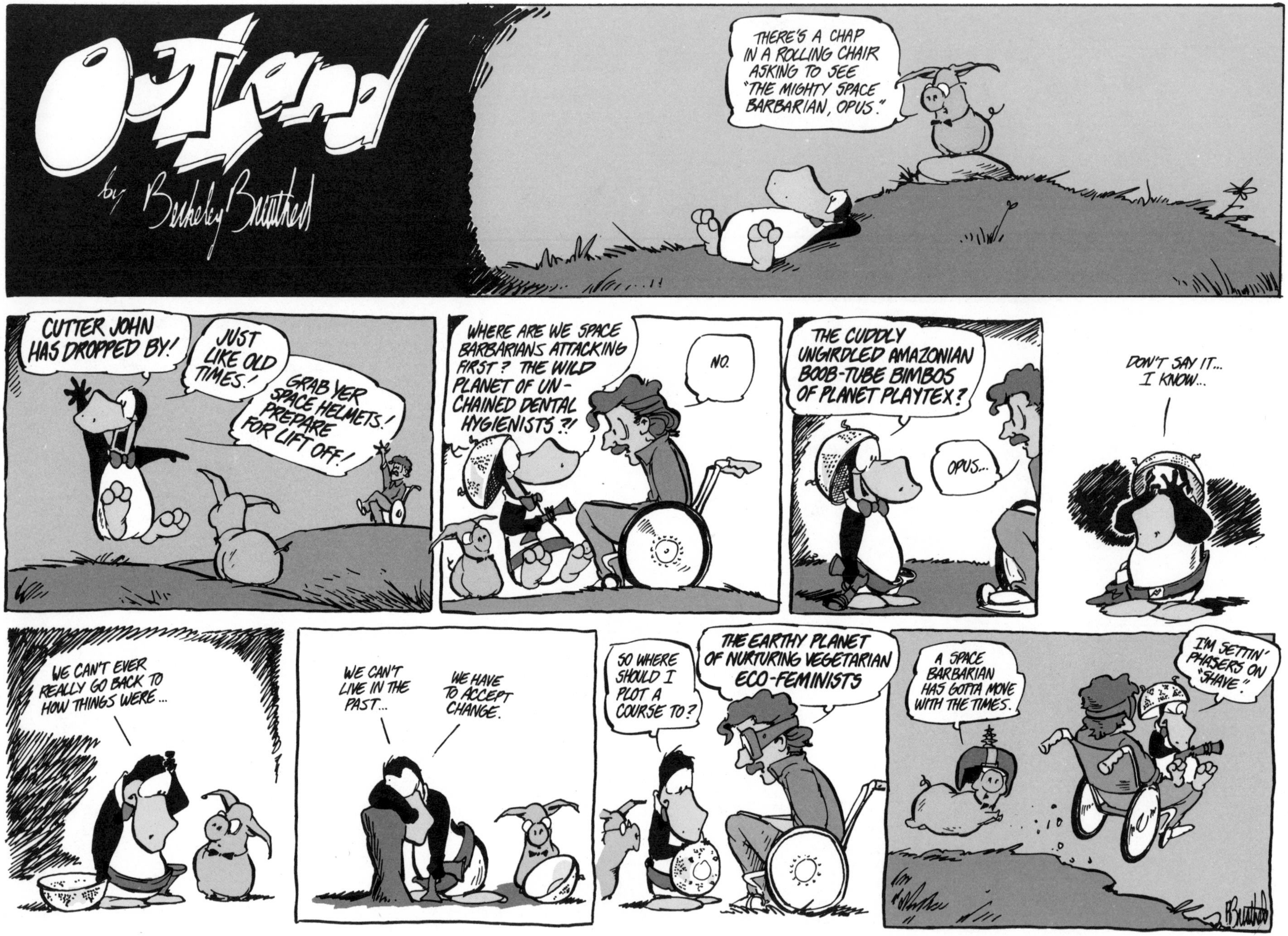
OUTLAND
by Berkeley Breathed
THERE'S A CHAP IN A ROLLING CHAIR ASKING TO SEE "THE MIGHTY SPACE BARBARIAN, OPUS."
CUTTER JOHN HAS DROPPED BY!
JUST LIKE OLD TIMES!
GRAB YER SPACE HELMETS! PREPARE FOR LIFT OFF!
WHERE ARE WE SPACE BARBARIANS ATTACKING FIRST? THE WILD PLANET OF UN-CHAINED DENTAL HYGIENISTS ?!
NO.
THE CUDDLY UNGIRDLED AMAZONIAN BOOB-TUBE BIMBOS OF PLANET PLAYTEX?
OPUS...
DON'T SAY IT... I KNOW...
WE CAN'T EVER REALLY GO BACK TO HOW THINGS WERE...
WE CAN'T LIVE IN THE PAST...
WE HAVE TO ACCEPT CHANGE.
SO WHERE SHOULD I PLOT A COURSE TO?
THE EARTHY PLANET OF NURTURING VEGETARIAN ECO-FEMINISTS
A SPACE BARBARIAN HAS GOTTA MOVE WITH THE TIMES.
I'M SETTIN' PHASERS ON "SHAVE."
B. Breathed

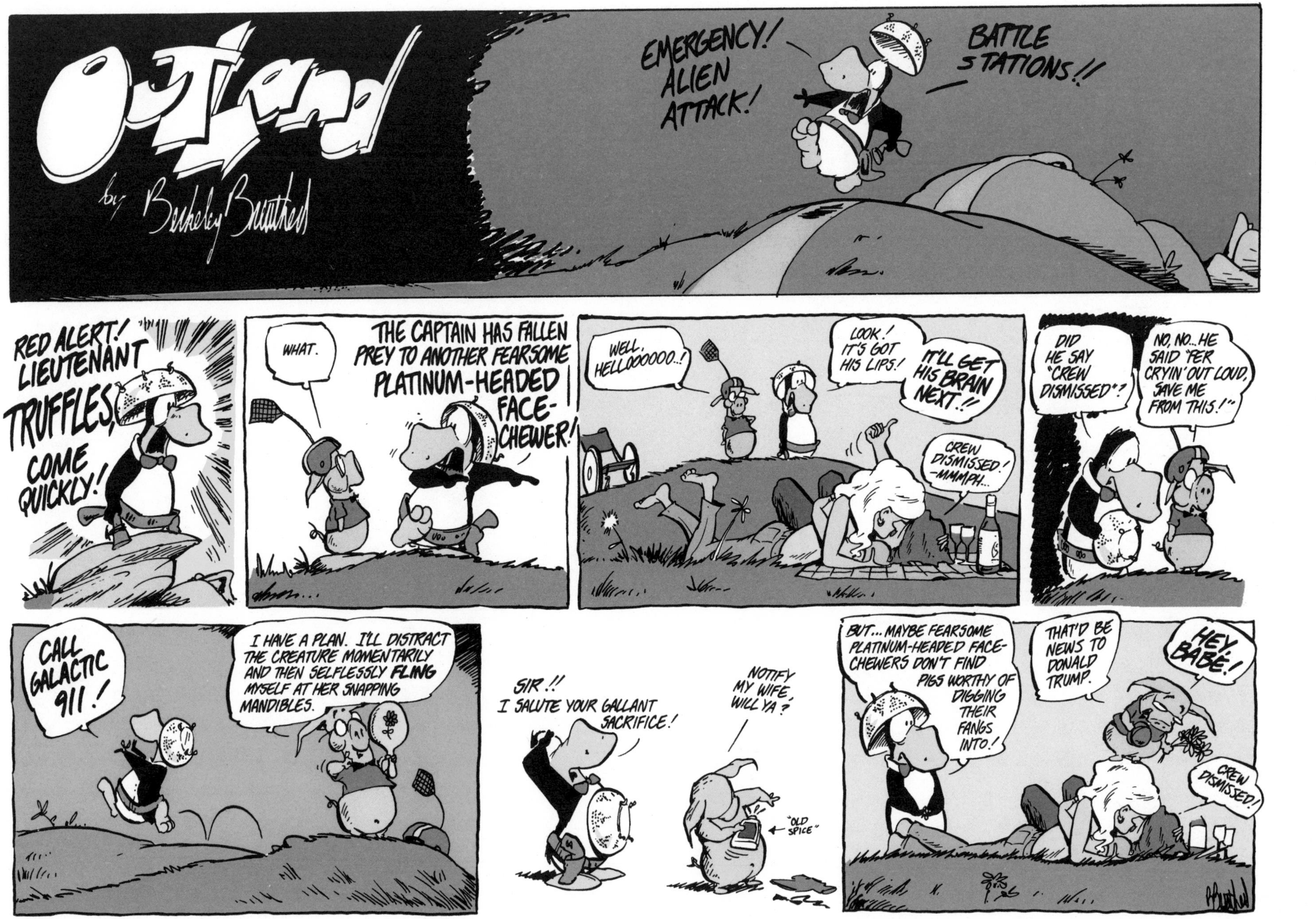
Outland
by Berkeley Breathed
EMERGENCY! ALIEN ATTACK!
BATTLE STATIONS!!
RED ALERT! LIEUTENANT TRUFFLES, COME QUICKLY!
WHAT.
THE CAPTAIN HAS FALLEN PREY TO ANOTHER FEARSOME PLATINUM-HEADED FACE-CHEWER!
WELL, HELLOOOOOO..!
LOOK! IT'S GOT HIS LIPS!
IT'LL GET HIS BRAIN NEXT!!
CREW DISMISSED! -MMMPH...
DID HE SAY "CREW DISMISSED"?
NO, NO...HE SAID 'FER CRYIN' OUT LOUD, SAVE ME FROM THIS!'"
CALL GALACTIC 911!
I HAVE A PLAN. I'LL DISTRACT THE CREATURE MOMENTARILY AND THEN SELFLESSLY FLING MYSELF AT HER SNAPPING MANDIBLES.
SIR!! I SALUTE YOUR GALLANT SACRIFICE!
NOTIFY MY WIFE, WILL YA?
"OLD SPICE"
BUT... MAYBE FEARSOME PLATINUM-HEADED FACE-CHEWERS DON'T FIND PIGS WORTHY OF DIGGING THEIR FANGS INTO!
THAT'D BE NEWS TO DONALD TRUMP.
HEY, BABE!
CREW DISMISSED!

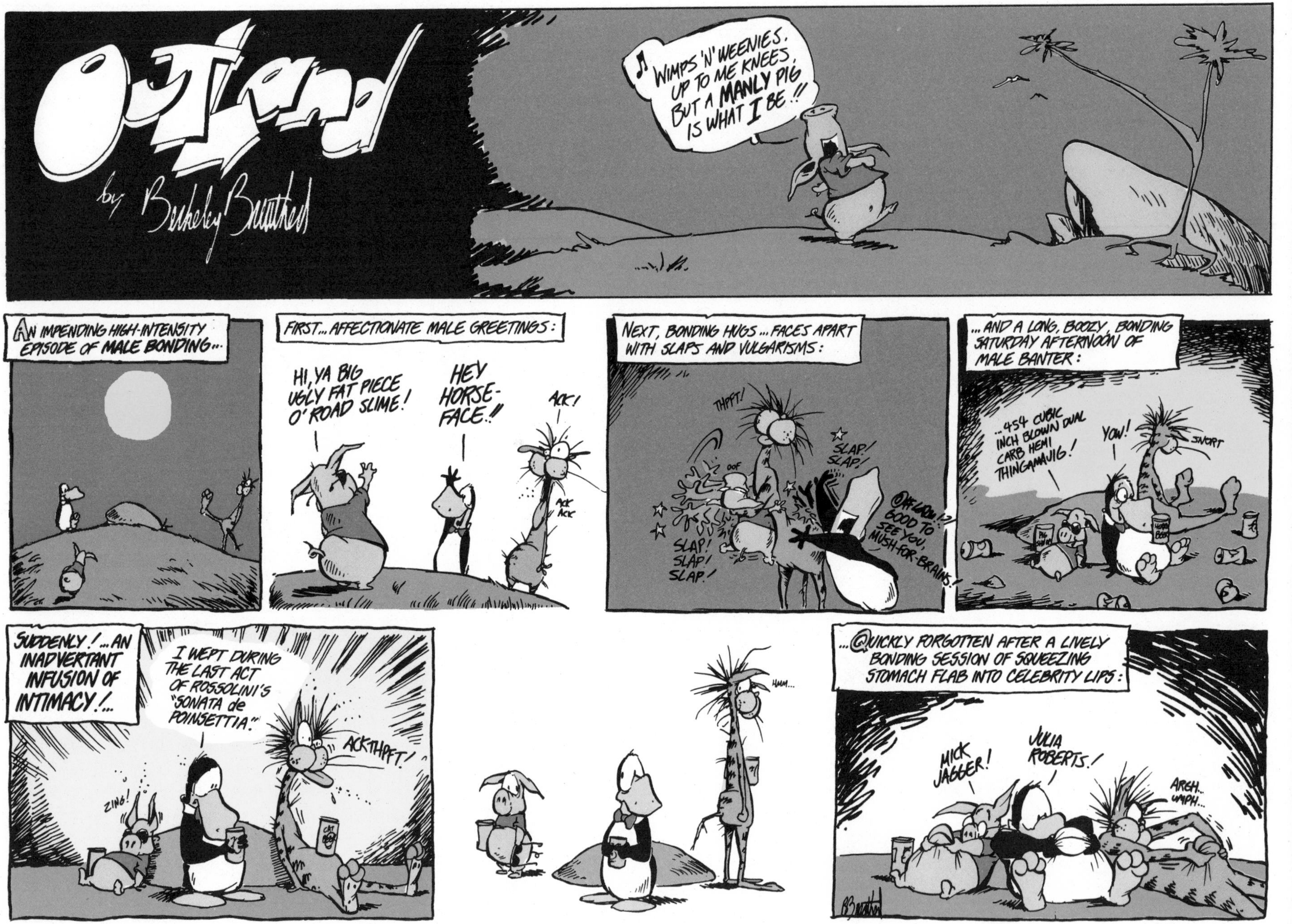
Outland
by Berkeley Breathed
♪ WIMPS 'N' WEENIES, UP TO ME KNEES, BUT A MANLY PIG IS WHAT I BE.!!
AN IMPENDING HIGH-INTENSITY EPISODE OF MALE BONDING...
FIRST... AFFECTIONATE MALE GREETINGS:
HI, YA BIG UGLY FAT PIECE O' ROAD SLIME!
HEY HORSE-FACE.!!
ACK!
ACK ACK
NEXT, BONDING HUGS... FACES APART WITH SLAPS AND VULGARISMS:
THPFT!
OOF
SLAP! SLAP!
SLAP! SLAP! SLAP!
GOOD TO SEE YOU, MUSH-FOR-BRAINS!
...AND A LONG, BOOZY, BONDING SATURDAY AFTERNOON OF MALE BANTER:
...454 CUBIC INCH BLOWN DUAL CARB HEMI THINGAMAJIG!
YOW!
SNORT
SUDDENLY!... AN INADVERTANT INFUSION OF INTIMACY!...
I WEPT DURING THE LAST ACT OF ROSSOLINI'S "SONATA de POINSETTIA."
ACKTHPFT!
ZING!
HMM...
...QUICKLY FORGOTTEN AFTER A LIVELY BONDING SESSION OF SQUEEZING STOMACH FLAB INTO CELEBRITY LIPS:
MICK JAGGER!
JULIA ROBERTS!
ARGH... UMPH...

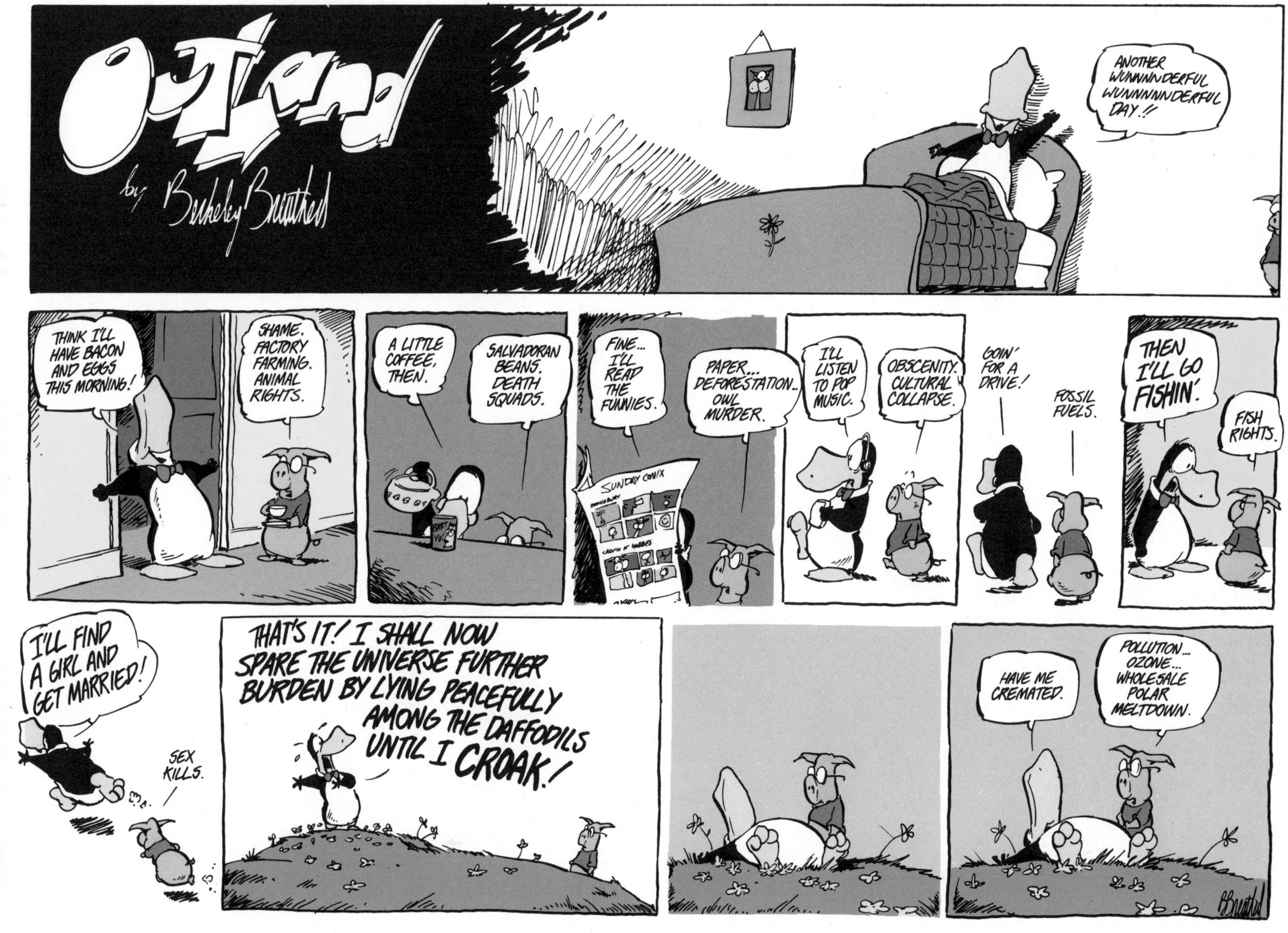
Outland
by Berkeley Breathed
ANOTHER WUNNNNDERFUL WUNNNNNDERFUL DAY.!!
THINK I'LL HAVE BACON AND EGGS THIS MORNING!
SHAME. FACTORY FARMING. ANIMAL RIGHTS.
A LITTLE COFFEE, THEN.
SALVADORAN BEANS. DEATH SQUADS.
FINE... I'LL READ THE FUNNIES.
SUNDAY COMIX
PAPER... DEFORESTATION... OWL MURDER.
I'LL LISTEN TO POP MUSIC.
OBSCENITY. CULTURAL COLLAPSE.
GOIN' FOR A DRIVE!
FOSSIL FUELS.
THEN I'LL GO FISHIN'.
FISH RIGHTS.
I'LL FIND A GIRL AND GET MARRIED!
SEX KILLS.
THAT'S IT! I SHALL NOW SPARE THE UNIVERSE FURTHER BURDEN BY LYING PEACEFULLY AMONG THE DAFFODILS UNTIL I CROAK!
HAVE ME CREMATED.
POLLUTION... OZONE... WHOLESALE POLAR MELTDOWN.
BBreathed

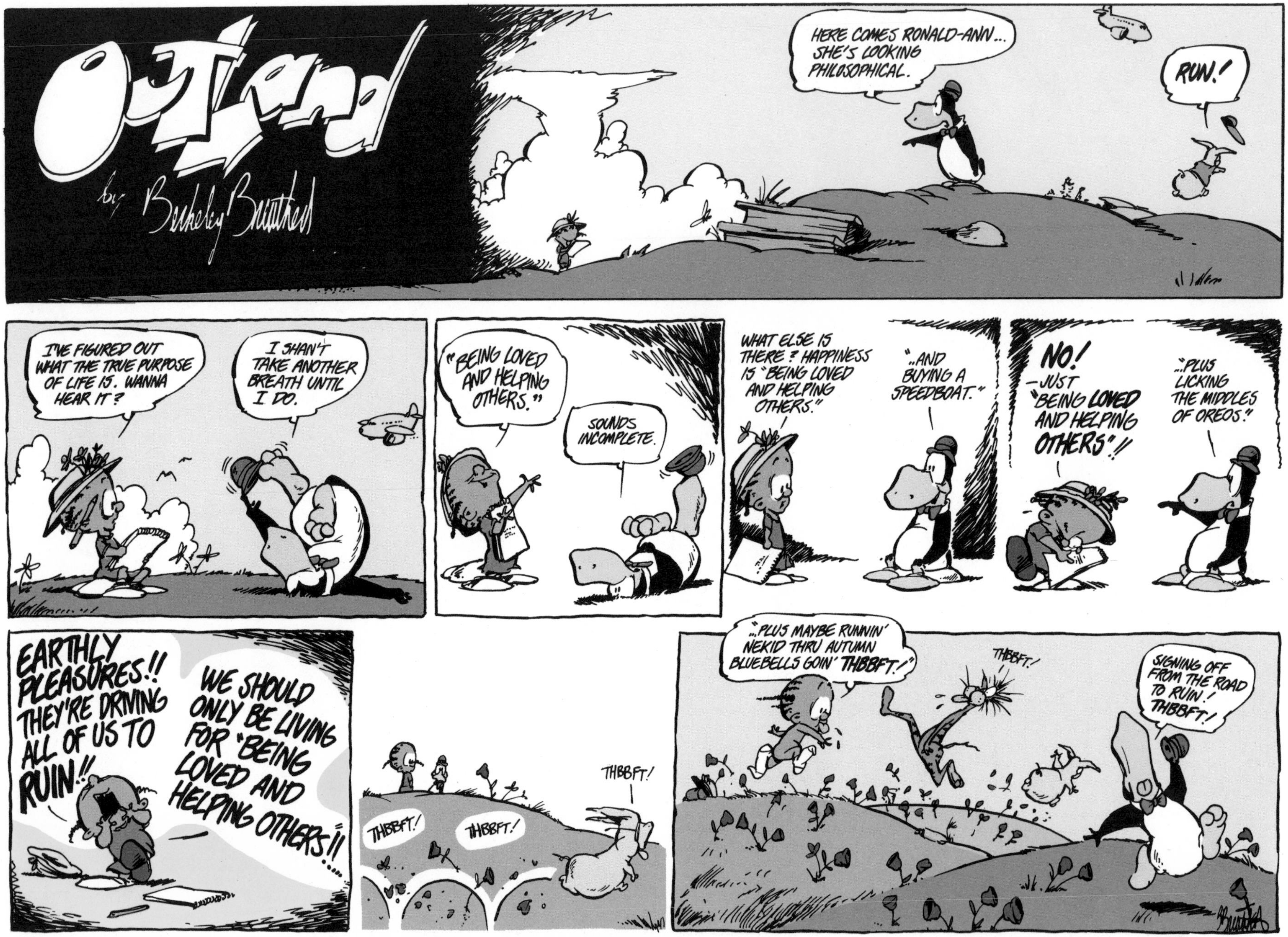
Outland
by Berkeley Breathed
HERE COMES RONALD-ANN... SHE'S LOOKING PHILOSOPHICAL.
RUN!
I'VE FIGURED OUT WHAT THE TRUE PURPOSE OF LIFE IS. WANNA HEAR IT?
I SHAN'T TAKE ANOTHER BREATH UNTIL I DO.
"BEING LOVED AND HELPING OTHERS."
SOUNDS INCOMPLETE.
WHAT ELSE IS THERE? HAPPINESS IS "BEING LOVED AND HELPING OTHERS."
"...AND BUYING A SPEEDBOAT."
NO! —JUST "BEING LOVED AND HELPING OTHERS"!!
"...PLUS LICKING THE MIDDLES OF OREOS."
EARTHLY PLEASURES!! THEY'RE DRIVING ALL OF US TO RUIN!!
WE SHOULD ONLY BE LIVING FOR "BEING LOVED AND HELPING OTHERS!!
THBBFT!
THBBFT!
THBBFT!
"...PLUS MAYBE RUNNIN' NEKID THRU AUTUMN BLUEBELLS GOIN' THBBFT!"
THBBFT!
SIGNING OFF FROM THE ROAD TO RUIN! THBBFT!

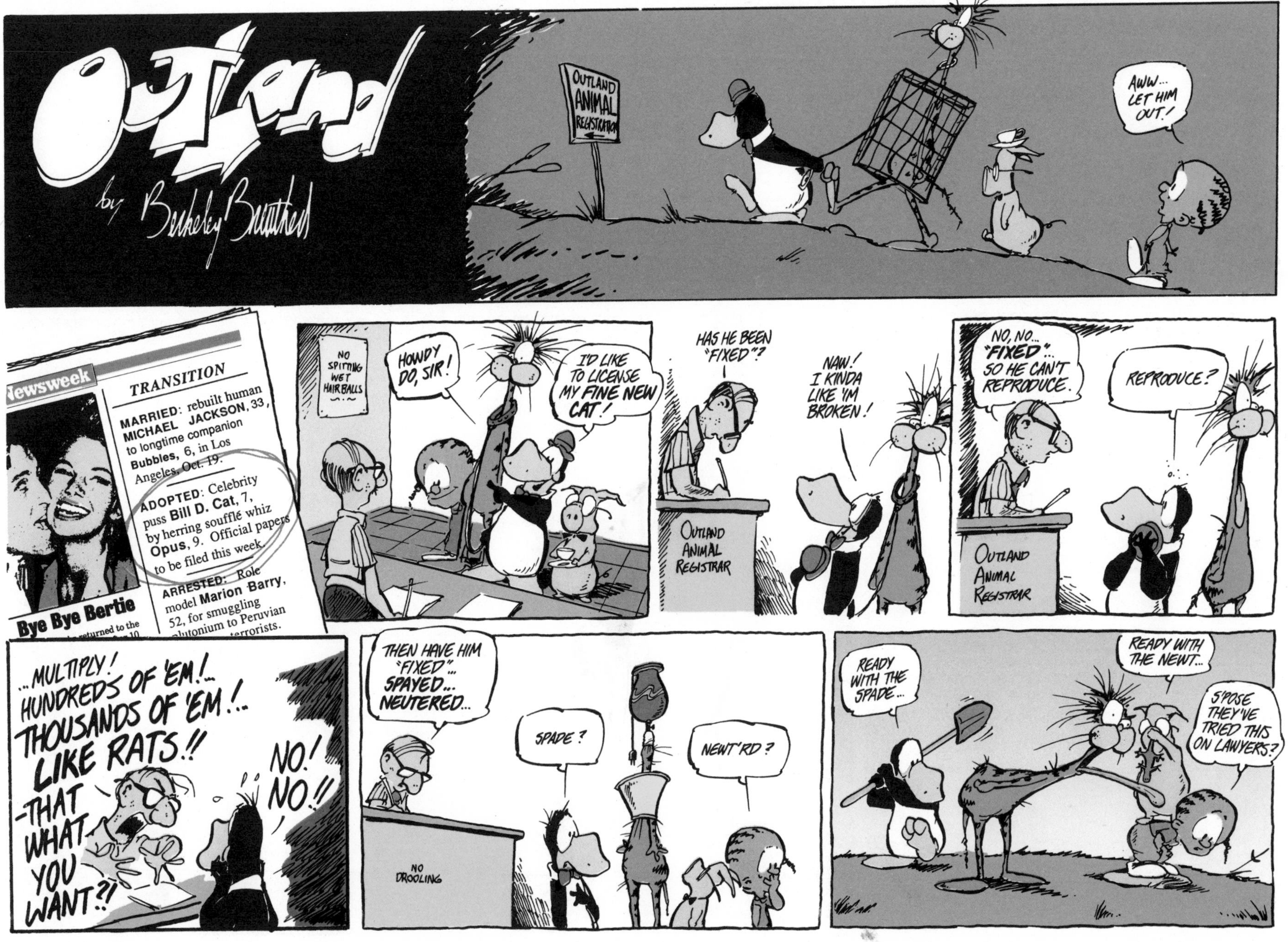
Outland
by Berkeley Breathed
OUTLAND ANIMAL REGISTRATION
AWW... LET HIM OUT!
Newsweek
TRANSITION
MARRIED: rebuilt human MICHAEL JACKSON, 33, to longtime companion Bubbles, 6, in Los Angeles, Oct. 19.
ADOPTED: Celebrity puss Bill D. Cat, 7, by herring soufflé whiz Opus, 9. Official papers to be filed this week.
ARRESTED: Role model Marion Barry, 52, for smuggling plutonium to Peruvian terrorists.
Bye Bye Bertie
NO SPITTING WET HAIRBALLS
HOWDY DO, SIR!
I'D LIKE TO LICENSE MY FINE NEW CAT!
HAS HE BEEN "FIXED"?
NAW! I KINDA LIKE 'IM BROKEN!
OUTLAND ANIMAL REGISTRAR
NO, NO... "FIXED"... SO HE CAN'T REPRODUCE.
REPRODUCE?
OUTLAND ANIMAL REGISTRAR
...MULTIPLY! HUNDREDS OF 'EM!... THOUSANDS OF 'EM!... LIKE RATS!! -THAT WHAT YOU WANT?!
NO! NO!!
THEN HAVE HIM "FIXED"... SPAYED... NEUTERED...
SPADE?
NEWT'RD?
NO DROOLING
READY WITH THE SPADE...
READY WITH THE NEWT...
S'POSE THEY'VE TRIED THIS ON LAWYERS?

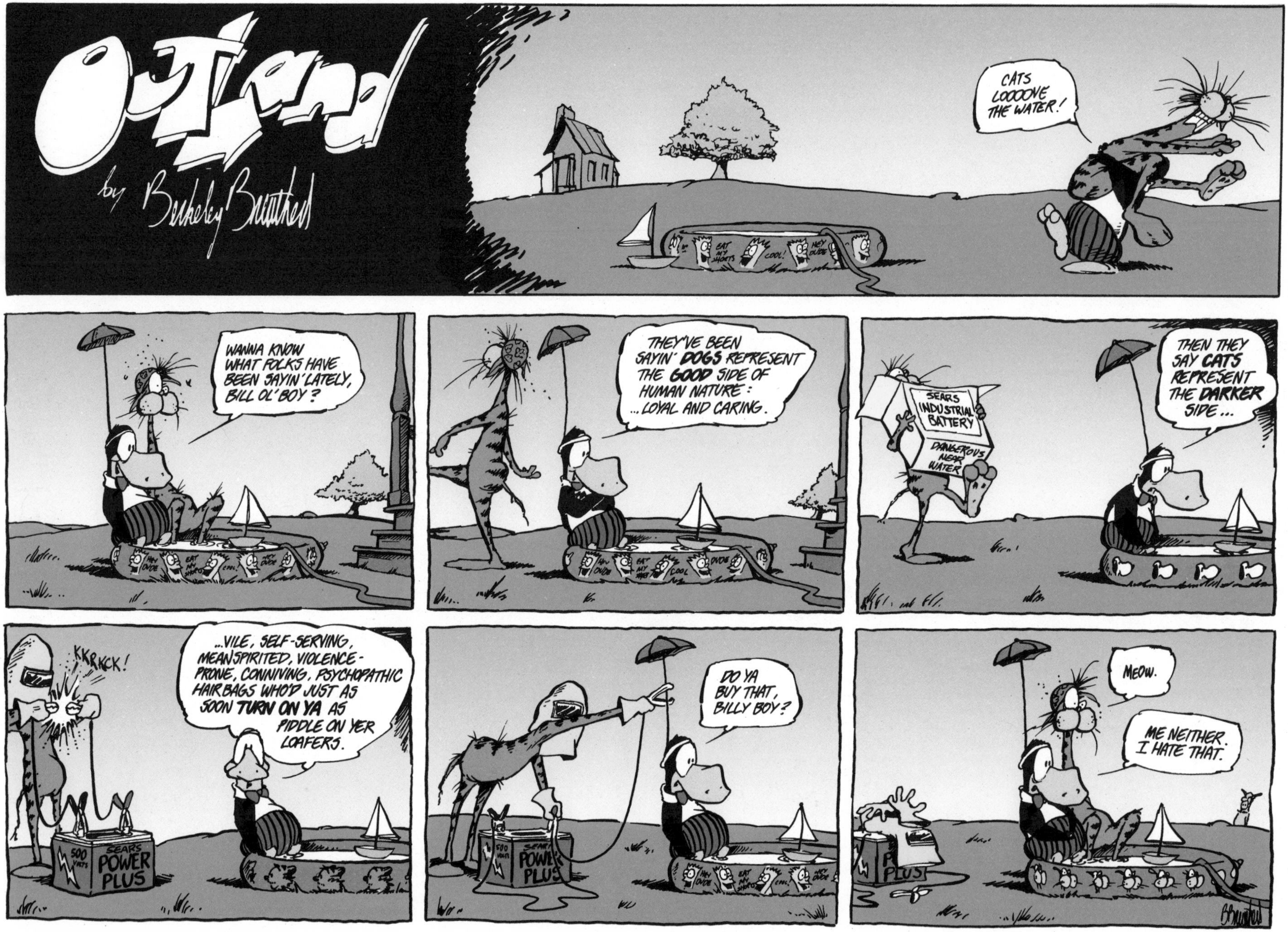

Outland
by Berkeley Breathed
EAT MY SHORTS
COOL!
HEY DUDE
CATS LOOOOVE THE WATER!
WANNA KNOW WHAT FOLKS HAVE BEEN SAYIN' LATELY, BILL OL' BOY?
THEY'VE BEEN SAYIN' DOGS REPRESENT THE GOOD SIDE OF HUMAN NATURE: ...LOYAL AND CARING.
SEARS INDUSTRIAL BATTERY
DANGEROUS NEAR WATER
THEN THEY SAY CATS REPRESENT THE DARKER SIDE...
KKRKCK!
...VILE, SELF-SERVING, MEANSPIRITED, VIOLENCE-PRONE, CONNIVING, PSYCHOPATHIC HAIRBAGS WHO'D JUST AS SOON TURN ON YA AS PIDDLE ON YER LOAFERS.
500 VOLTS
SEARS POWER PLUS
DO YA BUY THAT, BILLY BOY?
MEOW.
ME NEITHER. I HATE THAT.
BBreathed

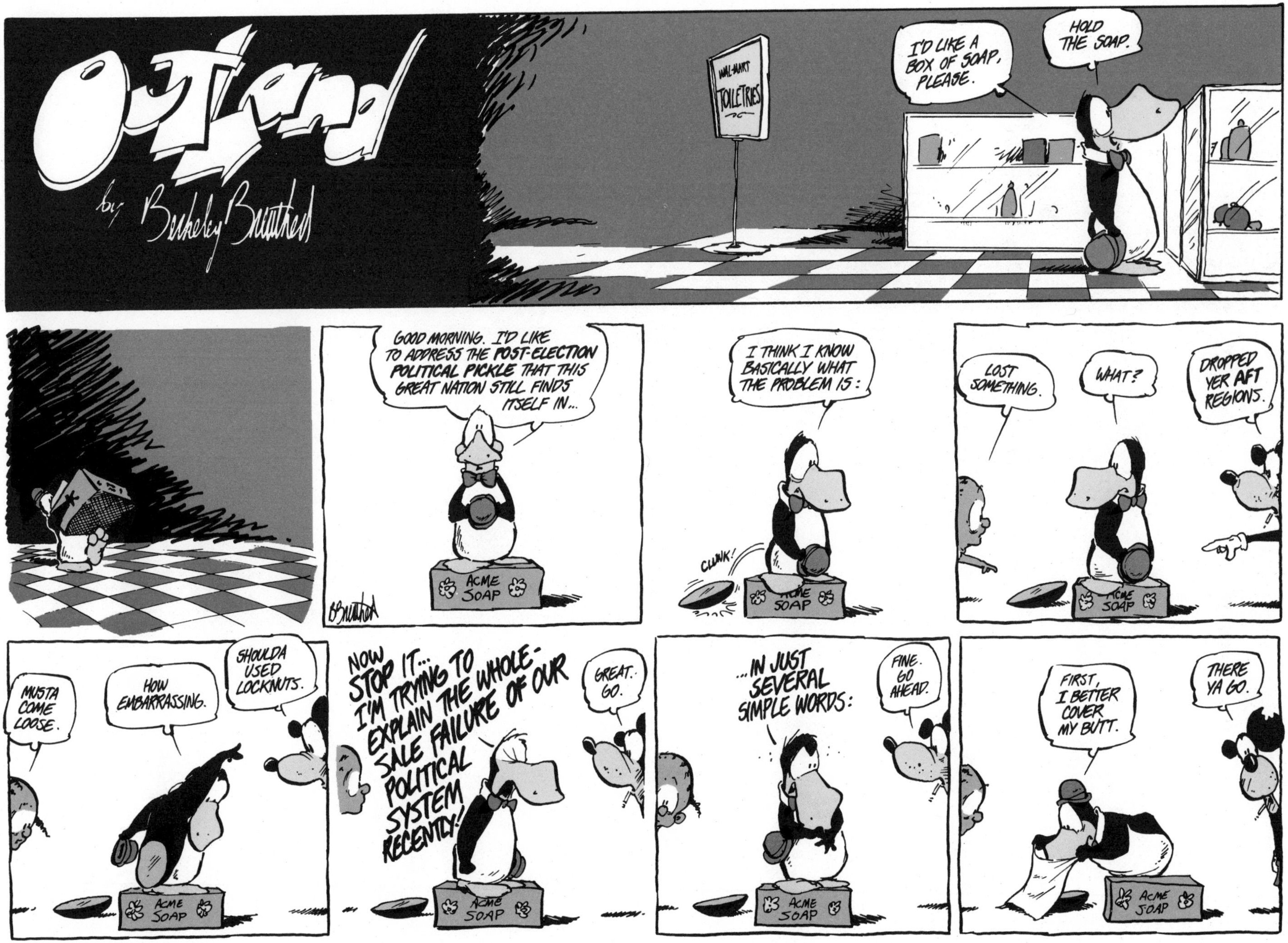
Outland
by Berkeley Breathed
WAL-MART
TOILETRIES
I'D LIKE A BOX OF SOAP, PLEASE.
HOLD THE SOAP.
GOOD MORNING. I'D LIKE TO ADDRESS THE POST-ELECTION POLITICAL PICKLE THAT THIS GREAT NATION STILL FINDS ITSELF IN...
ACME SOAP
I THINK I KNOW BASICALLY WHAT THE PROBLEM IS:
CLUNK!
LOST SOMETHING.
WHAT?
DROPPED YER AFT REGIONS.
MUSTA COME LOOSE.
HOW EMBARRASSING.
SHOULDA USED LOCKNUTS.
NOW STOP IT... I'M TRYING TO EXPLAIN THE WHOLE-SALE FAILURE OF OUR POLITICAL SYSTEM RECENTLY!
GREAT. GO.
...IN JUST SEVERAL SIMPLE WORDS:
FINE. GO AHEAD.
FIRST, I BETTER COVER MY BUTT.
THERE YA GO.

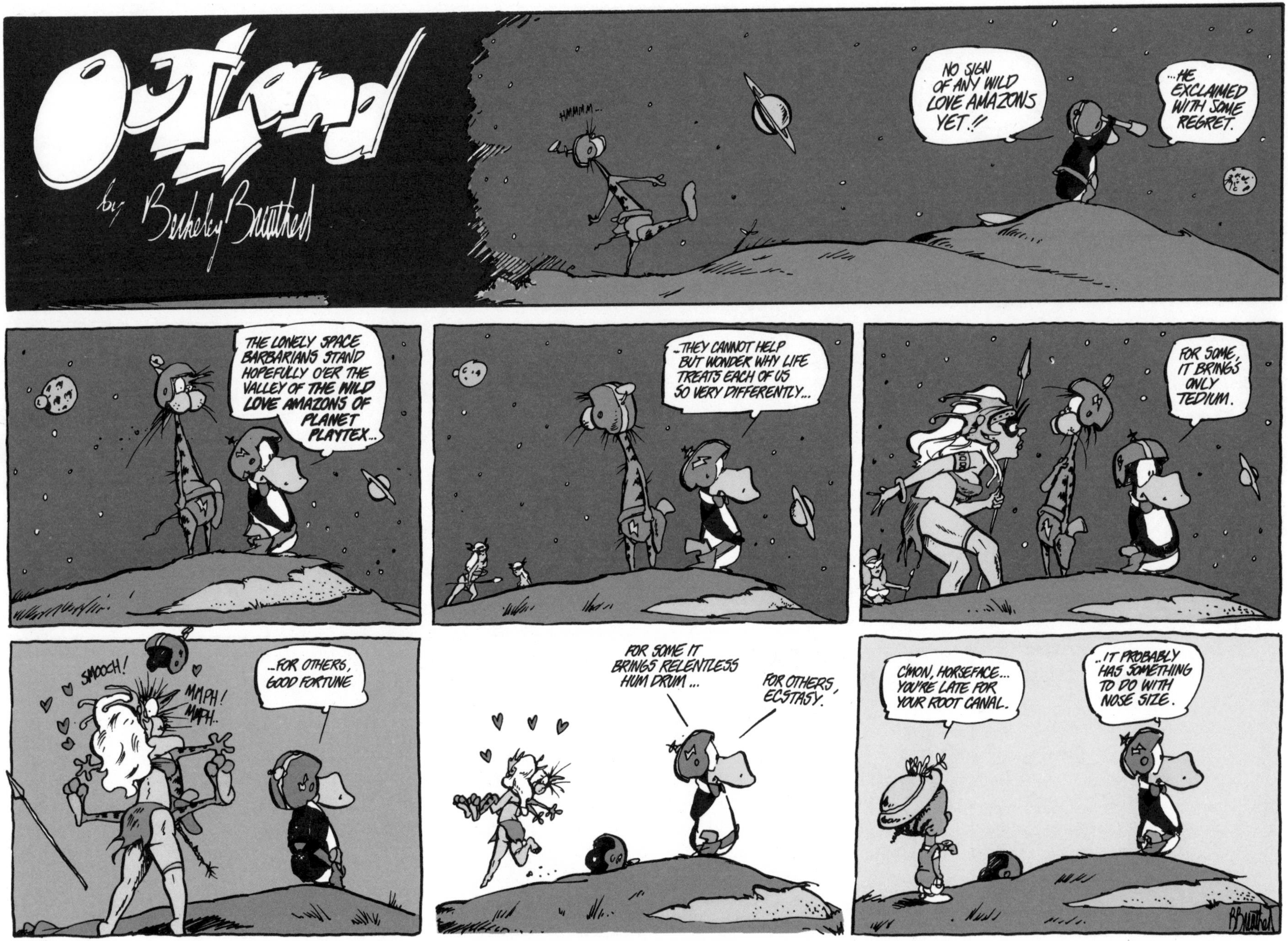

Outland
by Berkeley Breathed
HMMMM...
NO SIGN OF ANY WILD LOVE AMAZONS YET.!!
...HE EXCLAIMED WITH SOME REGRET.
THE LONELY SPACE BARBARIANS STAND HOPEFULLY O'ER THE VALLEY OF THE WILD LOVE AMAZONS OF PLANET PLAYTEX...
...THEY CANNOT HELP BUT WONDER WHY LIFE TREATS EACH OF US SO VERY DIFFERENTLY...
FOR SOME, IT BRINGS ONLY TEDIUM.
SMOOCH!
MMPH! MMPH..
...FOR OTHERS, GOOD FORTUNE
FOR SOME IT BRINGS RELENTLESS HUM DRUM ...
FOR OTHERS, ECSTASY.
C'MON, HORSEFACE... YOU'RE LATE FOR YOUR ROOT CANAL.
...IT PROBABLY HAS SOMETHING TO DO WITH NOSE SIZE.
B Breathed

# Outland
## by Berkeley Breathed

I THINK WE'RE FINISHED! LET'S RELEASE THE SHOCKING RESULTS TO THE CONSUMERS!

ACK

SNORT SNORT SNORT

FOR THE BENEFIT OF This Newspaper's **Valued** UPWARDLY-MOBILE READERS:

AN OUTLAND CONSUMER COMPARISON OF FAVORITE TAKE-HOME COMPANION/PETS

TODAY'S TRENDY OPTIONS:

A CAT — A VIETNAMESE POT-BELLIED PIG — A BABY

① WHAT ARE THEY LIKELY TO DRAG INTO THE HOUSE?

COMMUNICABLE DISEASE.

COUGH!

YOUR NEIGHBOR'S CANTALOUPE RINDS.

CHER.

② WHAT ARE THEIR MOST ENDEARING LITTLE HABITS?

CATS: DISAPPEARING FOR SEVERAL YEARS.

BABIES: PROJECTILE RAALPHING.

PIGS: MISTAKING IN-LAW EARS FOR EDIBLE TRUFFLES.

OLD HAIRBALL

HMM!

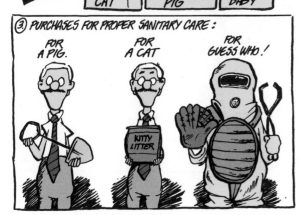

③ PURCHASES FOR PROPER SANITARY CARE:

FOR A PIG.

FOR A CAT

KITTY LITTER

FOR GUESS WHO!

④ SURE, THEY'RE CUDDLY NOW, BUT WHAT WILL THEY BE LIKE WHEN THEY GET OLDER?

WANTED: FOR ATTACKING PRESIDENT QUAYLE WITH WEED WHACKER

THE OUTLAND CONSUMER TESTING TEAM'S CHOICE FOR THE PREFERRED, TRENDY FAMILY ADDITION:

A SKI BOAT.

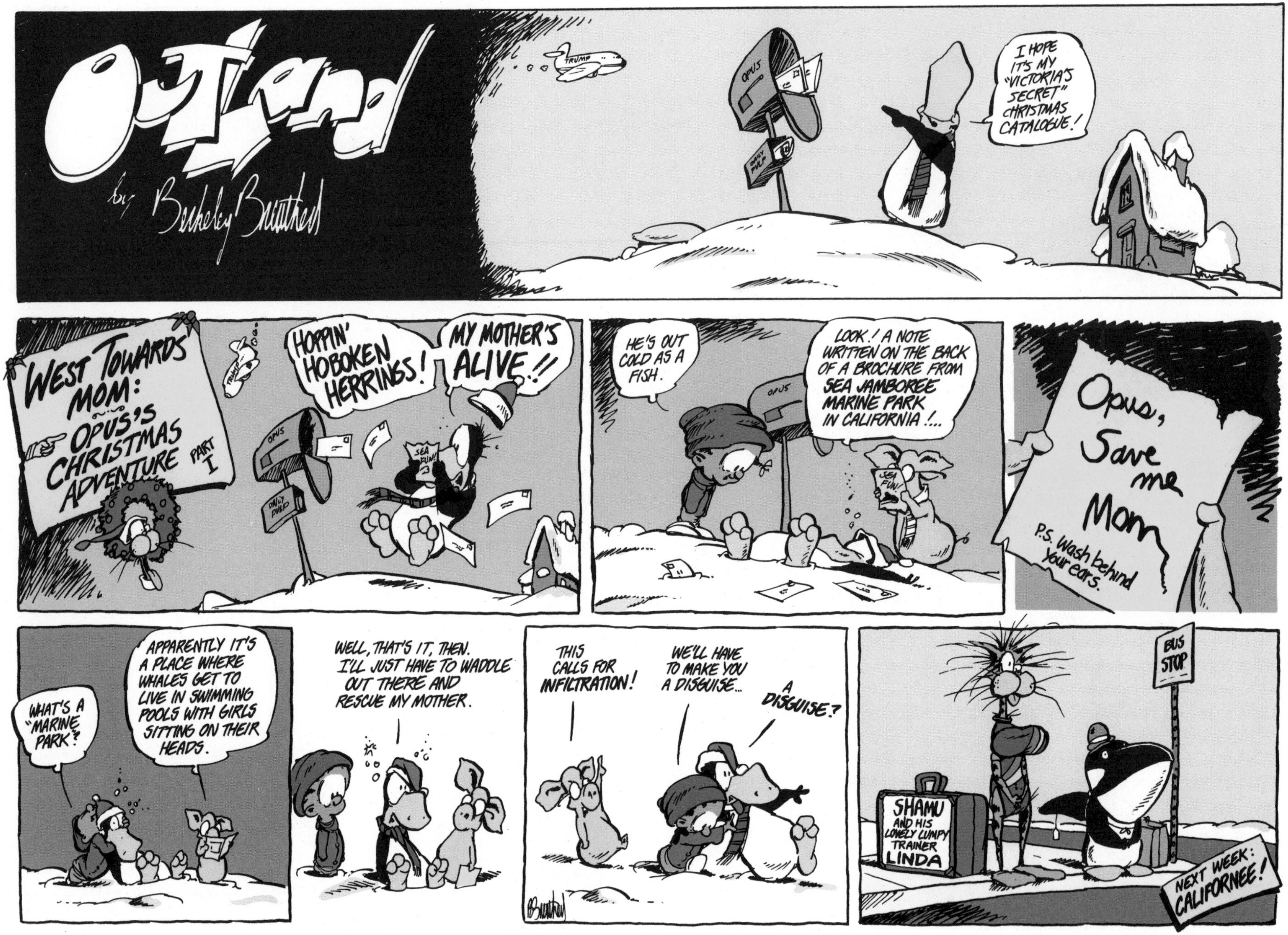
Outland
by Berkeley Breathed
TRUMP
OPUS
I HOPE IT'S MY "VICTORIA'S SECRET" CHRISTMAS CATALOGUE!
WEST TOWARDS MOM: OPUS'S CHRISTMAS ADVENTURE PART I
TRUMP
OPUS
HOPPIN' HOBOKEN HERRINGS!
MY MOTHER'S ALIVE!!
SEA FUN!
HE'S OUT COLD AS A FISH.
OPUS
LOOK! A NOTE WRITTEN ON THE BACK OF A BROCHURE FROM SEA JAMBOREE MARINE PARK IN CALIFORNIA!...
SEA FUN!
Opus, Save me Mom
P.S. Wash behind your ears.
WHAT'S A "MARINE PARK"?
APPARENTLY IT'S A PLACE WHERE WHALES GET TO LIVE IN SWIMMING POOLS WITH GIRLS SITTING ON THEIR HEADS.
WELL, THAT'S IT, THEN. I'LL JUST HAVE TO WADDLE OUT THERE AND RESCUE MY MOTHER.
THIS CALLS FOR INFILTRATION!
WE'LL HAVE TO MAKE YOU A DISGUISE...
A DISGUISE?
BUS STOP
SHAMU AND HIS LOVELY LUMPY TRAINER LINDA
NEXT WEEK: CALIFORNEE!

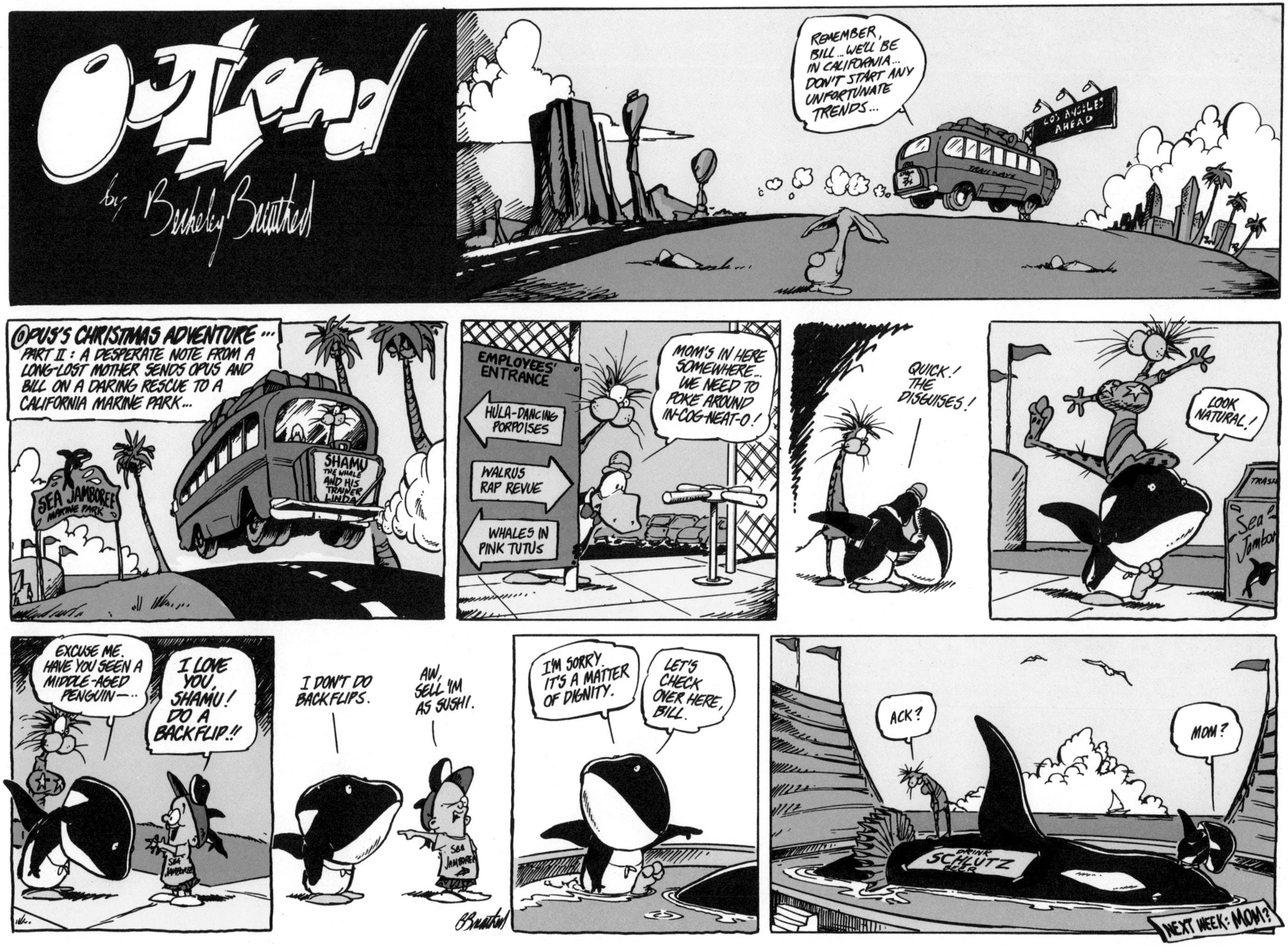

Outland
by Berkeley Breathed
REMEMBER, BILL... WE'LL BE IN CALIFORNIA... DON'T START ANY UNFORTUNATE TRENDS...
LOS ANGELES AHEAD
OPUS'S CHRISTMAS ADVENTURE... PART II: A DESPERATE NOTE FROM A LONG-LOST MOTHER SENDS OPUS AND BILL ON A DARING RESCUE TO A CALIFORNIA MARINE PARK...
SEA JAMBOREE MARINE PARK
SHAMU THE WHALE AND HIS TRAINER LINDA
EMPLOYEES' ENTRANCE
HULA-DANCING PORPOISES
WALRUS RAP REVUE
WHALES IN PINK TUTUS
MOM'S IN HERE SOMEWHERE... WE NEED TO POKE AROUND IN-COG-NEAT-O!
QUICK! THE DISGUISES!
LOOK NATURAL!
TRASH
EXCUSE ME. HAVE YOU SEEN A MIDDLE-AGED PENGUIN—...
I LOVE YOU, SHAMU! DO A BACKFLIP!!
SEA JAMBOREE
I DON'T DO BACKFLIPS.
AW, SELL 'IM AS SUSHI.
I'M SORRY. IT'S A MATTER OF DIGNITY.
LET'S CHECK OVER HERE, BILL.
ACK?
MOM?
DRINK SCHLUTZ BEER
NEXT WEEK: MOM?

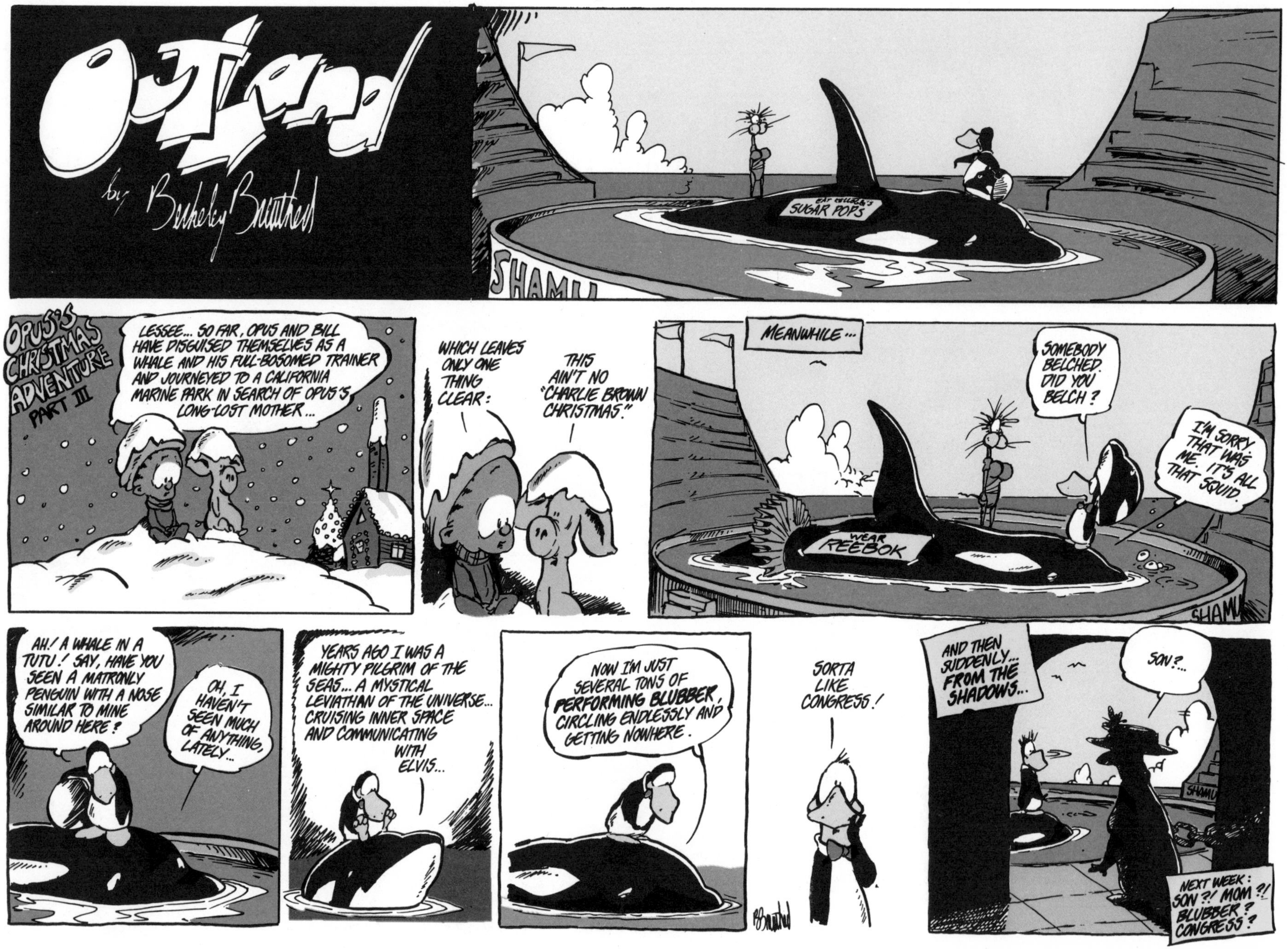 
Outland
by Berkeley Breathed
EAT KELLOGG'S SUGAR POPS
SHAMU
OPUS'S CHRISTMAS ADVENTURE PART III
LESSEE... SO FAR, OPUS AND BILL HAVE DISGUISED THEMSELVES AS A WHALE AND HIS FULL-BOSOMED TRAINER AND JOURNEYED TO A CALIFORNIA MARINE PARK IN SEARCH OF OPUS'S LONG-LOST MOTHER...
WHICH LEAVES ONLY ONE THING CLEAR:
THIS AIN'T NO "CHARLIE BROWN CHRISTMAS."
MEANWHILE...
SOMEBODY BELCHED. DID YOU BELCH?
I'M SORRY. THAT WAS ME. IT'S ALL THAT SQUID.
WEAR REEBOK
SHAMU
AH! A WHALE IN A TUTU! SAY, HAVE YOU SEEN A MATRONLY PENGUIN WITH A NOSE SIMILAR TO MINE AROUND HERE?
OH, I HAVEN'T SEEN MUCH OF ANYTHING, LATELY...
YEARS AGO I WAS A MIGHTY PILGRIM OF THE SEAS... A MYSTICAL LEVIATHAN OF THE UNIVERSE... CRUISING INNER SPACE AND COMMUNICATING WITH ELVIS...
NOW I'M JUST SEVERAL TONS OF PERFORMING BLUBBER, CIRCLING ENDLESSLY AND GETTING NOWHERE.
SORTA LIKE CONGRESS!
AND THEN SUDDENLY... FROM THE SHADOWS...
SON?...
SHAMU
NEXT WEEK: SON?! MOM?! BLUBBER? CONGRESS?

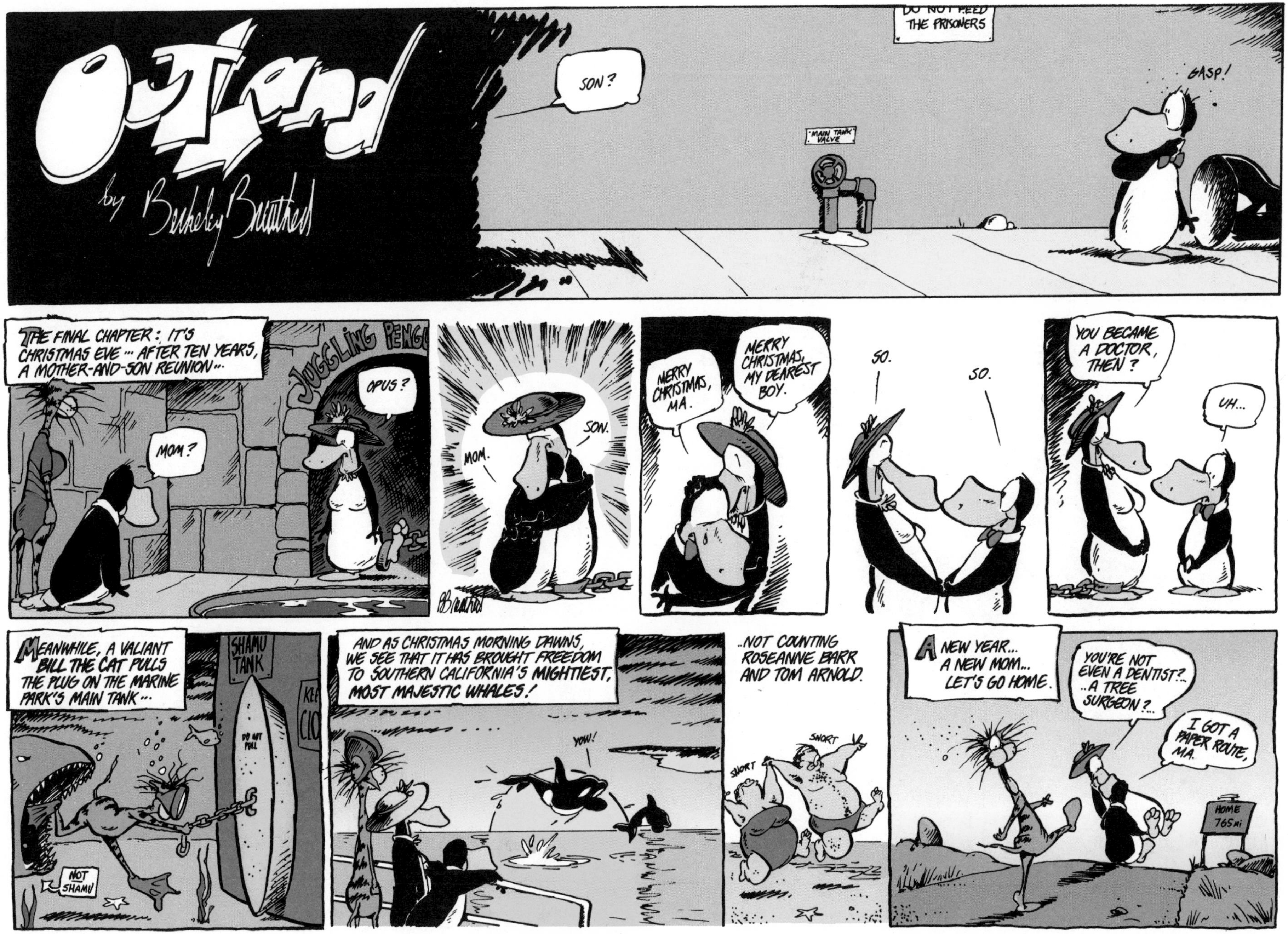
Outland
by Berkeley Breathed
SON?
DO NOT FEED THE PRISONERS
"MAIN TANK" VALVE
GASP!
THE FINAL CHAPTER: IT'S CHRISTMAS EVE... AFTER TEN YEARS, A MOTHER-AND-SON REUNION...
JUGGLING PENGU
OPUS?
MOM?
MOM.
SON.
MERRY CHRISTMAS, MA.
MERRY CHRISTMAS, MY DEAREST BOY.
SO.
SO.
YOU BECAME A DOCTOR, THEN?
UH...
MEANWHILE, A VALIANT BILL THE CAT PULLS THE PLUG ON THE MARINE PARK'S MAIN TANK...
SHAMU TANK
DO NOT PULL
NOT SHAMU
AND AS CHRISTMAS MORNING DAWNS, WE SEE THAT IT HAS BROUGHT FREEDOM TO SOUTHERN CALIFORNIA'S MIGHTIEST, MOST MAJESTIC WHALES!
YOW!
..NOT COUNTING ROSEANNE BARR AND TOM ARNOLD.
SNORT
SNORT
A NEW YEAR... A NEW MOM... LET'S GO HOME.
YOU'RE NOT EVEN A DENTIST?... ..A TREE SURGEON?...
I GOT A PAPER ROUTE, MA.
HOME 765 mi

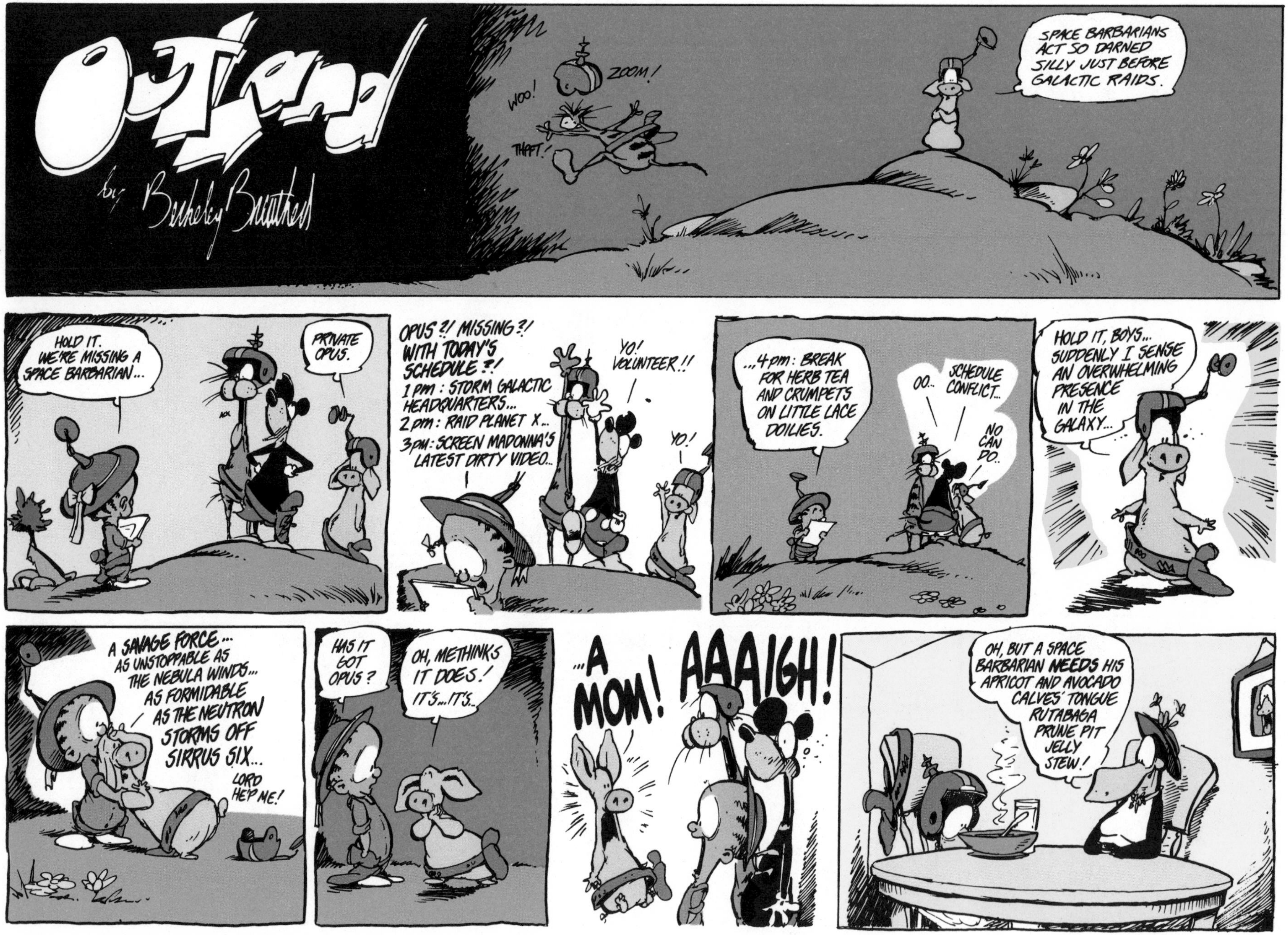
Outland
by Berkeley Breathed
WOO!
ZOOM!
THFFT!
SPACE BARBARIANS ACT SO DARNED SILLY JUST BEFORE GALACTIC RAIDS.
HOLD IT. WE'RE MISSING A SPACE BARBARIAN...
PRIVATE OPUS.
OPUS?! MISSING?! WITH TODAY'S SCHEDULE?! 1 pm: STORM GALACTIC HEADQUARTERS... 2 pm: RAID PLANET X... 3pm: SCREEN MADONNA'S LATEST DIRTY VIDEO...
YO! VOLUNTEER!!
YO!
...4pm: BREAK FOR HERB TEA AND CRUMPETS ON LITTLE LACE DOILIES.
OO...
SCHEDULE CONFLICT...
NO CAN DO..
HOLD IT, BOYS... SUDDENLY I SENSE AN OVERWHELMING PRESENCE IN THE GALAXY...
A SAVAGE FORCE... AS UNSTOPPABLE AS THE NEBULA WINDS... AS FORMIDABLE AS THE NEUTRON STORMS OFF SIRRUS SIX...
LORD HE'P ME!
HAS IT GOT OPUS?
OH, METHINKS IT DOES! IT'S...IT'S...
...A MOM!
AAAIGH!
OH, BUT A SPACE BARBARIAN NEEDS HIS APRICOT AND AVOCADO CALVES' TONGUE RUTABAGA PRUNE PIT JELLY STEW!

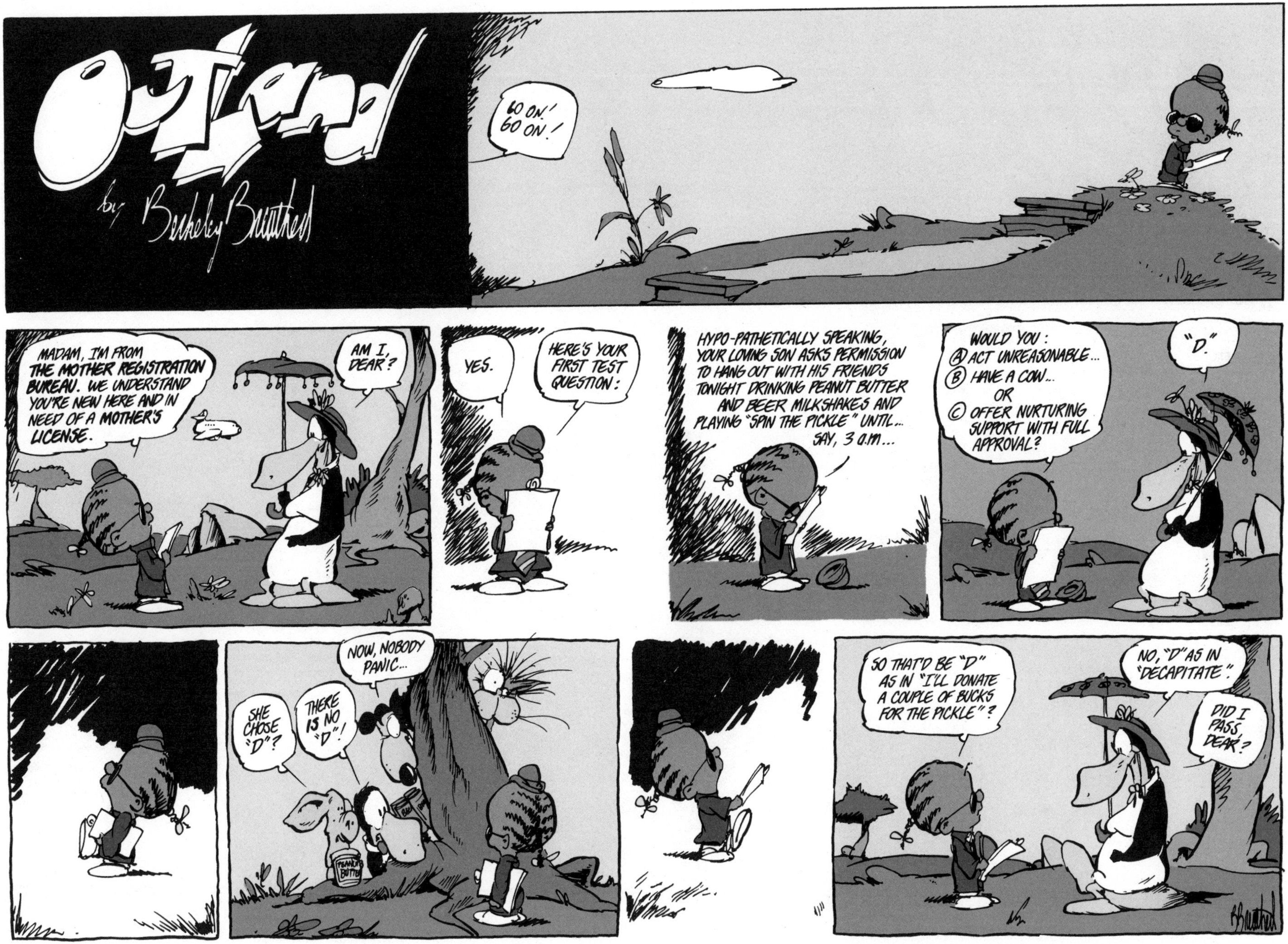
Outland
by Berkeley Breathed
GO ON! GO ON!
MADAM, I'M FROM THE MOTHER REGISTRATION BUREAU. WE UNDERSTAND YOU'RE NEW HERE AND IN NEED OF A MOTHER'S LICENSE.
AM I, DEAR?
YES.
HERE'S YOUR FIRST TEST QUESTION:
HYPO-PATHETICALLY SPEAKING, YOUR LOVING SON ASKS PERMISSION TO HANG OUT WITH HIS FRIENDS TONIGHT DRINKING PEANUT BUTTER AND BEER MILKSHAKES AND PLAYING "SPIN THE PICKLE" UNTIL... SAY, 3 a.m...
WOULD YOU: (A) ACT UNREASONABLE... (B) HAVE A COW... OR (C) OFFER NURTURING SUPPORT WITH FULL APPROVAL?
"D."
NOW, NOBODY PANIC...
SHE CHOSE "D"?
THERE IS NO "D"!
SO THAT'D BE "D" AS IN "I'LL DONATE A COUPLE OF BUCKS FOR THE PICKLE"?
NO, "D" AS IN "DECAPITATE".
DID I PASS, DEAR?
BBreathed

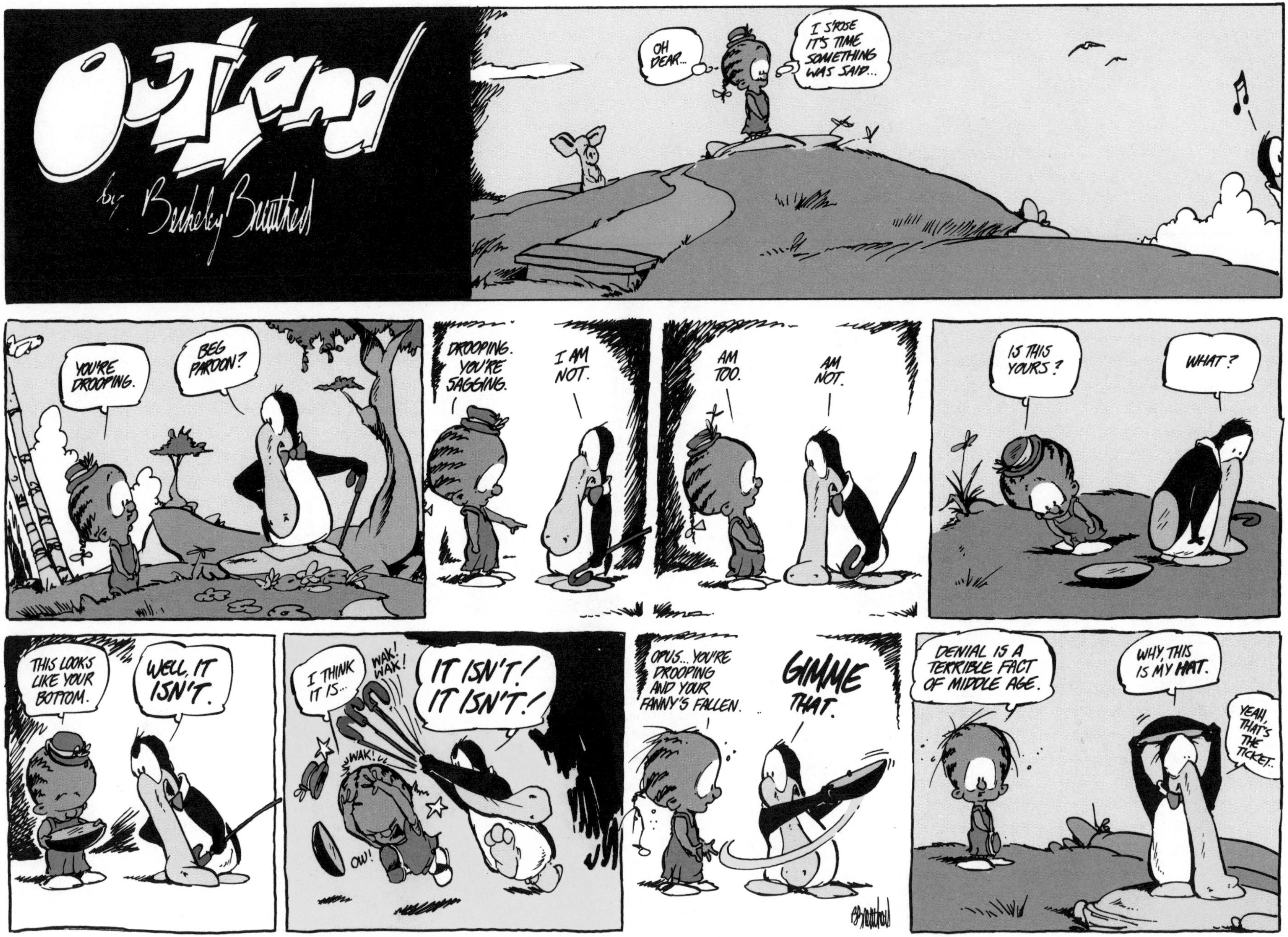
Outland
by Berkeley Breathed
OH DEAR...
I S'POSE IT'S TIME SOMETHING WAS SAID...
YOU'RE DROOPING.
BEG PARDON?
DROOPING. YOU'RE SAGGING.
I AM NOT.
AM TOO.
AM NOT.
IS THIS YOURS?
WHAT?
THIS LOOKS LIKE YOUR BOTTOM.
WELL, IT ISN'T.
I THINK IT IS...
WAK! WAK!
IT ISN'T! IT ISN'T!
WAK!
OW!
OPUS... YOU'RE DROOPING AND YOUR FANNY'S FALLEN.
GIMME THAT.
DENIAL IS A TERRIBLE FACT OF MIDDLE AGE.
WHY, THIS IS MY HAT.
YEAH, THAT'S THE TICKET...

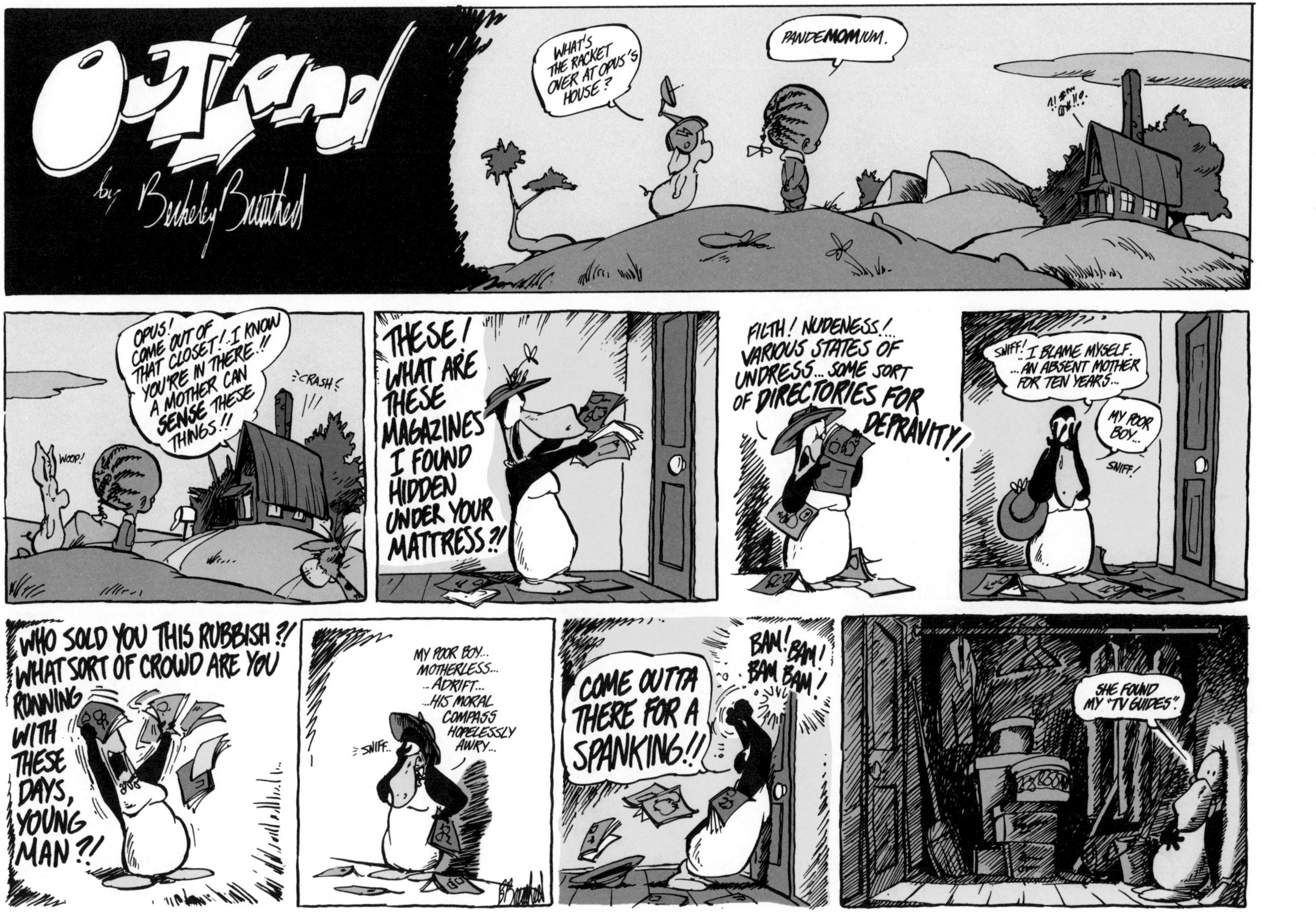
OUTLAND
by Berkeley Breathed
WHAT'S THE RACKET OVER AT OPUS'S HOUSE?
PANDEMOMIUM.
OPUS! COME OUT OF THAT CLOSET! I KNOW YOU'RE IN THERE!! A MOTHER CAN SENSE THESE THINGS!!
CRASH
WOOP!
THESE! WHAT ARE THESE MAGAZINES I FOUND HIDDEN UNDER YOUR MATTRESS?!
FILTH! NUDENESS!... VARIOUS STATES OF UNDRESS... SOME SORT OF DIRECTORIES FOR DEPRAVITY!!
SNIFF! I BLAME MYSELF. ...AN ABSENT MOTHER FOR TEN YEARS...
MY POOR BOY...
SNIFF!
WHO SOLD YOU THIS RUBBISH?! WHAT SORT OF CROWD ARE YOU RUNNING WITH THESE DAYS, YOUNG MAN?!
MY POOR BOY... MOTHERLESS... ...ADRIFT... ...HIS MORAL COMPASS HOPELESSLY AWRY...
SNIFF..
COME OUTTA THERE FOR A SPANKING!!
BAM! BAM! BAM BAM!
SHE FOUND MY "TV GUIDES".

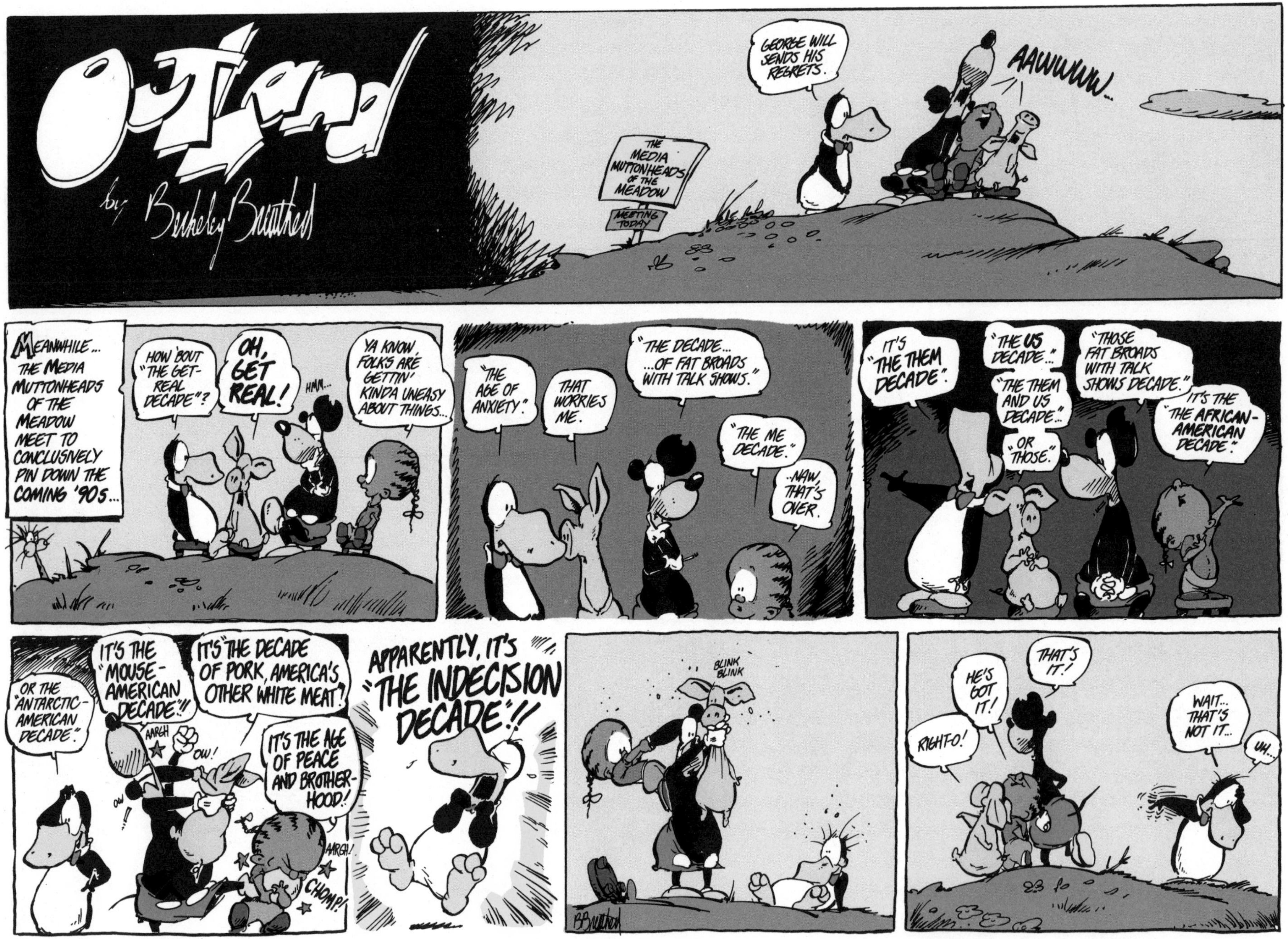
Outland
by Berkeley Breathed
THE MEDIA MUTTONHEADS OF THE MEADOW
MEETING TODAY
GEORGE WILL SENDS HIS REGRETS.
AAWWWW...
MEANWHILE... THE MEDIA MUTTONHEADS OF THE MEADOW MEET TO CONCLUSIVELY PIN DOWN THE COMING '90s...
HOW 'BOUT "THE GET-REAL DECADE"?
OH, GET REAL!
HMM...
YA KNOW, FOLKS ARE GETTIN' KINDA UNEASY ABOUT THINGS...
"THE AGE OF ANXIETY".
THAT WORRIES ME.
"THE DECADE... ...OF FAT BROADS WITH TALK SHOWS."
"THE ME DECADE."
...NAW, THAT'S OVER.
IT'S "THE THEM DECADE".
"THE US DECADE."...
"THE THEM AND US DECADE."...
"OR THOSE."
"THOSE FAT BROADS WITH TALK SHOWS DECADE."
IT'S THE "THE AFRICAN-AMERICAN DECADE."
...OR THE "ANTARCTIC-AMERICAN DECADE."
IT'S THE "MOUSE-AMERICAN DECADE"!!
IT'S "THE DECADE OF PORK, AMERICA'S OTHER WHITE MEAT"!
AARGH
OW!
OW
IT'S THE AGE OF PEACE AND BROTHERHOOD!
AARGH!
CHOMP!
APPARENTLY, IT'S "THE INDECISION DECADE"!!
BLINK BLINK
B Breathed
THAT'S IT!
HE'S GOT IT!
RIGHT-O!
WAIT... THAT'S NOT IT...
UH...

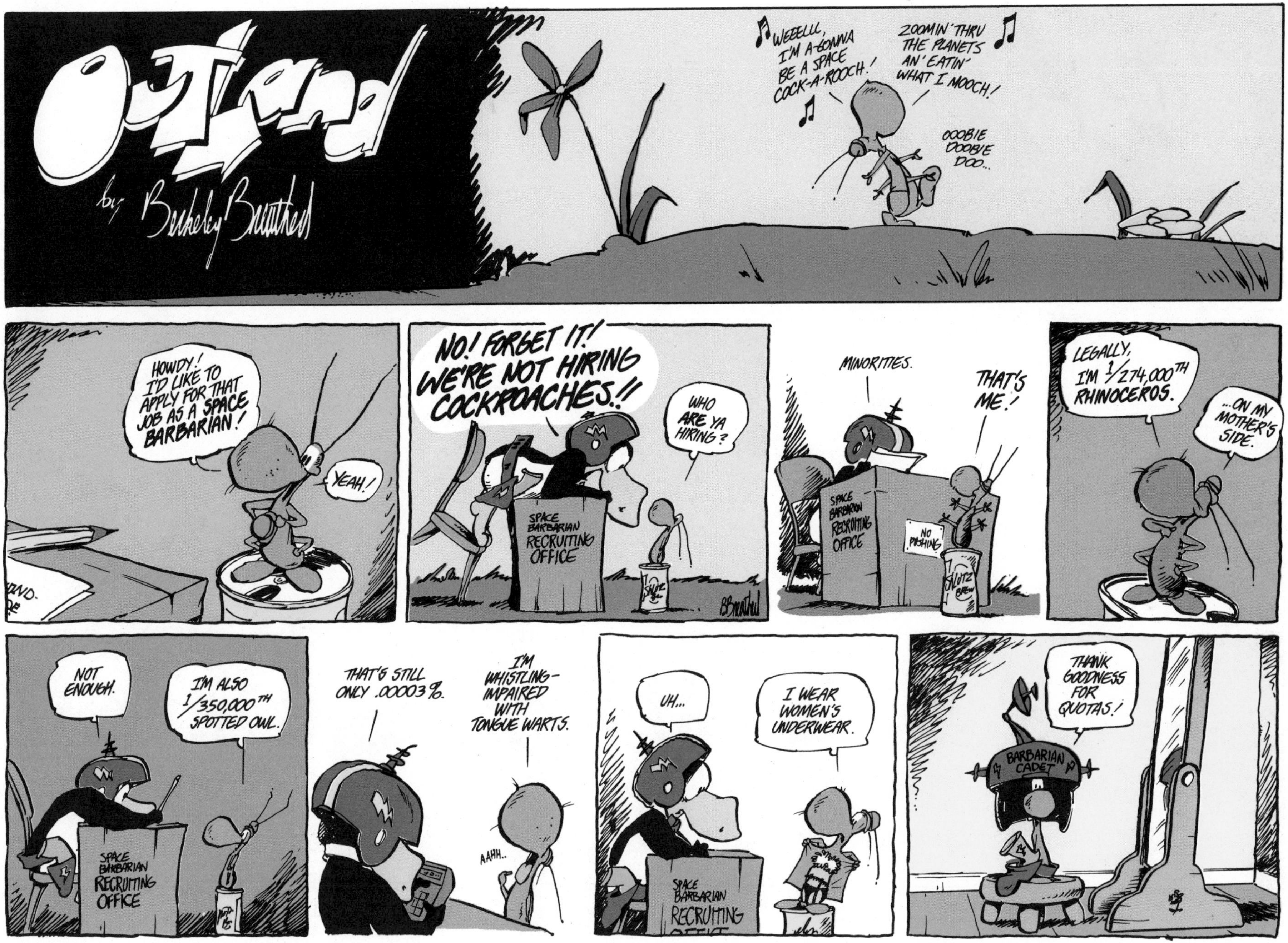
Outland
by Berkeley Breathed
WEEELLL, I'M A-GONNA BE A SPACE COCK-A-ROOCH!
ZOOMIN' THRU THE PLANETS AN' EATIN' WHAT I MOOCH!
OOOBIE DOOBIE DOO...
HOWDY! I'D LIKE TO APPLY FOR THAT JOB AS A SPACE BARBARIAN!
YEAH!
NO! FORGET IT! WE'RE NOT HIRING COCKROACHES!!
SPACE BARBARIAN RECRUITING OFFICE
WHO ARE YA HIRING?
MINORITIES.
THAT'S ME!
NO PUSHING
LEGALLY, I'M 1/274,000TH RHINOCEROS.
...ON MY MOTHER'S SIDE.
NOT ENOUGH.
I'M ALSO 1/350,000TH SPOTTED OWL.
SPACE BARBARIAN RECRUITING OFFICE
THAT'S STILL ONLY .00003%.
I'M WHISTLING-IMPAIRED WITH TONGUE WARTS.
AAHH..
UH...
I WEAR WOMEN'S UNDERWEAR.
SPACE BARBARIAN RECRUITING
THANK GOODNESS FOR QUOTAS!
BARBARIAN CADET

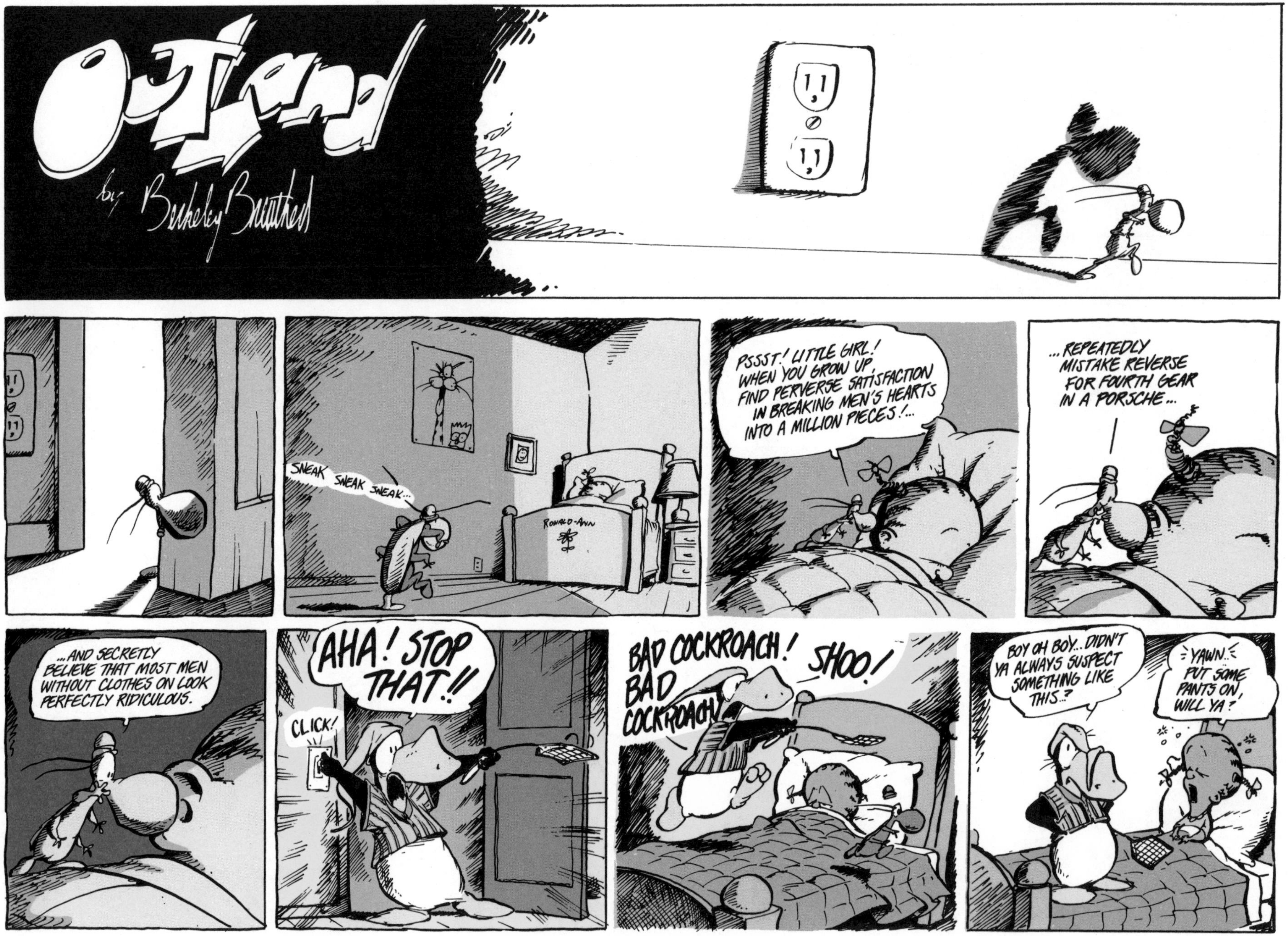

Outland
by Berkeley Breathed
SNEAK SNEAK SNEAK...
RONALD-ANN
PSSST! LITTLE GIRL! WHEN YOU GROW UP, FIND PERVERSE SATISFACTION IN BREAKING MEN'S HEARTS INTO A MILLION PIECES!...
...REPEATEDLY MISTAKE REVERSE FOR FOURTH GEAR IN A PORSCHE...
...AND SECRETLY BELIEVE THAT MOST MEN WITHOUT CLOTHES ON LOOK PERFECTLY RIDICULOUS.
CLICK!
AHA! STOP THAT!!
BAD COCKROACH! BAD COCKROACH!
BAD COCKROACH!
SHOO!
BOY OH BOY... DIDN'T YA ALWAYS SUSPECT SOMETHING LIKE THIS..?
YAWN.. PUT SOME PANTS ON, WILL YA?

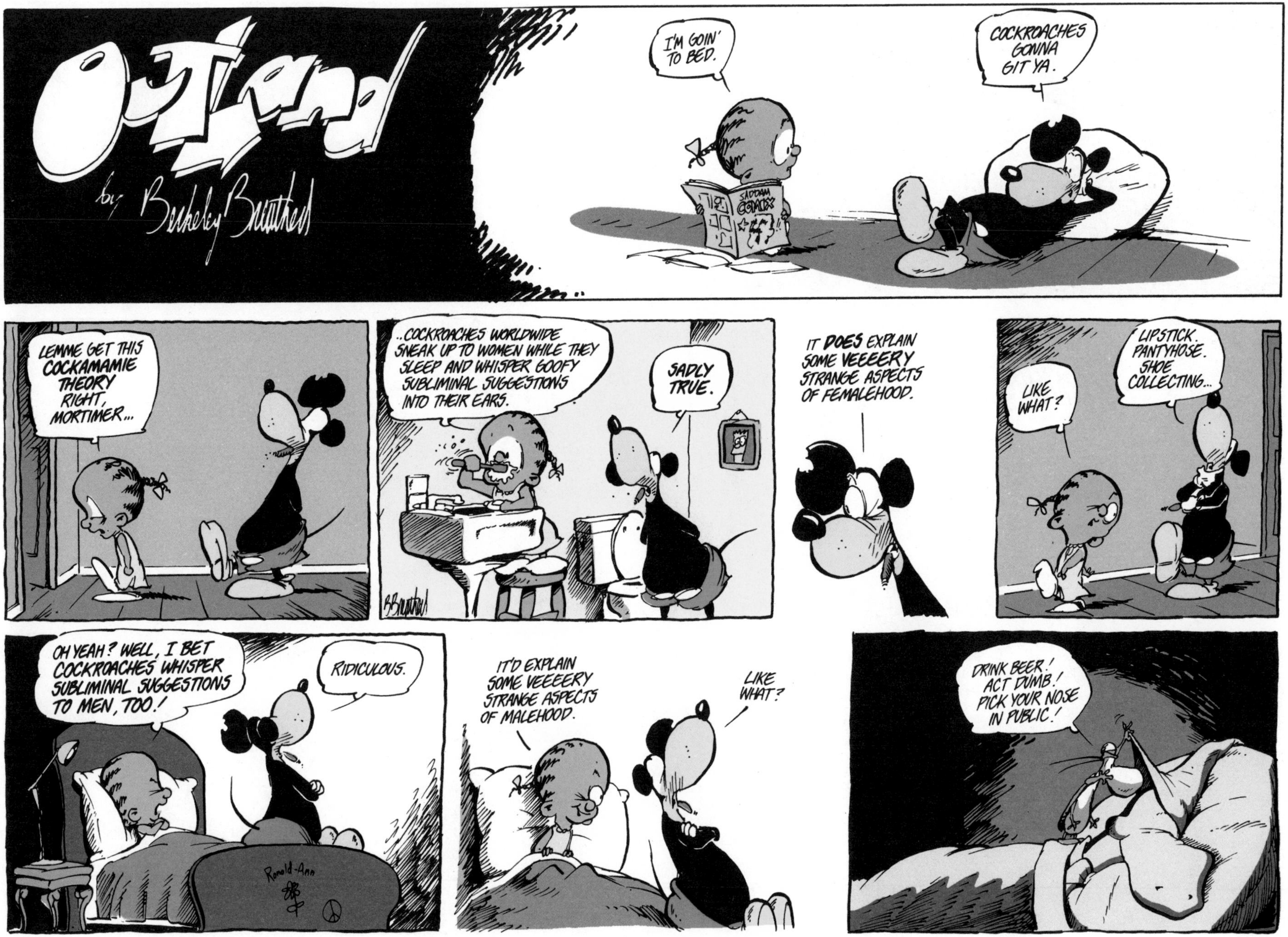

Outland
by Berkeley Breathed
I'M GOIN' TO BED.
COCKROACHES GONNA GIT YA.
SADDAM COMIX
LEMME GET THIS COCKAMAMIE THEORY RIGHT, MORTIMER...
...COCKROACHES WORLDWIDE SNEAK UP TO WOMEN WHILE THEY SLEEP AND WHISPER GOOFY SUBLIMINAL SUGGESTIONS INTO THEIR EARS.
SADLY TRUE.
IT DOES EXPLAIN SOME VEEEERY STRANGE ASPECTS OF FEMALEHOOD.
LIKE WHAT?
LIPSTICK. PANTYHOSE. SHOE COLLECTING...
OH YEAH? WELL, I BET COCKROACHES WHISPER SUBLIMINAL SUGGESTIONS TO MEN, TOO!
RIDICULOUS.
Ronald-Ann
IT'D EXPLAIN SOME VEEEERY STRANGE ASPECTS OF MALEHOOD.
LIKE WHAT?
DRINK BEER! ACT DUMB! PICK YOUR NOSE IN PUBLIC!

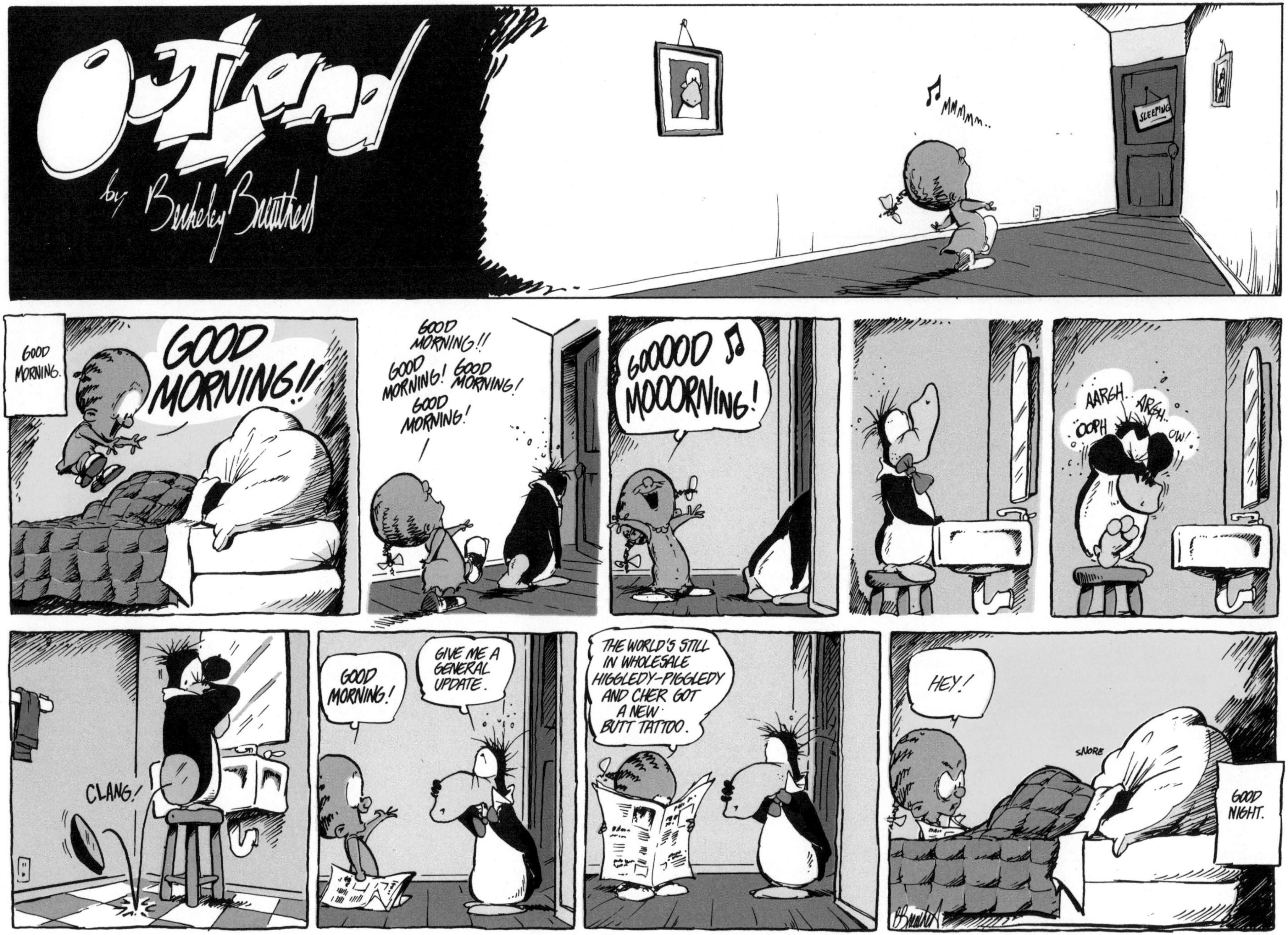

Outland
by Berkeley Breathed
MMMMM..
SLEEPING
GOOD MORNING.
GOOD MORNING!!
GOOD MORNING!!
GOOD MORNING! GOOD MORNING!
GOOD MORNING!
GOOD MORNING!
GOOOOD MOOORNING!
AARGH ARGH
OOPH
OW!
CLANG!
GOOD MORNING!
GIVE ME A GENERAL UPDATE.
THE WORLD'S STILL IN WHOLESALE HIGGLEDY-PIGGLEDY AND CHER GOT A NEW BUTT TATTOO.
HEY!
SNORE
GOOD NIGHT.

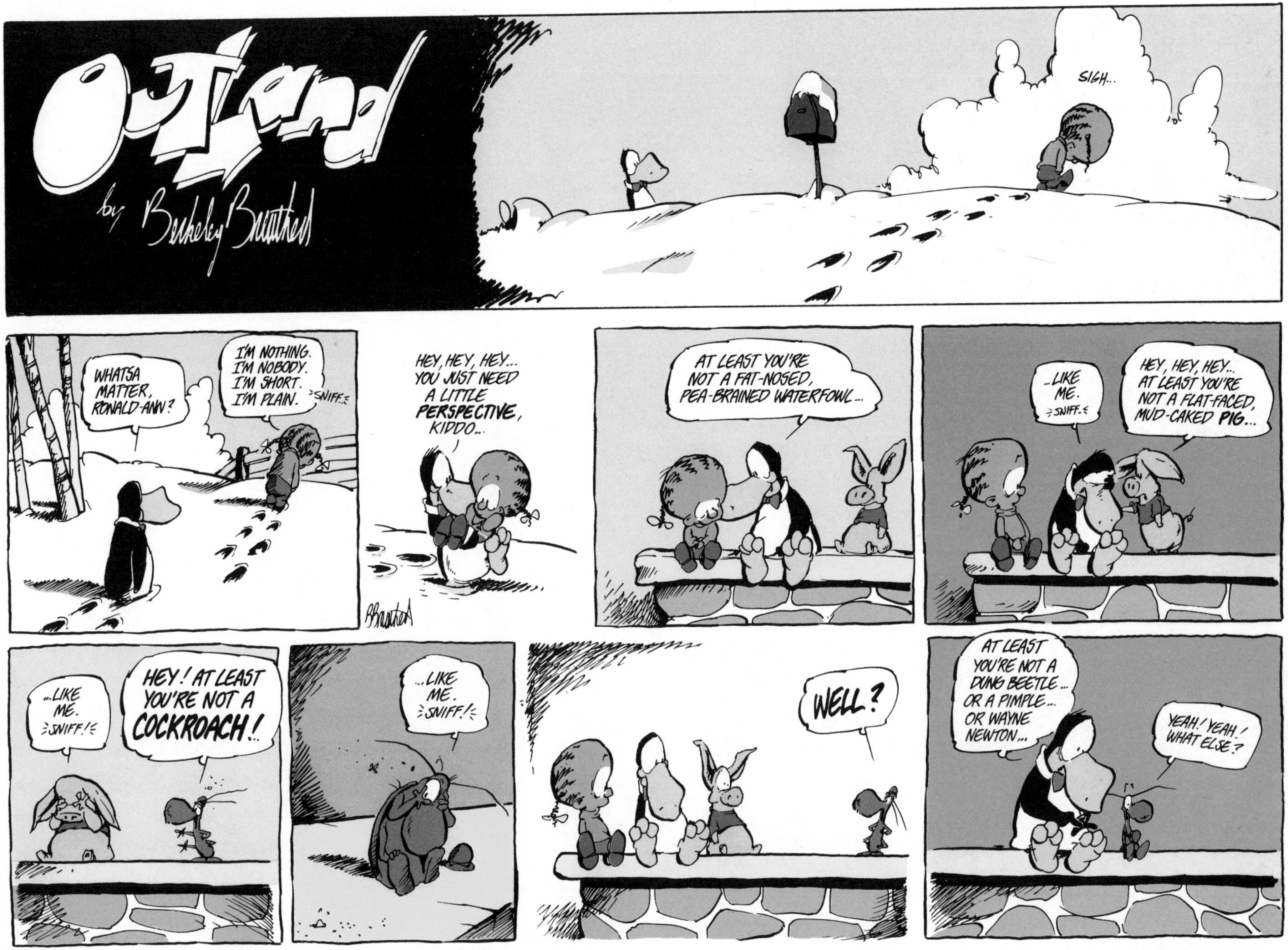
Outland
by Berkeley Breathed
SIGH...
WHATSA MATTER, RONALD-ANN?
I'M NOTHING. I'M NOBODY. I'M SHORT. I'M PLAIN.
SNIFF
HEY, HEY, HEY... YOU JUST NEED A LITTLE PERSPECTIVE, KIDDO...
AT LEAST YOU'RE NOT A FAT-NOSED, PEA-BRAINED WATERFOWL...
...LIKE ME.
SNIFF.
HEY, HEY, HEY... AT LEAST YOU'RE NOT A FLAT-FACED, MUD-CAKED PIG...
...LIKE ME.
SNIFF!
HEY! AT LEAST YOU'RE NOT A COCKROACH!
...LIKE ME.
SNIFF!
WELL?
AT LEAST YOU'RE NOT A DUNG BEETLE... OR A PIMPLE... OR WAYNE NEWTON...
YEAH! YEAH! WHAT ELSE?

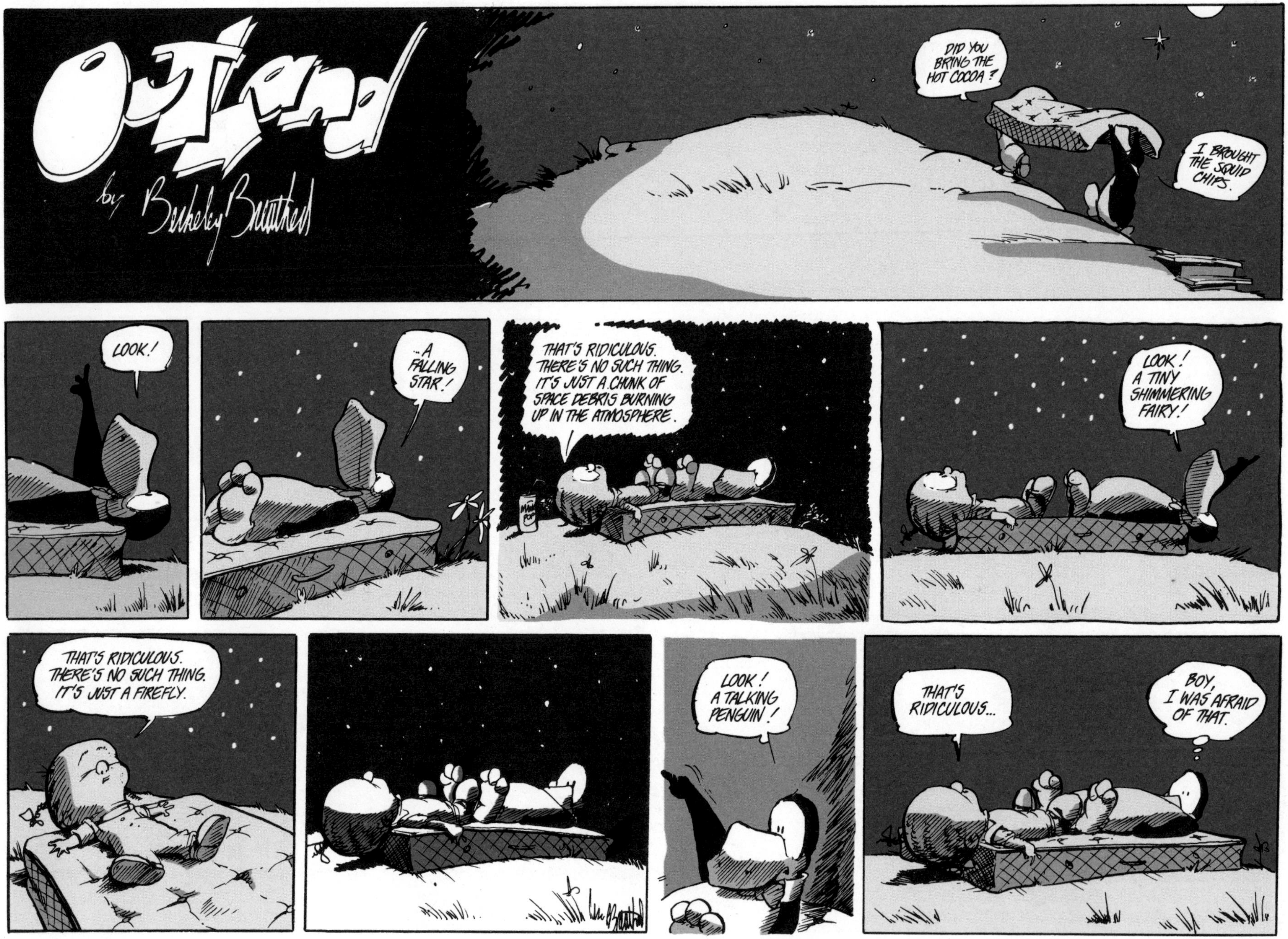

Outland
by Berkeley Breathed
DID YOU BRING THE HOT COCOA?
I BROUGHT THE SQUID CHIPS.
LOOK!
...A FALLING STAR!
THAT'S RIDICULOUS. THERE'S NO SUCH THING. IT'S JUST A CHUNK OF SPACE DEBRIS BURNING UP IN THE ATMOSPHERE.
LOOK! A TINY SHIMMERING FAIRY!
THAT'S RIDICULOUS. THERE'S NO SUCH THING. IT'S JUST A FIREFLY.
LOOK! A TALKING PENGUIN!
THAT'S RIDICULOUS...
BOY, I WAS AFRAID OF THAT.

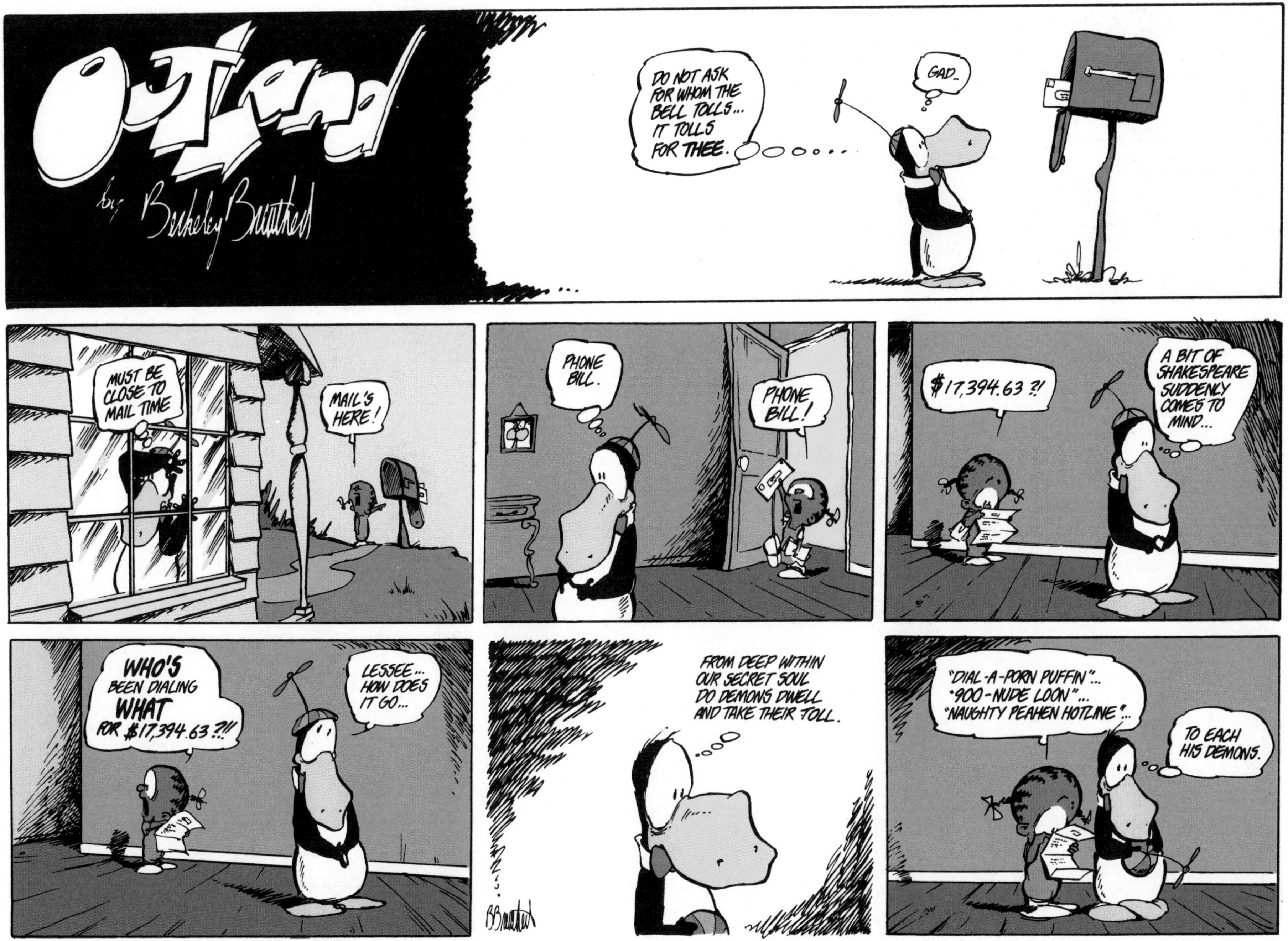
OUTLAND
by Berkeley Breathed
DO NOT ASK FOR WHOM THE BELL TOLLS... IT TOLLS FOR THEE.
GAD..
MUST BE CLOSE TO MAIL TIME
MAIL'S HERE!
PHONE BILL.
PHONE BILL!
$17,394.63 ?!
A BIT OF SHAKESPEARE SUDDENLY COMES TO MIND...
WHO'S BEEN DIALING WHAT FOR $17,394.63 ?!!
LESSEE... HOW DOES IT GO...
FROM DEEP WITHIN OUR SECRET SOUL DO DEMONS DWELL AND TAKE THEIR TOLL.
"DIAL-A-PORN PUFFIN"... "900-NUDE LOON"... "NAUGHTY PEAHEN HOTLINE"...
TO EACH HIS DEMONS.

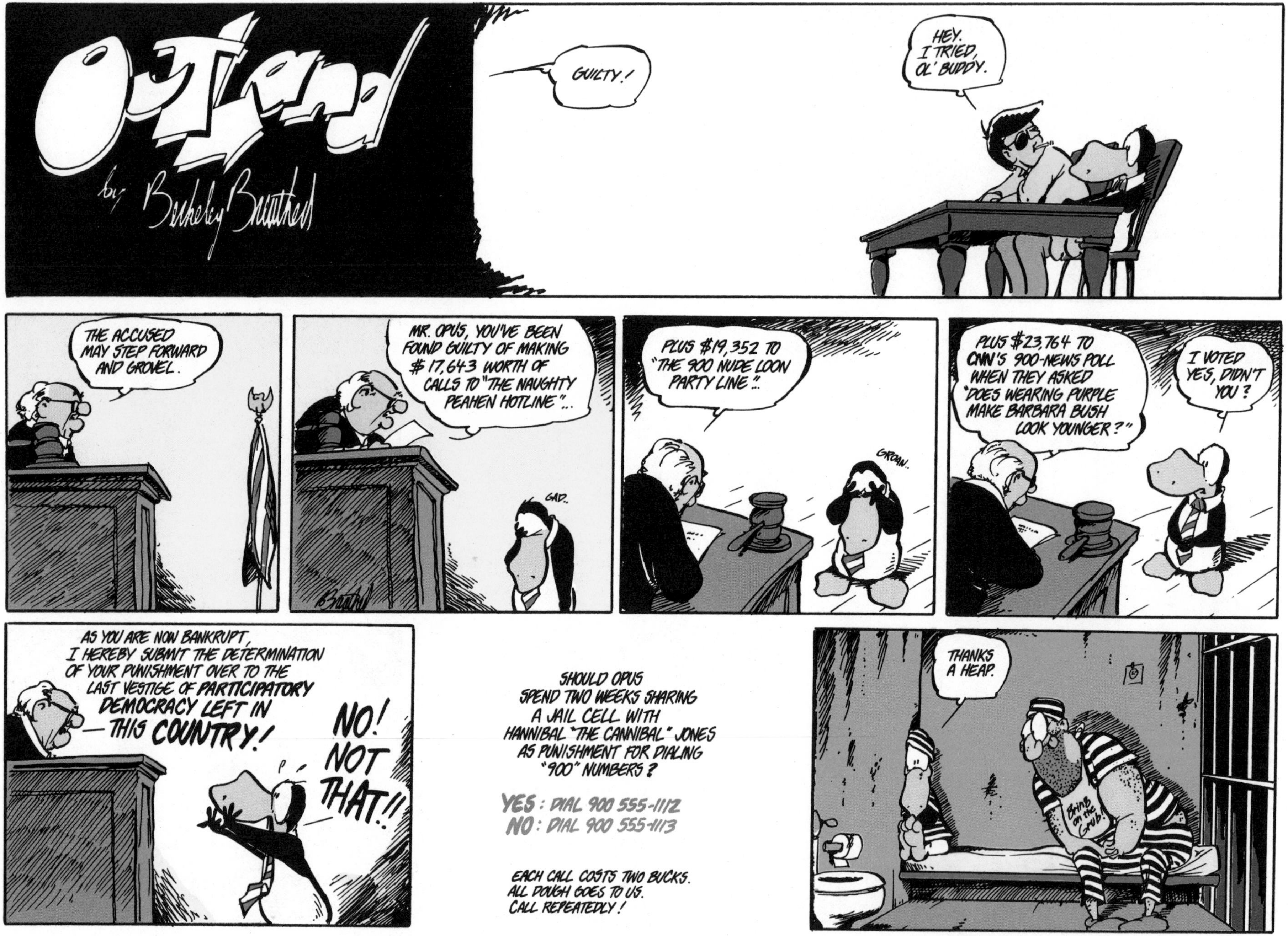
Outland
by Berkeley Breathed
GUILTY!
HEY. I TRIED, OL' BUDDY.
THE ACCUSED MAY STEP FORWARD AND GROVEL.
MR. OPUS, YOU'VE BEEN FOUND GUILTY OF MAKING $17,643 WORTH OF CALLS TO "THE NAUGHTY PEAHEN HOTLINE"...
GAD..
PLUS $19,352 TO "THE 900 NUDE LOON PARTY LINE"..
GROAN..
PLUS $23,764 TO CNN'S 900-NEWS POLL WHEN THEY ASKED "DOES WEARING PURPLE MAKE BARBARA BUSH LOOK YOUNGER?"
I VOTED YES, DIDN'T YOU?
AS YOU ARE NOW BANKRUPT, I HEREBY SUBMIT THE DETERMINATION OF YOUR PUNISHMENT OVER TO THE LAST VESTIGE OF PARTICIPATORY DEMOCRACY LEFT IN THIS COUNTRY!
NO! NOT THAT!!
SHOULD OPUS SPEND TWO WEEKS SHARING A JAIL CELL WITH HANNIBAL "THE CANNIBAL" JONES AS PUNISHMENT FOR DIALING "900" NUMBERS?
YES: DIAL 900 555-1112
NO: DIAL 900 555-1113
EACH CALL COSTS TWO BUCKS. ALL DOUGH GOES TO US. CALL REPEATEDLY!
THANKS A HEAP.
Bring on the Grub!

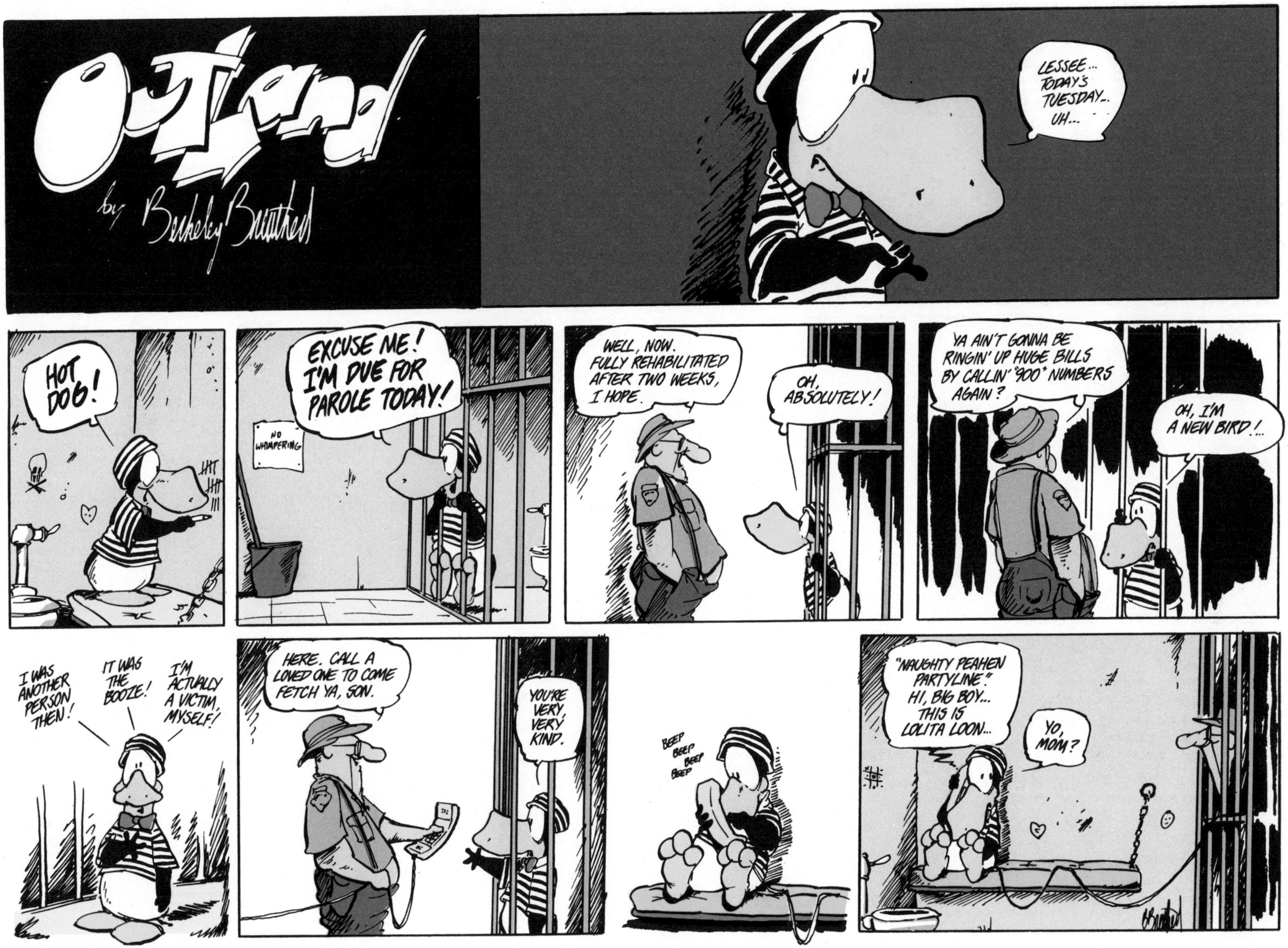
Outland
by Berkeley Breathed
LESSEE... TODAY'S TUESDAY... UH...
HOT DOG!
NO WHIMPERING
EXCUSE ME! I'M DUE FOR PAROLE TODAY!
WELL, NOW. FULLY REHABILITATED AFTER TWO WEEKS, I HOPE.
OH, ABSOLUTELY!
YA AIN'T GONNA BE RINGIN' UP HUGE BILLS BY CALLIN' "900" NUMBERS AGAIN?
OH, I'M A NEW BIRD!...
I WAS ANOTHER PERSON THEN!
IT WAS THE BOOZE!
I'M ACTUALLY A VICTIM, MYSELF!
HERE. CALL A LOVED ONE TO COME FETCH YA, SON.
YOU'RE VERY, VERY KIND.
BEEP BEEP BEEP BEEP
"NAUGHTY PEAHEN PARTYLINE." HI, BIG BOY... THIS IS LOLITA LOON...
YO, MOM?

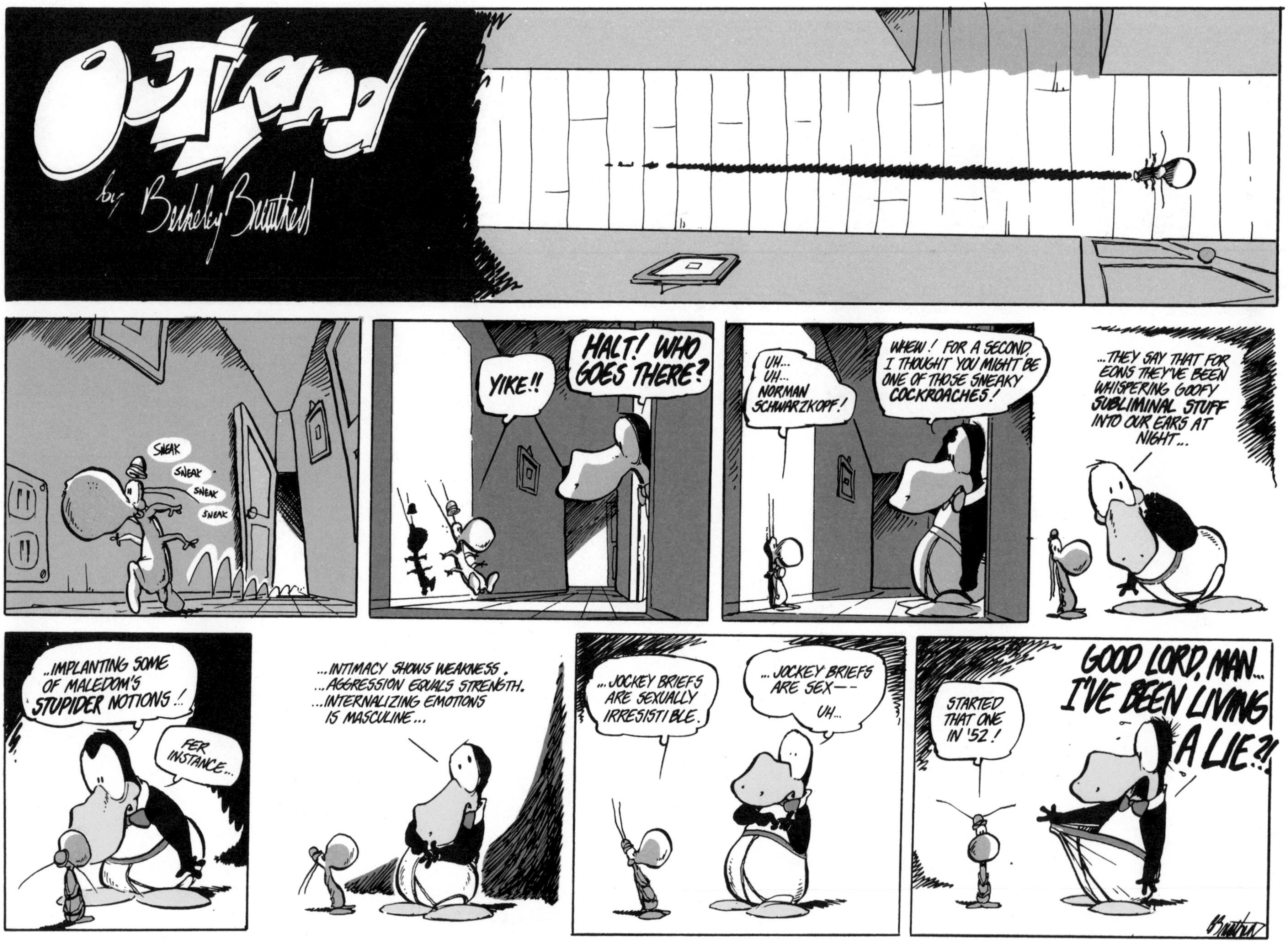

Outland
by Berkeley Breathed
SNEAK
SNEAK
SNEAK
SNEAK
YIKE!!
HALT! WHO GOES THERE?
UH... UH... NORMAN SCHWARZKOPF!
WHEW! FOR A SECOND, I THOUGHT YOU MIGHT BE ONE OF THOSE SNEAKY COCKROACHES!
...THEY SAY THAT FOR EONS THEY'VE BEEN WHISPERING GOOFY SUBLIMINAL STUFF INTO OUR EARS AT NIGHT...
..IMPLANTING SOME OF MALEDOM'S STUPIDER NOTIONS!
FER INSTANCE...
...INTIMACY SHOWS WEAKNESS.
...AGGRESSION EQUALS STRENGTH.
...INTERNALIZING EMOTIONS IS MASCULINE...
...JOCKEY BRIEFS ARE SEXUALLY IRRESISTIBLE.
...JOCKEY BRIEFS ARE SEX--
UH...
STARTED THAT ONE IN '52!
GOOD LORD, MAN... I'VE BEEN LIVING A LIE?!

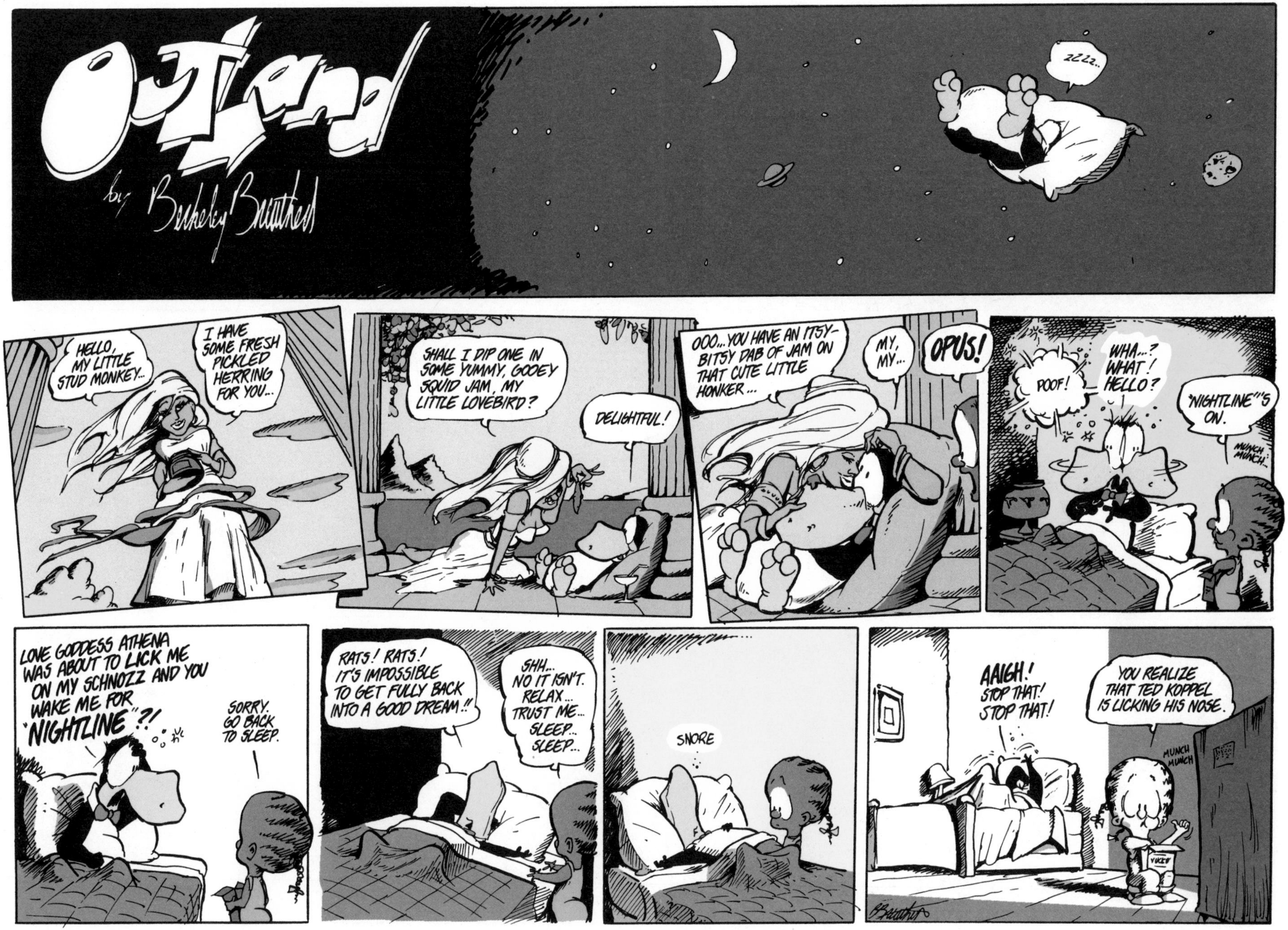

Outland
by Berkeley Breathed
ZZZZ..
HELLO, MY LITTLE STUD MONKEY...
I HAVE SOME FRESH PICKLED HERRING FOR YOU...
SHALL I DIP ONE IN SOME YUMMY, GOOEY SQUID JAM, MY LITTLE LOVEBIRD?
DELIGHTFUL!
OOO... YOU HAVE AN ITSY-BITSY DAB OF JAM ON THAT CUTE LITTLE HONKER...
MY, MY...
OPUS!
POOF!
WHA...? WHAT! HELLO?
"NIGHTLINE"'S ON.
MUNCH MUNCH
LOVE GODDESS ATHENA WAS ABOUT TO LICK ME ON MY SCHNOZZ AND YOU WAKE ME FOR "NIGHTLINE"?!
SORRY. GO BACK TO SLEEP.
RATS! RATS! IT'S IMPOSSIBLE TO GET FULLY BACK INTO A GOOD DREAM!!
SHH... NO IT ISN'T. RELAX... TRUST ME... SLEEP... SLEEP...
SNORE
AAIGH! STOP THAT! STOP THAT!
YOU REALIZE THAT TED KOPPEL IS LICKING HIS NOSE.
MUNCH MUNCH

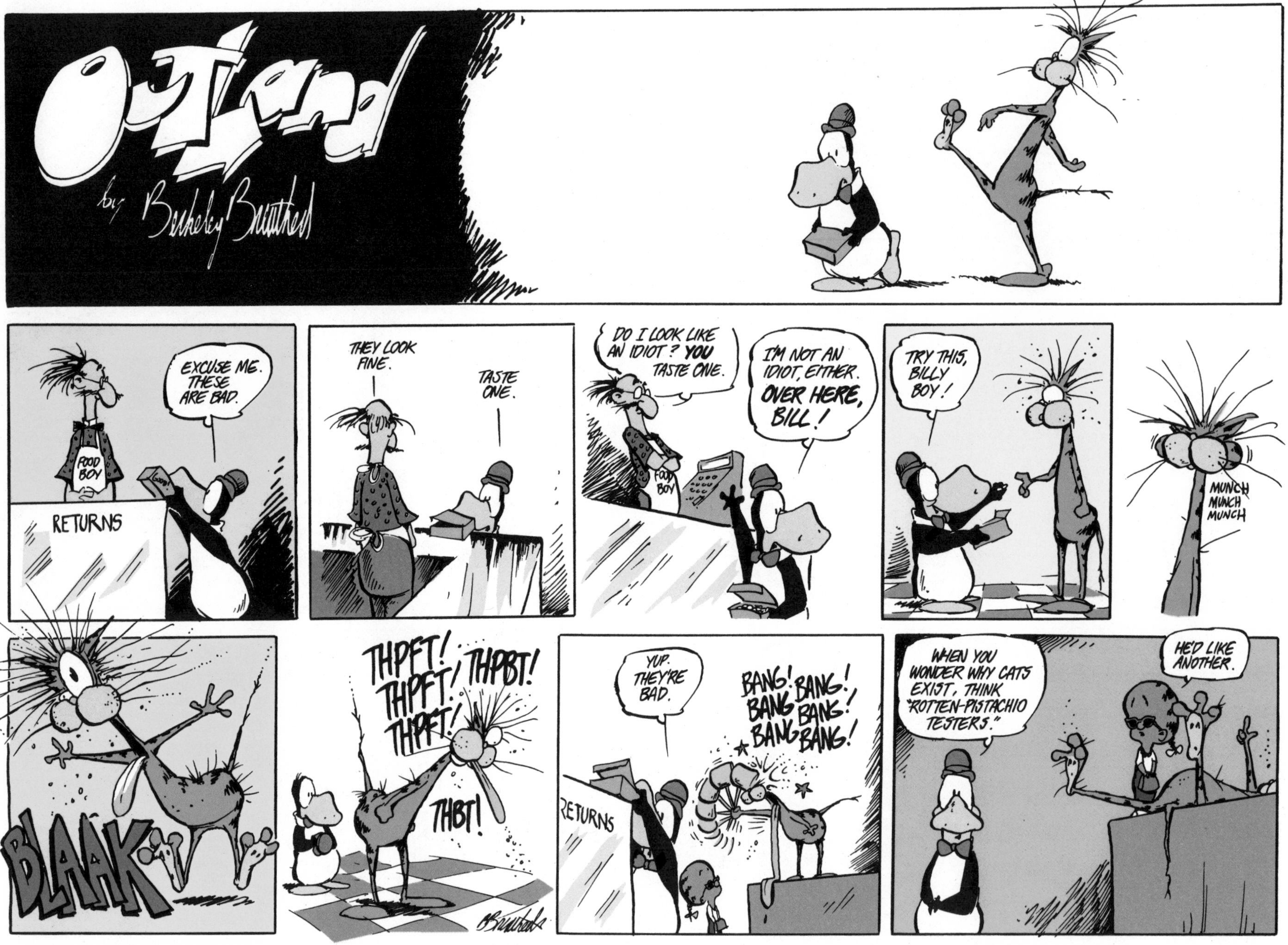

Outland
by Berkeley Breathed
EXCUSE ME. THESE ARE BAD.
FOOD BOY
RETURNS
THEY LOOK FINE.
TASTE ONE.
DO I LOOK LIKE AN IDIOT? YOU TASTE ONE.
I'M NOT AN IDIOT, EITHER. OVER HERE, BILL!
TRY THIS, BILLY BOY!
MUNCH MUNCH MUNCH
BLAAK
THPFT! THPFT! THPFT! THPBT!
THBT!
YUP. THEY'RE BAD.
BANG! BANG! BANG! BANG! BANG! BANG!
RETURNS
WHEN YOU WONDER WHY CATS EXIST, THINK "ROTTEN-PISTACHIO TESTERS."
HE'D LIKE ANOTHER.

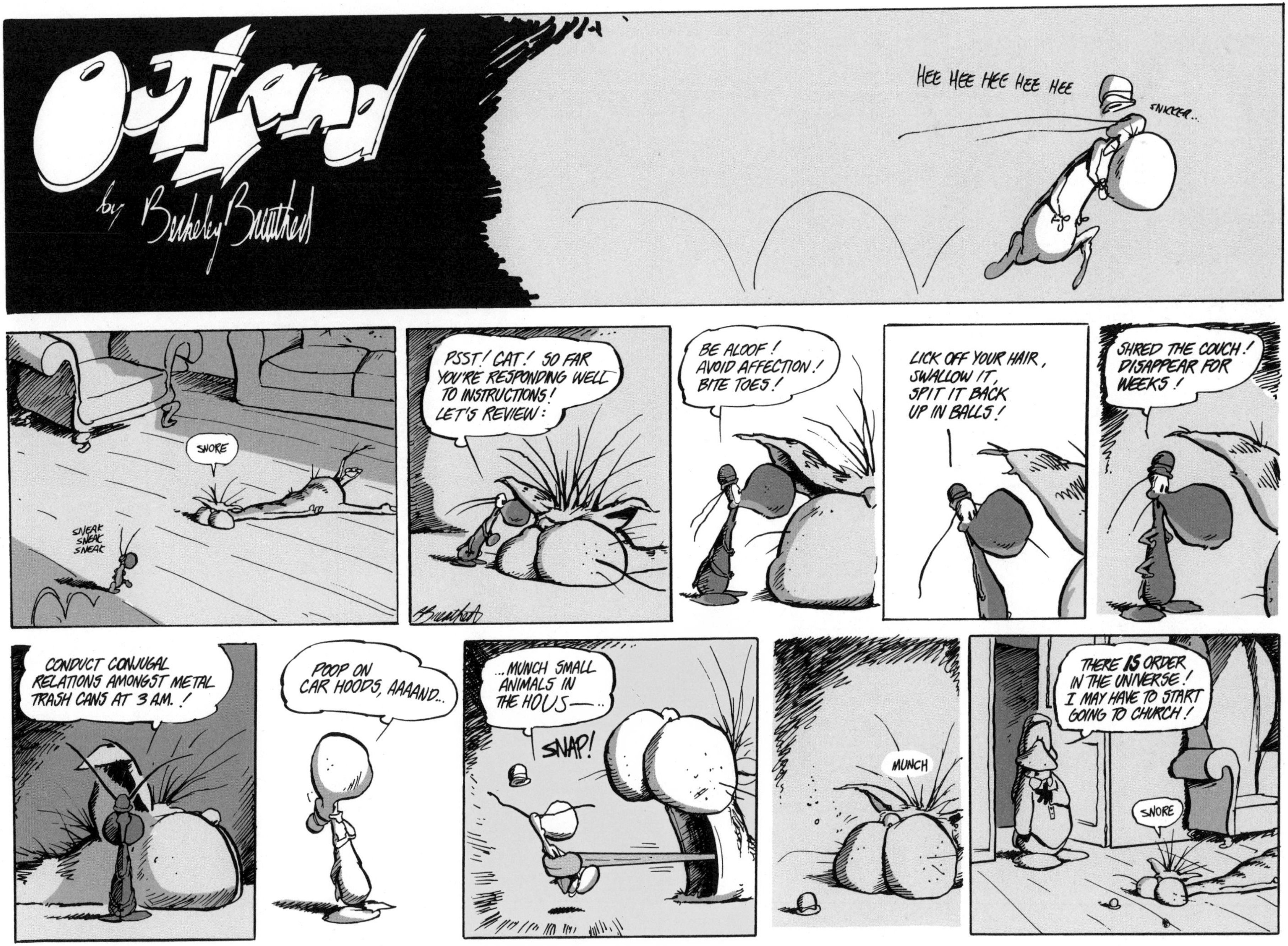
Outland
by Berkeley Breathed
HEE HEE HEE HEE HEE
SNICKER...
SNORE
SNEAK SNEAK SNEAK
PSST! CAT! SO FAR YOU'RE RESPONDING WELL TO INSTRUCTIONS! LET'S REVIEW:
BE ALOOF! AVOID AFFECTION! BITE TOES!
LICK OFF YOUR HAIR, SWALLOW IT, SPIT IT BACK UP IN BALLS!
SHRED THE COUCH! DISAPPEAR FOR WEEKS!
CONDUCT CONJUGAL RELATIONS AMONGST METAL TRASH CANS AT 3 A.M.!
POOP ON CAR HOODS, AAAAND...
...MUNCH SMALL ANIMALS IN THE HOUS——...
SNAP!
MUNCH
THERE IS ORDER IN THE UNIVERSE! I MAY HAVE TO START GOING TO CHURCH!
SNORE

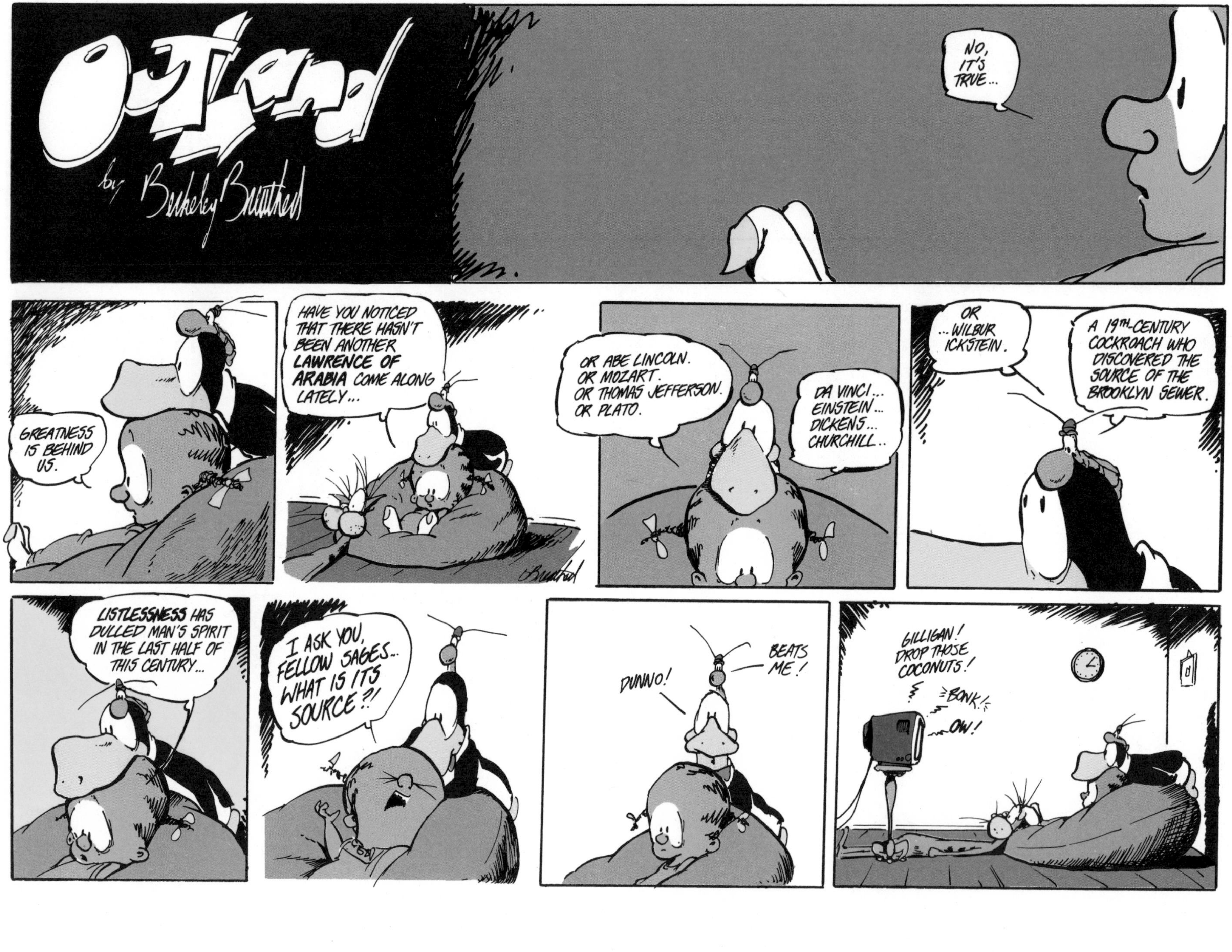
Outland
by Berkeley Breathed
NO, IT'S TRUE...
GREATNESS IS BEHIND US.
HAVE YOU NOTICED THAT THERE HASN'T BEEN ANOTHER LAWRENCE OF ARABIA COME ALONG LATELY...
OR ABE LINCOLN. OR MOZART. OR THOMAS JEFFERSON. OR PLATO.
DA VINCI... EINSTEIN... DICKENS... CHURCHILL...
OR ...WILBUR ICKSTEIN.
A 19TH-CENTURY COCKROACH WHO DISCOVERED THE SOURCE OF THE BROOKLYN SEWER.
LISTLESSNESS HAS DULLED MAN'S SPIRIT IN THE LAST HALF OF THIS CENTURY...
I ASK YOU, FELLOW SAGES... WHAT IS ITS SOURCE?!
DUNNO!
BEATS ME!
GILLIGAN! DROP THOSE COCONUTS!
BONK!
OW!

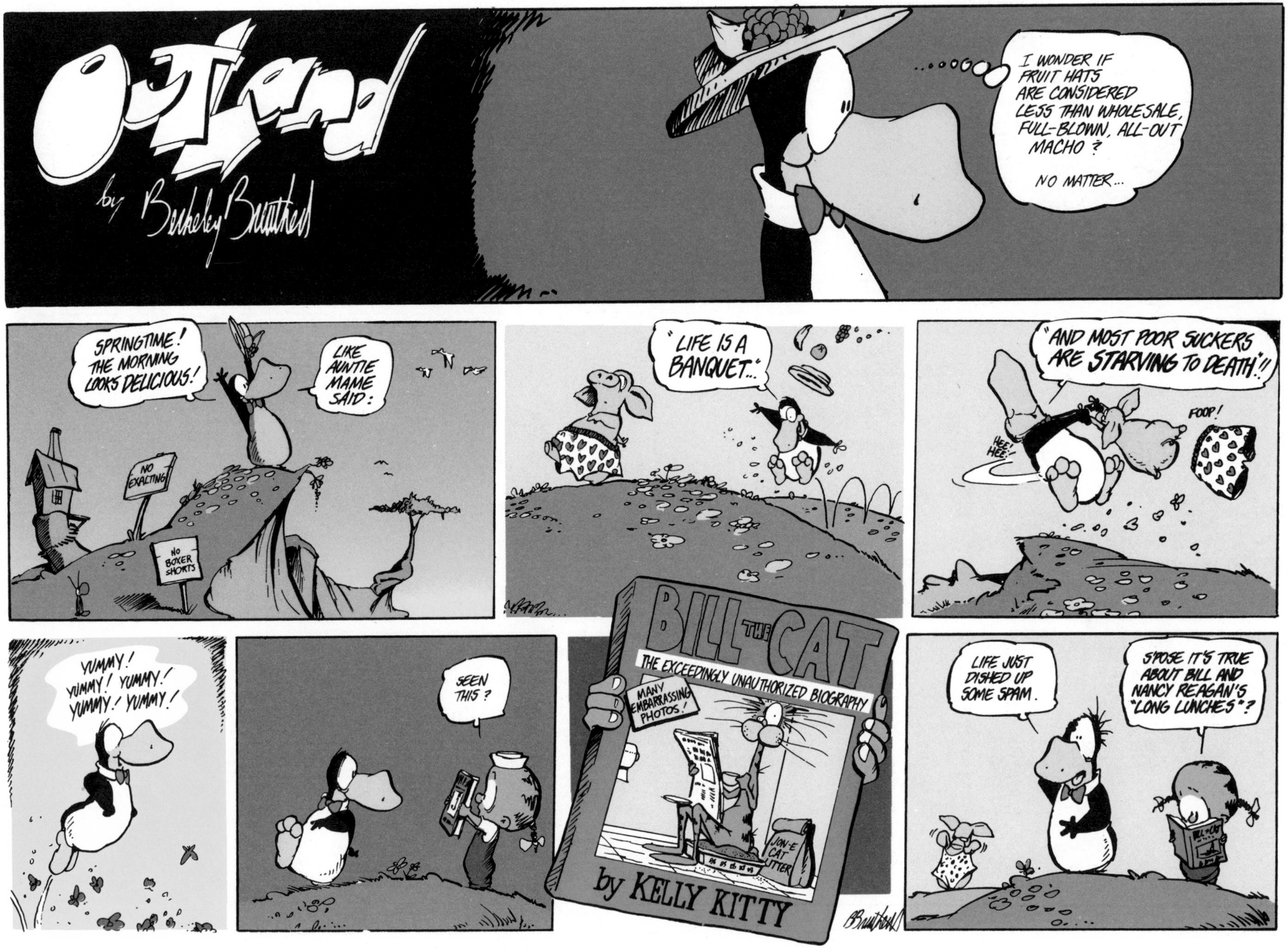

Outland
by Berkeley Breathed
I WONDER IF FRUIT HATS ARE CONSIDERED LESS THAN WHOLESALE, FULL-BLOWN, ALL-OUT MACHO ?
NO MATTER...
SPRINGTIME! THE MORNING LOOKS DELICIOUS!
LIKE AUNTIE MAME SAID:
NO EXALTING
NO BOXER SHORTS
"LIFE IS A BANQUET..."
"AND MOST POOR SUCKERS ARE STARVING TO DEATH"!!
HEE! HEE!
FOOP!
YUMMY! YUMMY! YUMMY! YUMMY! YUMMY!
SEEN THIS ?
BILL THE CAT
THE EXCEEDINGLY UNAUTHORIZED BIOGRAPHY
MANY EMBARRASSING PHOTOS!
by KELLY KITTY
LIFE JUST DISHED UP SOME SPAM.
S'POSE IT'S TRUE ABOUT BILL AND NANCY REAGAN'S "LONG LUNCHES"?
BBreathed

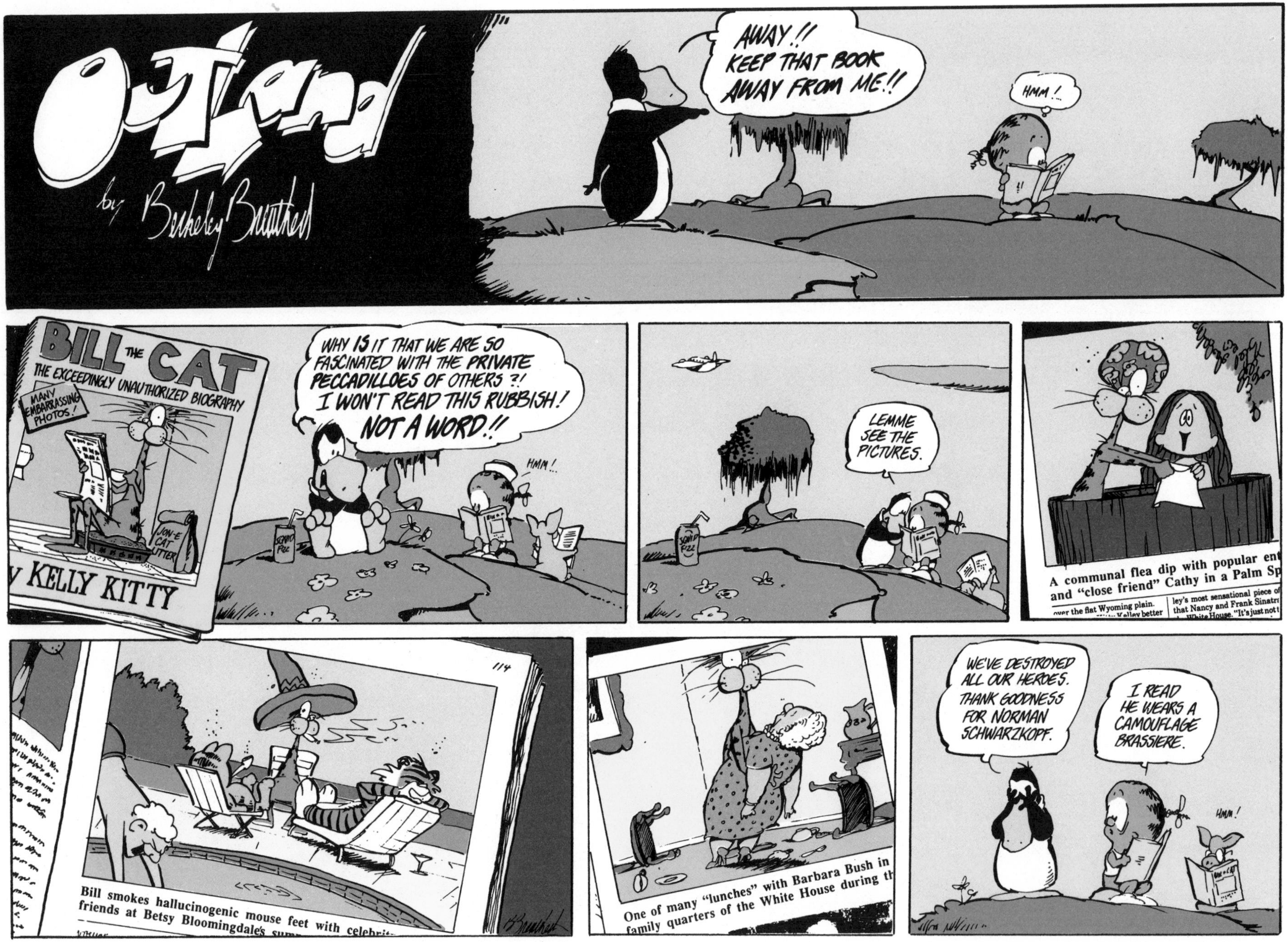
Outland
by Berkeley Breathed
AWAY!! KEEP THAT BOOK AWAY FROM ME!!
HMM!.
BILL THE CAT
THE EXCEEDINGLY UNAUTHORIZED BIOGRAPHY
MANY EMBARRASSING PHOTOS!
JON-E CAT LITTER
y KELLY KITTY
SQUID FIZZ
WHY IS IT THAT WE ARE SO FASCINATED WITH THE PRIVATE PECCADILLOES OF OTHERS ?! I WON'T READ THIS RUBBISH! NOT A WORD!!
HMM!.
LEMME SEE THE PICTURES.
SQUID FIZZ
A communal flea dip with popular ent
and "close friend" Cathy in a Palm Sp
over the flat Wyoming plain.
ley's most sensational piece of
that Nancy and Frank Sinatr
114
Bill smokes hallucinogenic mouse feet with celebrit
friends at Betsy Bloomingdale's sum
One of many "lunches" with Barbara Bush in
family quarters of the White House during th
WE'VE DESTROYED ALL OUR HEROES. THANK GOODNESS FOR NORMAN SCHWARZKOPF.
I READ HE WEARS A CAMOUFLAGE BRASSIERE.
HMM!

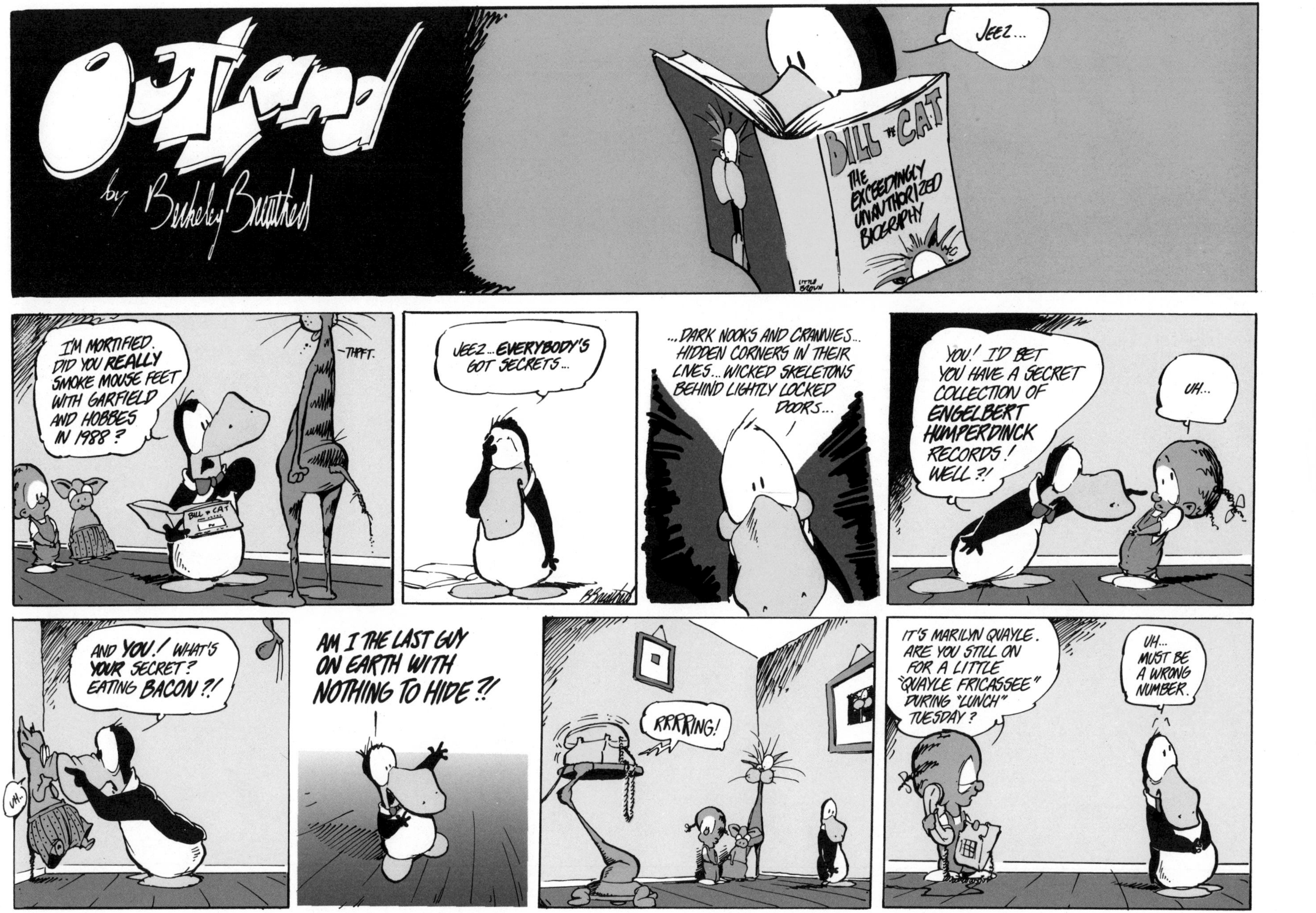
Outland
by Berkeley Breathed
JEEZ...
BILL THE CAT
THE EXCEEDINGLY UNAUTHORIZED BIOGRAPHY
LITTLE BROWN
I'M MORTIFIED. DID YOU REALLY SMOKE MOUSE FEET WITH GARFIELD AND HOBBES IN 1988?
-THPFT.
JEEZ... EVERYBODY'S GOT SECRETS...
...DARK NOOKS AND CRANNIES... HIDDEN CORNERS IN THEIR LIVES... WICKED SKELETONS BEHIND LIGHTLY LOCKED DOORS...
YOU! I'D BET YOU HAVE A SECRET COLLECTION OF ENGELBERT HUMPERDINCK RECORDS! WELL?!
UH...
AND YOU! WHAT'S YOUR SECRET? EATING BACON?!
UH...
AM I THE LAST GUY ON EARTH WITH NOTHING TO HIDE?!
RRRRING!
IT'S MARILYN QUAYLE. ARE YOU STILL ON FOR A LITTLE "QUAYLE FRICASSEE" DURING "LUNCH" TUESDAY?
UH... MUST BE A WRONG NUMBER.

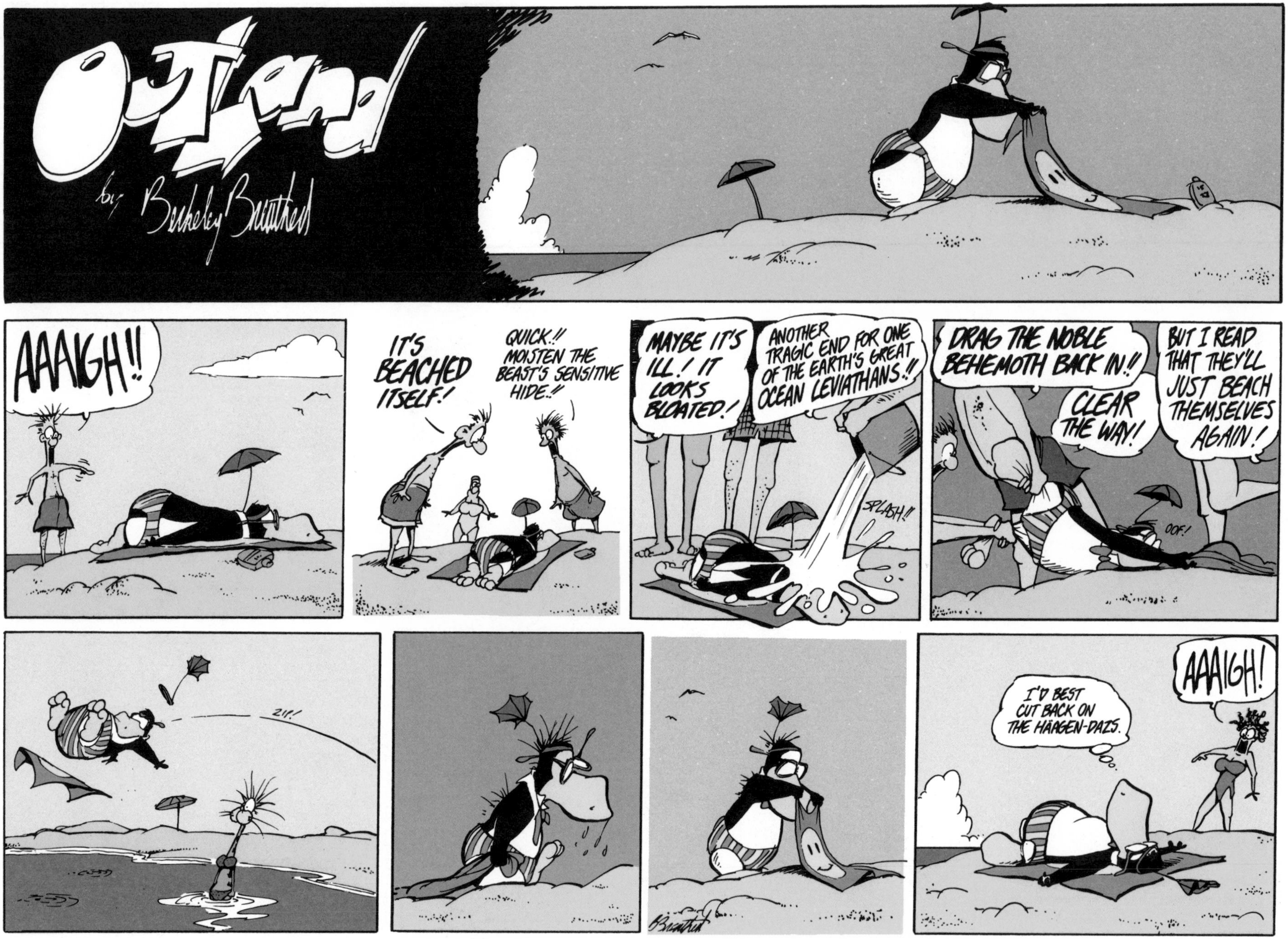
Outland
by Berkeley Breathed
AAAIGH!!
IT'S BEACHED ITSELF!
QUICK.!! MOISTEN THE BEAST'S SENSITIVE HIDE.!!
MAYBE IT'S ILL! IT LOOKS BLOATED!
ANOTHER TRAGIC END FOR ONE OF THE EARTH'S GREAT OCEAN LEVIATHANS.!!
SPLASH!!
DRAG THE NOBLE BEHEMOTH BACK IN!!
CLEAR THE WAY!
BUT I READ THAT THEY'LL JUST BEACH THEMSELVES AGAIN!
OOF!
ZIP!
I'D BEST CUT BACK ON THE HÄAGEN-DAZS.
AAAIGH!
BBreathed

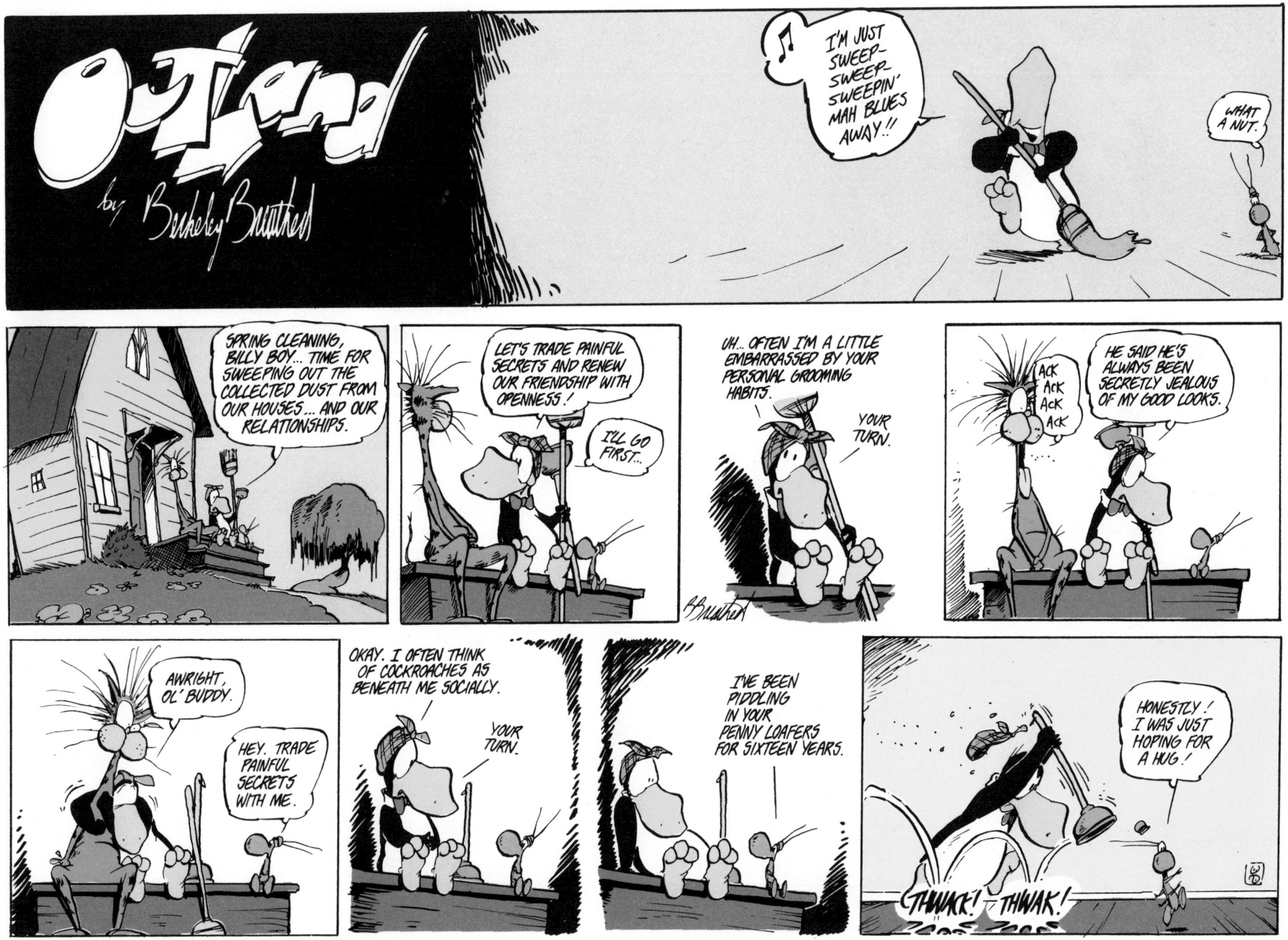
Outland
by Berkeley Breathed
I'M JUST SWEEP-SWEEP-SWEEPIN' MAH BLUES AWAY!!
WHAT A NUT.
SPRING CLEANING, BILLY BOY... TIME FOR SWEEPING OUT THE COLLECTED DUST FROM OUR HOUSES... AND OUR RELATIONSHIPS.
LET'S TRADE PAINFUL SECRETS AND RENEW OUR FRIENDSHIP WITH OPENNESS!
I'LL GO FIRST...
UH... OFTEN I'M A LITTLE EMBARRASSED BY YOUR PERSONAL GROOMING HABITS.
YOUR TURN.
ACK ACK ACK ACK
HE SAID HE'S ALWAYS BEEN SECRETLY JEALOUS OF MY GOOD LOOKS.
AWRIGHT, OL' BUDDY.
HEY. TRADE PAINFUL SECRETS WITH ME.
OKAY. I OFTEN THINK OF COCKROACHES AS BENEATH ME SOCIALLY.
YOUR TURN.
I'VE BEEN PIDDLING IN YOUR PENNY LOAFERS FOR SIXTEEN YEARS.
HONESTLY! I WAS JUST HOPING FOR A HUG!
THWACK! THWAK!

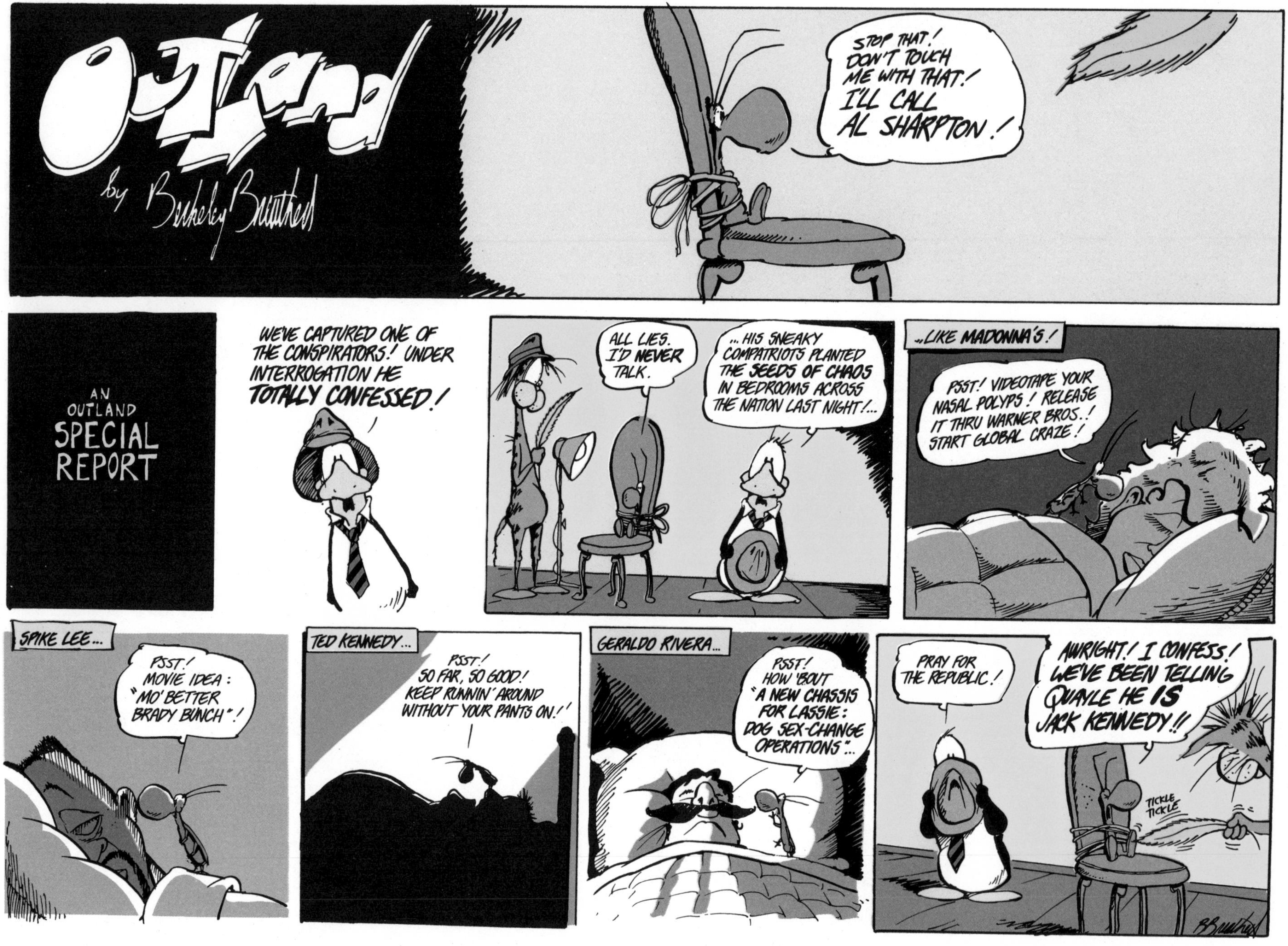
Outland
by Berkeley Breathed
STOP THAT! DON'T TOUCH ME WITH THAT! I'LL CALL AL SHARPTON!
AN OUTLAND SPECIAL REPORT
WE'VE CAPTURED ONE OF THE CONSPIRATORS! UNDER INTERROGATION HE TOTALLY CONFESSED!
ALL LIES. I'D NEVER TALK.
...HIS SNEAKY COMPATRIOTS PLANTED THE SEEDS OF CHAOS IN BEDROOMS ACROSS THE NATION LAST NIGHT!...
...LIKE MADONNA'S!
PSST! VIDEOTAPE YOUR NASAL POLYPS! RELEASE IT THRU WARNER BROS.! START GLOBAL CRAZE!
SPIKE LEE...
PSST! MOVIE IDEA: "MO' BETTER BRADY BUNCH"!
TED KENNEDY...
PSST! SO FAR, SO GOOD! KEEP RUNNIN' AROUND WITHOUT YOUR PANTS ON!
GERALDO RIVERA...
PSST! HOW 'BOUT "A NEW CHASSIS FOR LASSIE: DOG SEX-CHANGE OPERATIONS"...
PRAY FOR THE REPUBLIC!
AWRIGHT! I CONFESS! WE'VE BEEN TELLING QUAYLE HE IS JACK KENNEDY!!
TICKLE TICKLE

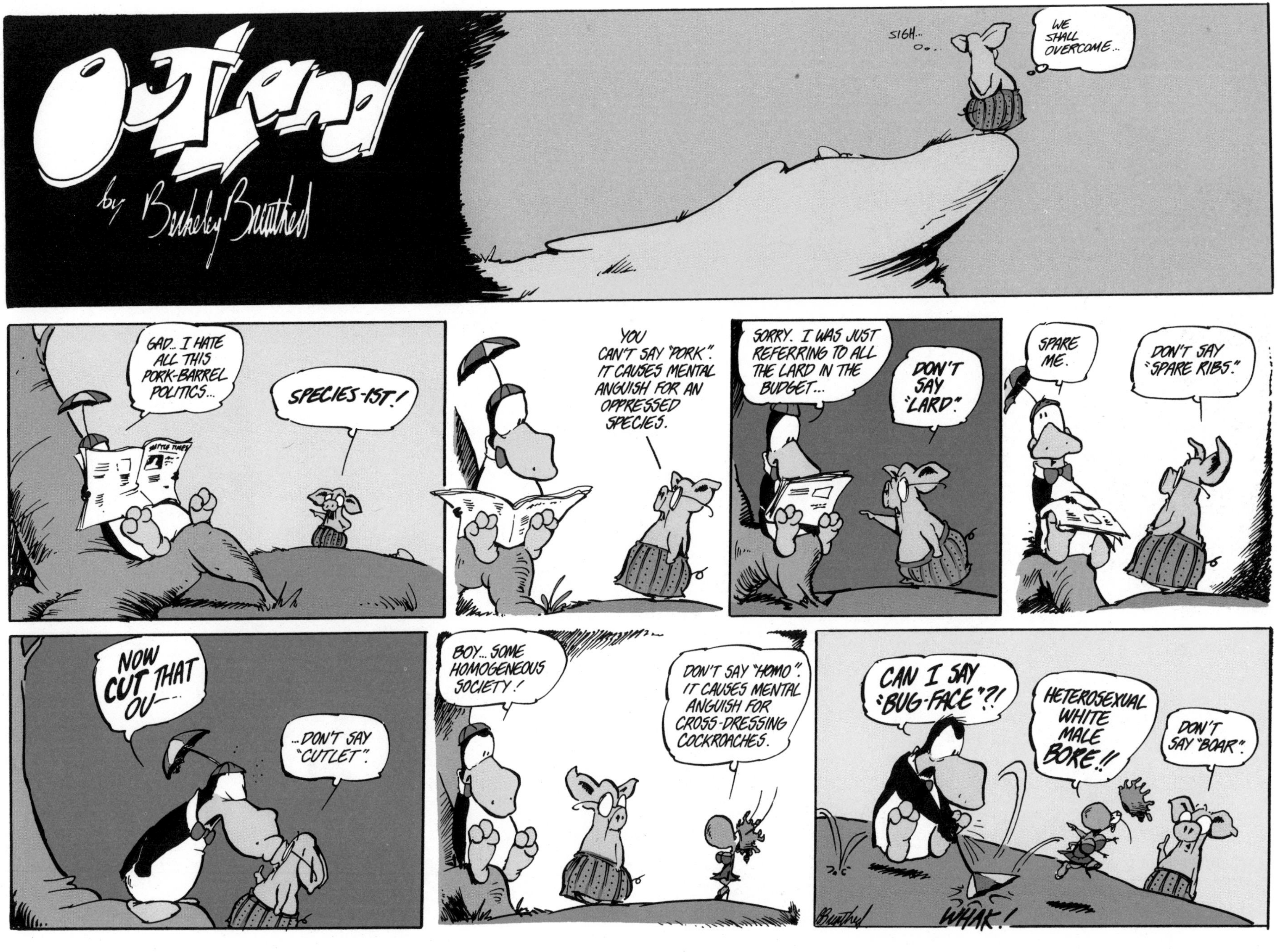
Outland
by Berkeley Breathed
SIGH...
WE SHALL OVERCOME...
GAD... I HATE ALL THIS PORK-BARREL POLITICS...
SPECIES-IST!
YOU CAN'T SAY "PORK". IT CAUSES MENTAL ANGUISH FOR AN OPPRESSED SPECIES.
SORRY. I WAS JUST REFERRING TO ALL THE LARD IN THE BUDGET...
DON'T SAY "LARD".
SPARE ME.
DON'T SAY "SPARE RIBS."
NOW CUT THAT OU—
...DON'T SAY "CUTLET".
BOY... SOME HOMOGENEOUS SOCIETY!
DON'T SAY "HOMO". IT CAUSES MENTAL ANGUISH FOR CROSS-DRESSING COCKROACHES.
CAN I SAY "BUG-FACE"?!
HETEROSEXUAL WHITE MALE BORE!!
DON'T SAY "BOAR".
WHAK!

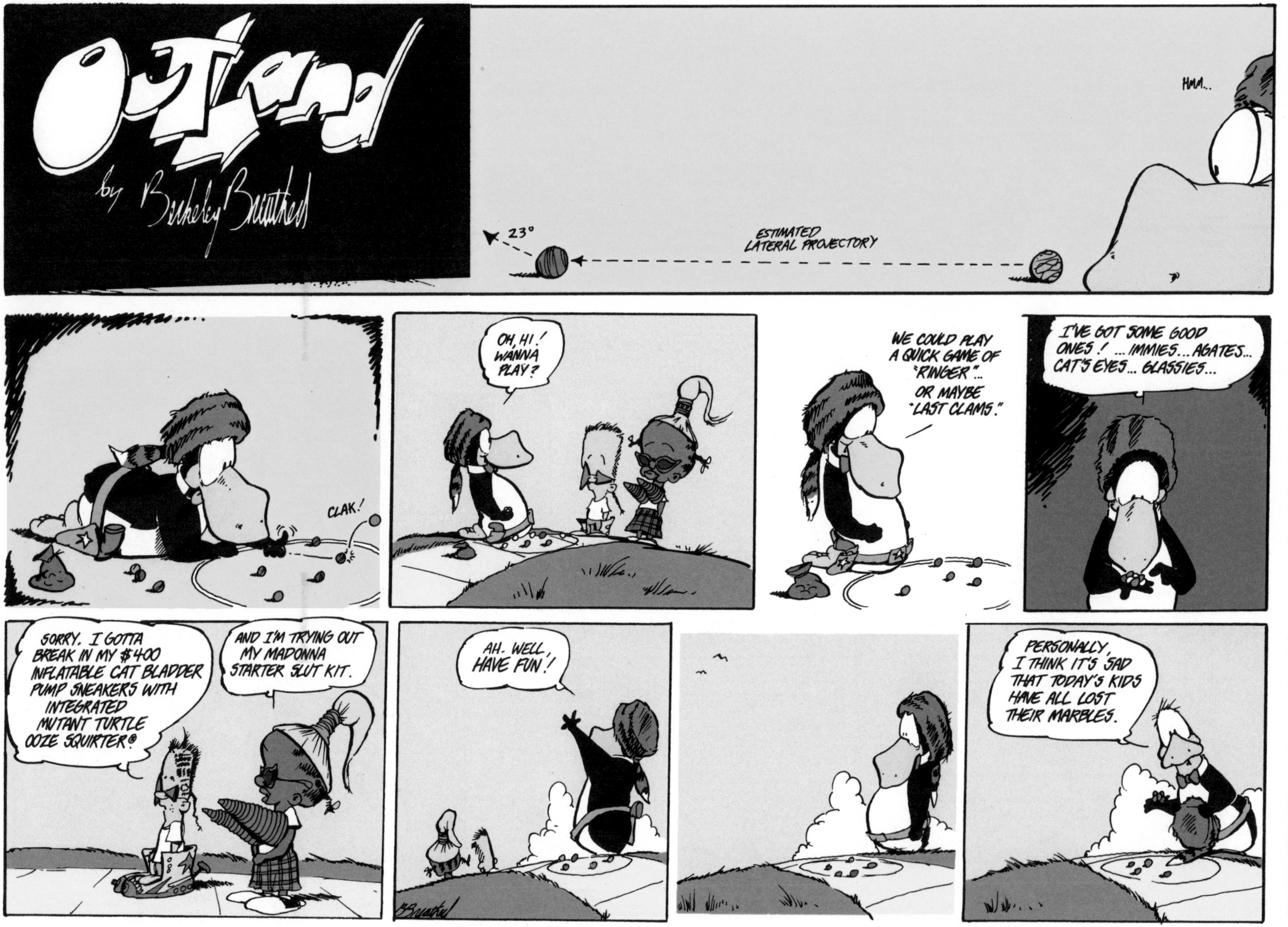
Outland
by Berkeley Breathed
HMM...
23°
ESTIMATED LATERAL PROJECTORY
CLAK!
OH, HI! WANNA PLAY?
WE COULD PLAY A QUICK GAME OF "RINGER"... OR MAYBE "LAST CLAMS."
I'VE GOT SOME GOOD ONES! ... IMMIES... AGATES... CAT'S EYES... GLASSIES...
SORRY. I GOTTA BREAK IN MY $400 INFLATABLE CAT BLADDER PUMP SNEAKERS WITH INTEGRATED MUTANT TURTLE OOZE SQUIRTER®
AND I'M TRYING OUT MY MADONNA STARTER SLUT KIT.
AH. WELL, HAVE FUN!
PERSONALLY, I THINK IT'S SAD THAT TODAY'S KIDS HAVE ALL LOST THEIR MARBLES.
BBreathed

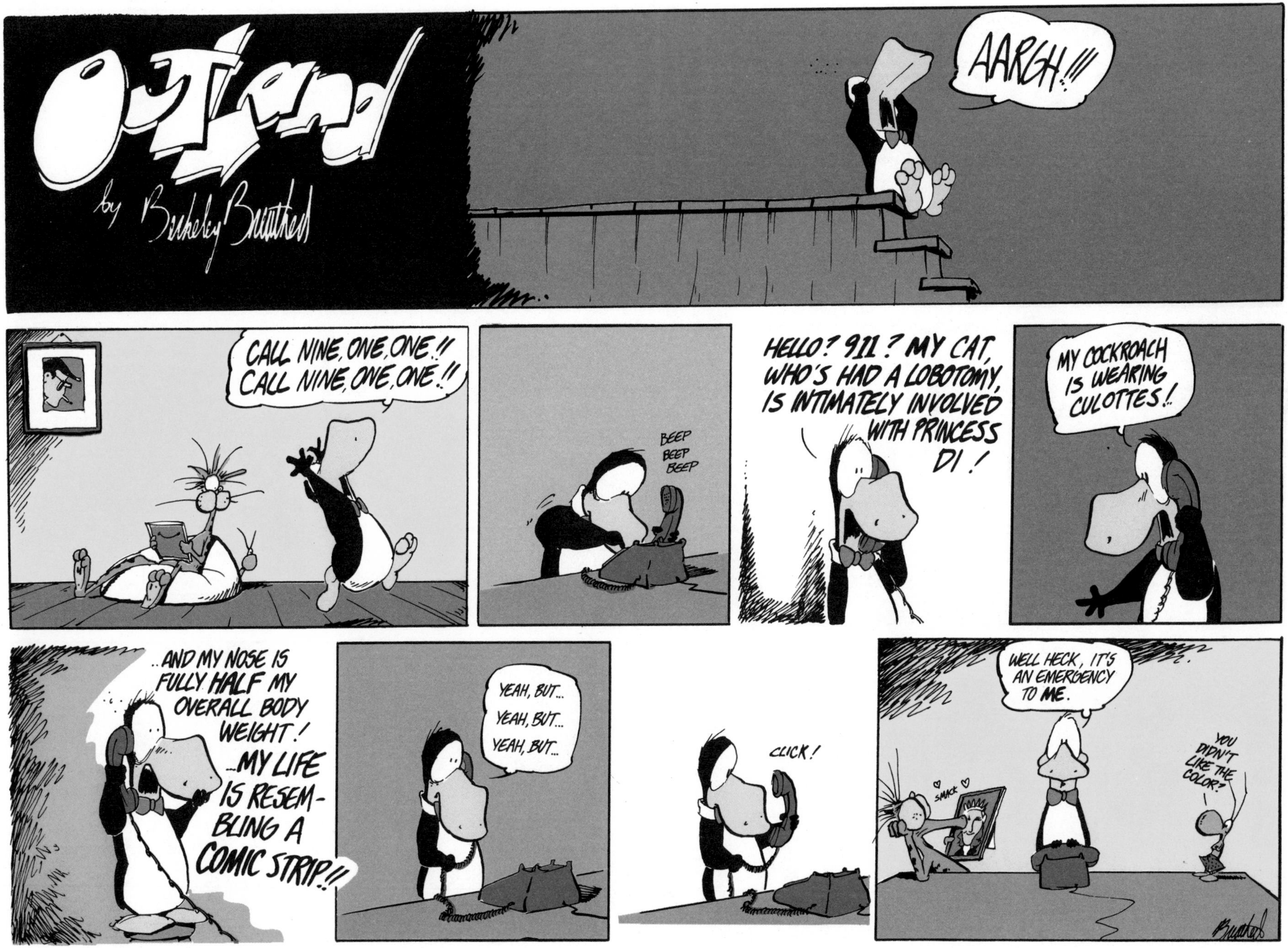
Outland
by Berkeley Breathed
AARGH!!!
CALL NINE, ONE, ONE!! CALL NINE, ONE, ONE!!
BEEP BEEP BEEP
HELLO? 911? MY CAT, WHO'S HAD A LOBOTOMY, IS INTIMATELY INVOLVED WITH PRINCESS DI!
MY COCKROACH IS WEARING CULOTTES!
..AND MY NOSE IS FULLY HALF MY OVERALL BODY WEIGHT! ...MY LIFE IS RESEMBLING A COMIC STRIP!!
YEAH, BUT...
YEAH, BUT...
YEAH, BUT...
CLICK!
WELL HECK, IT'S AN EMERGENCY TO ME.
SMACK
YOU DIDN'T LIKE THE COLOR?
Breathed

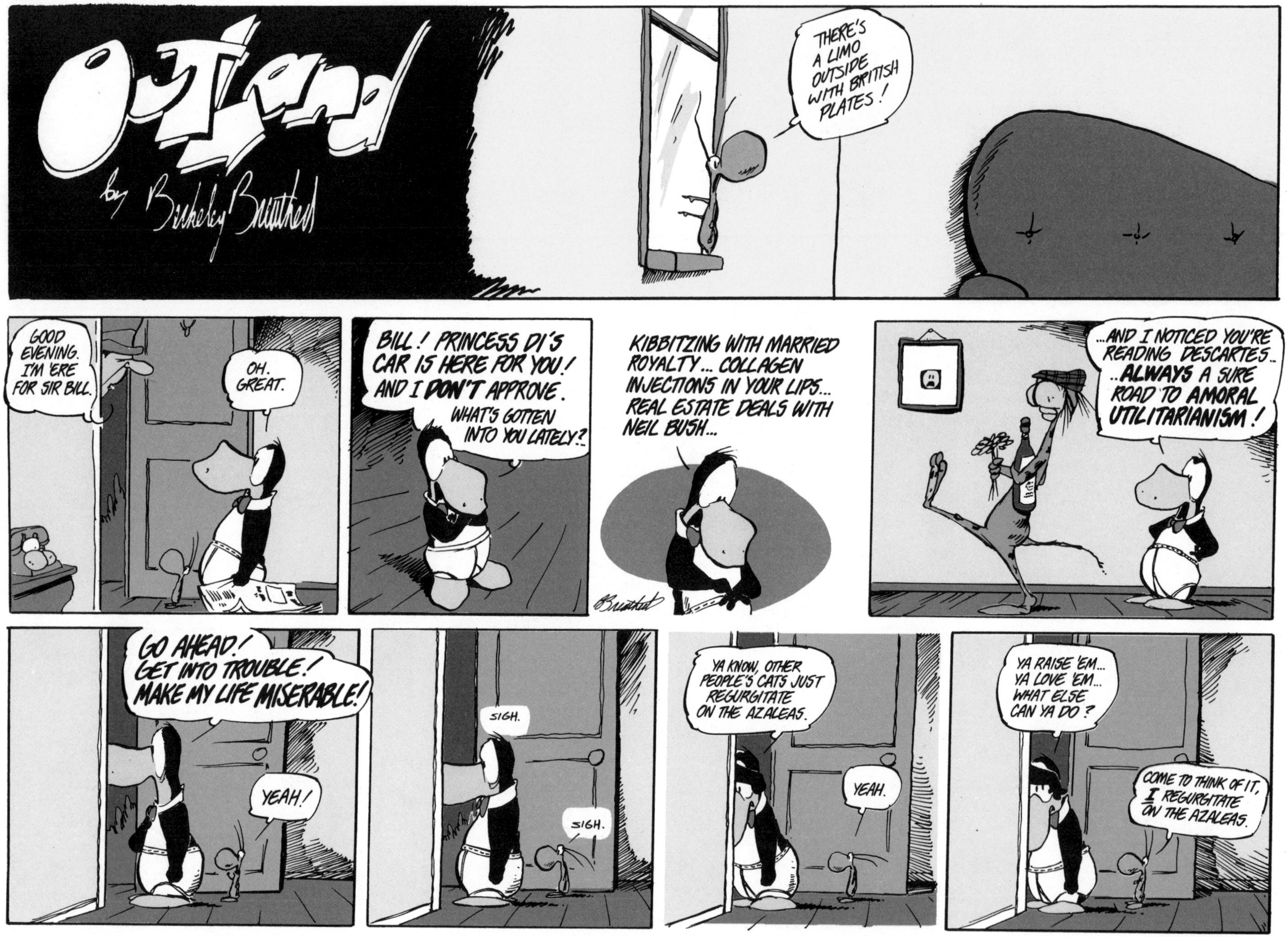
OUTLAND
by Berkeley Breathed
THERE'S A LIMO OUTSIDE WITH BRITISH PLATES!
GOOD EVENING. I'M 'ERE FOR SIR BILL.
OH. GREAT.
BILL! PRINCESS DI'S CAR IS HERE FOR YOU! AND I DON'T APPROVE.
WHAT'S GOTTEN INTO YOU LATELY?
KIBBITZING WITH MARRIED ROYALTY... COLLAGEN INJECTIONS IN YOUR LIPS... REAL ESTATE DEALS WITH NEIL BUSH...
...AND I NOTICED YOU'RE READING DESCARTES... ...ALWAYS A SURE ROAD TO AMORAL UTILITARIANISM!
GO AHEAD! GET INTO TROUBLE! MAKE MY LIFE MISERABLE!
YEAH!
SIGH.
SIGH.
YA KNOW, OTHER PEOPLE'S CATS JUST REGURGITATE ON THE AZALEAS.
YEAH.
YA RAISE 'EM... YA LOVE 'EM... WHAT ELSE CAN YA DO?
COME TO THINK OF IT, I REGURGITATE ON THE AZALEAS.

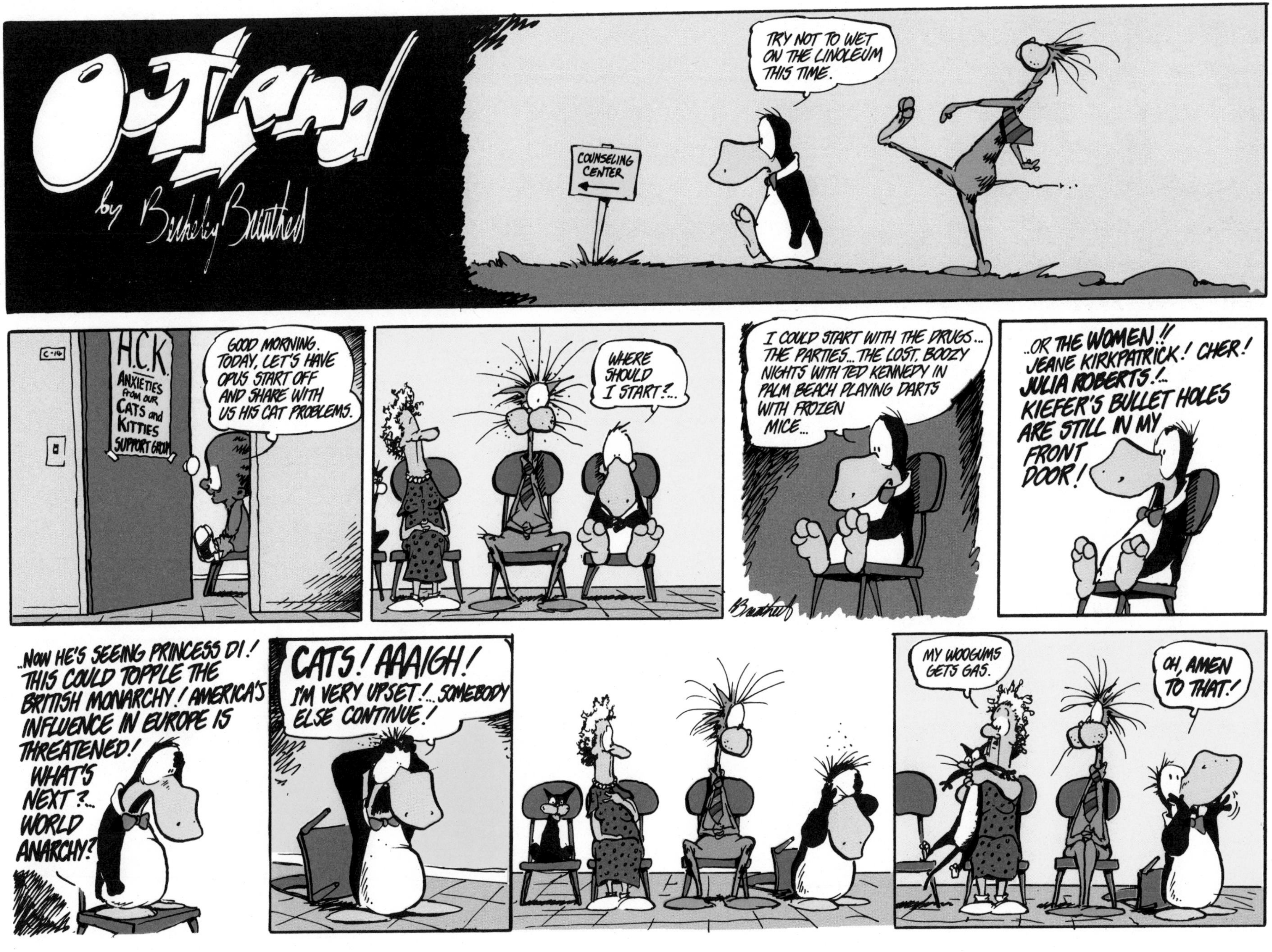
Outland
by Berkeley Breathed
TRY NOT TO WET ON THE LINOLEUM THIS TIME.
COUNSELING CENTER
H.C.K. ANXIETIES from our CATS and KITTIES SUPPORT GROUP
GOOD MORNING. TODAY, LET'S HAVE OPUS START OFF AND SHARE WITH US HIS CAT PROBLEMS.
WHERE SHOULD I START?...
I COULD START WITH THE DRUGS... THE PARTIES... THE LOST, BOOZY NIGHTS WITH TED KENNEDY IN PALM BEACH PLAYING DARTS WITH FROZEN MICE...
...OR THE WOMEN!! JEANE KIRKPATRICK! CHER! JULIA ROBERTS!... KIEFER'S BULLET HOLES ARE STILL IN MY FRONT DOOR!
...NOW HE'S SEEING PRINCESS DI! THIS COULD TOPPLE THE BRITISH MONARCHY! AMERICA'S INFLUENCE IN EUROPE IS THREATENED! WHAT'S NEXT?... WORLD ANARCHY?
CATS! AAAIGH! I'M VERY UPSET!... SOMEBODY ELSE CONTINUE!
MY WOOGUMS GETS GAS.
OH, AMEN TO THAT!

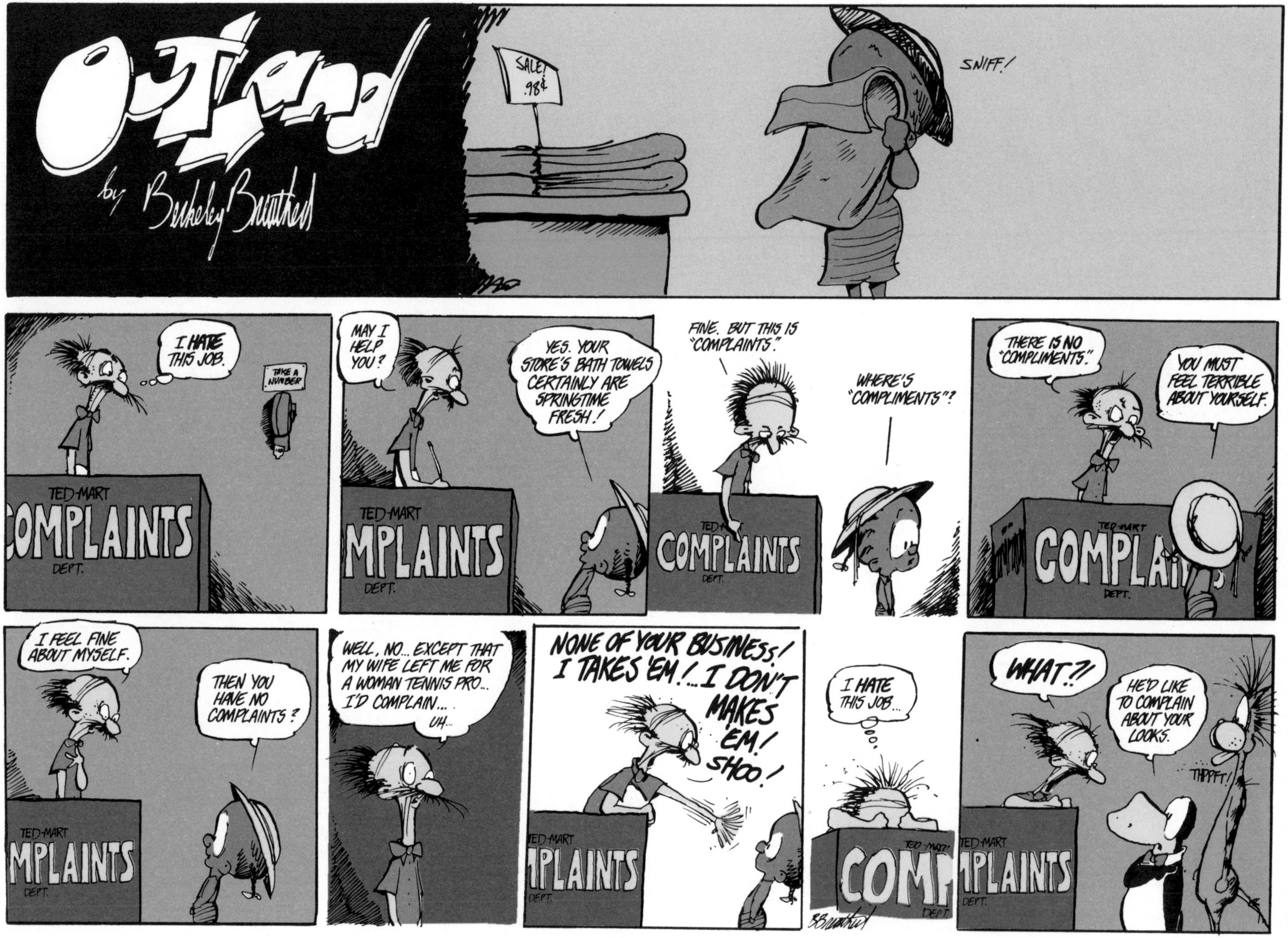
Outland
by Berkeley Breathed
SALE! .98¢
SNIFF!
I HATE THIS JOB.
TAKE A NUMBER
TED-MART
COMPLAINTS
DEPT.
MAY I HELP YOU?
YES. YOUR STORE'S BATH TOWELS CERTAINLY ARE SPRINGTIME FRESH!
FINE. BUT THIS IS "COMPLAINTS."
WHERE'S "COMPLIMENTS"?
THERE IS NO "COMPLIMENTS."
YOU MUST FEEL TERRIBLE ABOUT YOURSELF.
I FEEL FINE ABOUT MYSELF.
THEN YOU HAVE NO COMPLAINTS?
WELL, NO... EXCEPT THAT MY WIFE LEFT ME FOR A WOMAN TENNIS PRO... I'D COMPLAIN... UH...
NONE OF YOUR BUSINESS! I TAKES 'EM!... I DON'T MAKES 'EM! SHOO!
I HATE THIS JOB...
WHAT?!
HE'D LIKE TO COMPLAIN ABOUT YOUR LOOKS.
THPPFT!

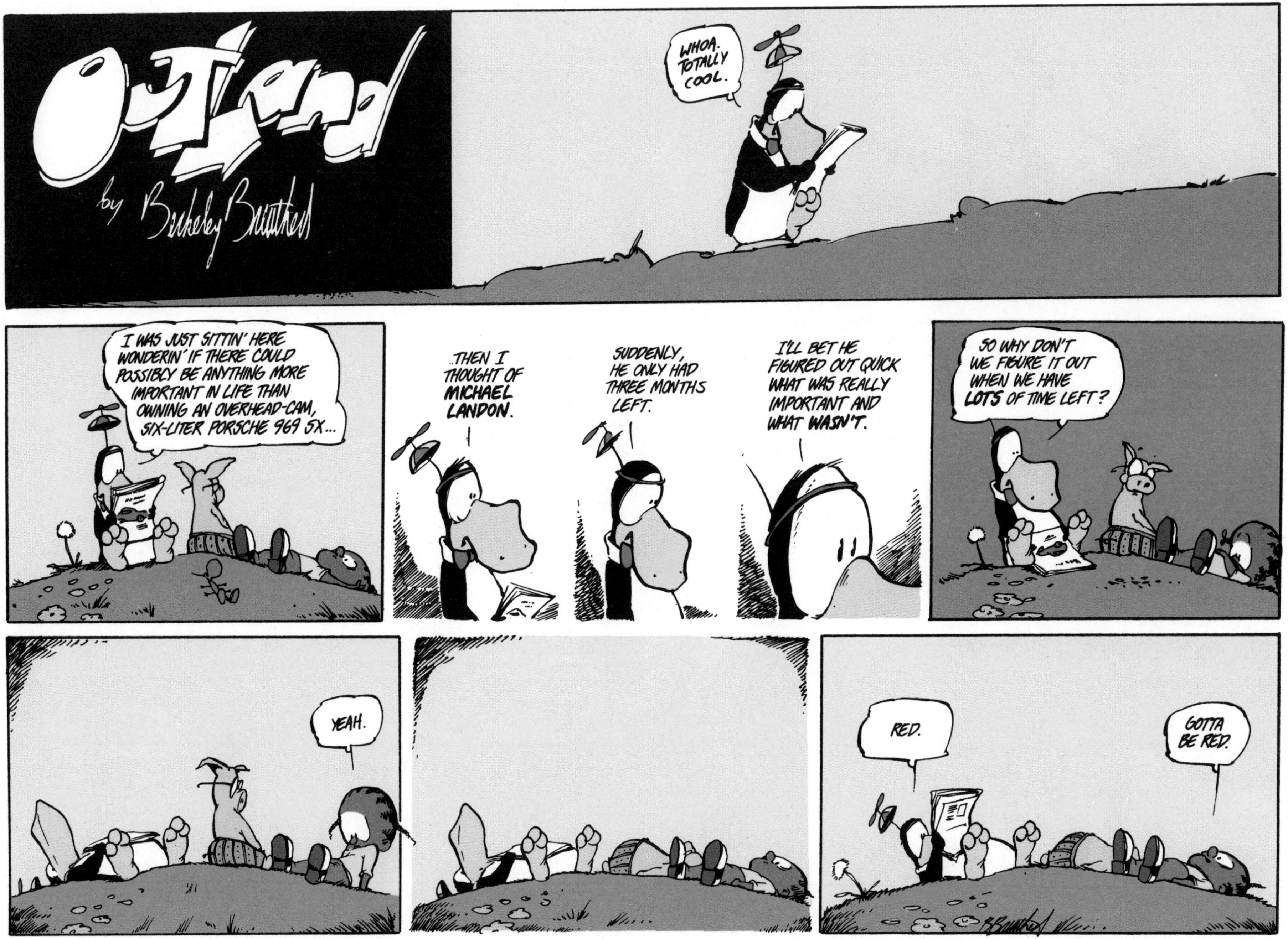
Outland
by Berkeley Breathed
WHOA. TOTALLY COOL.
I WAS JUST SITTIN' HERE WONDERIN' IF THERE COULD POSSIBLY BE ANYTHING MORE IMPORTANT IN LIFE THAN OWNING AN OVERHEAD-CAM, SIX-LITER PORSCHE 969 SX...
...THEN I THOUGHT OF MICHAEL LANDON.
SUDDENLY, HE ONLY HAD THREE MONTHS LEFT.
I'LL BET HE FIGURED OUT QUICK WHAT WAS REALLY IMPORTANT AND WHAT WASN'T.
SO WHY DON'T WE FIGURE IT OUT WHEN WE HAVE LOTS OF TIME LEFT?
YEAH.
RED.
GOTTA BE RED.
B. Breathed

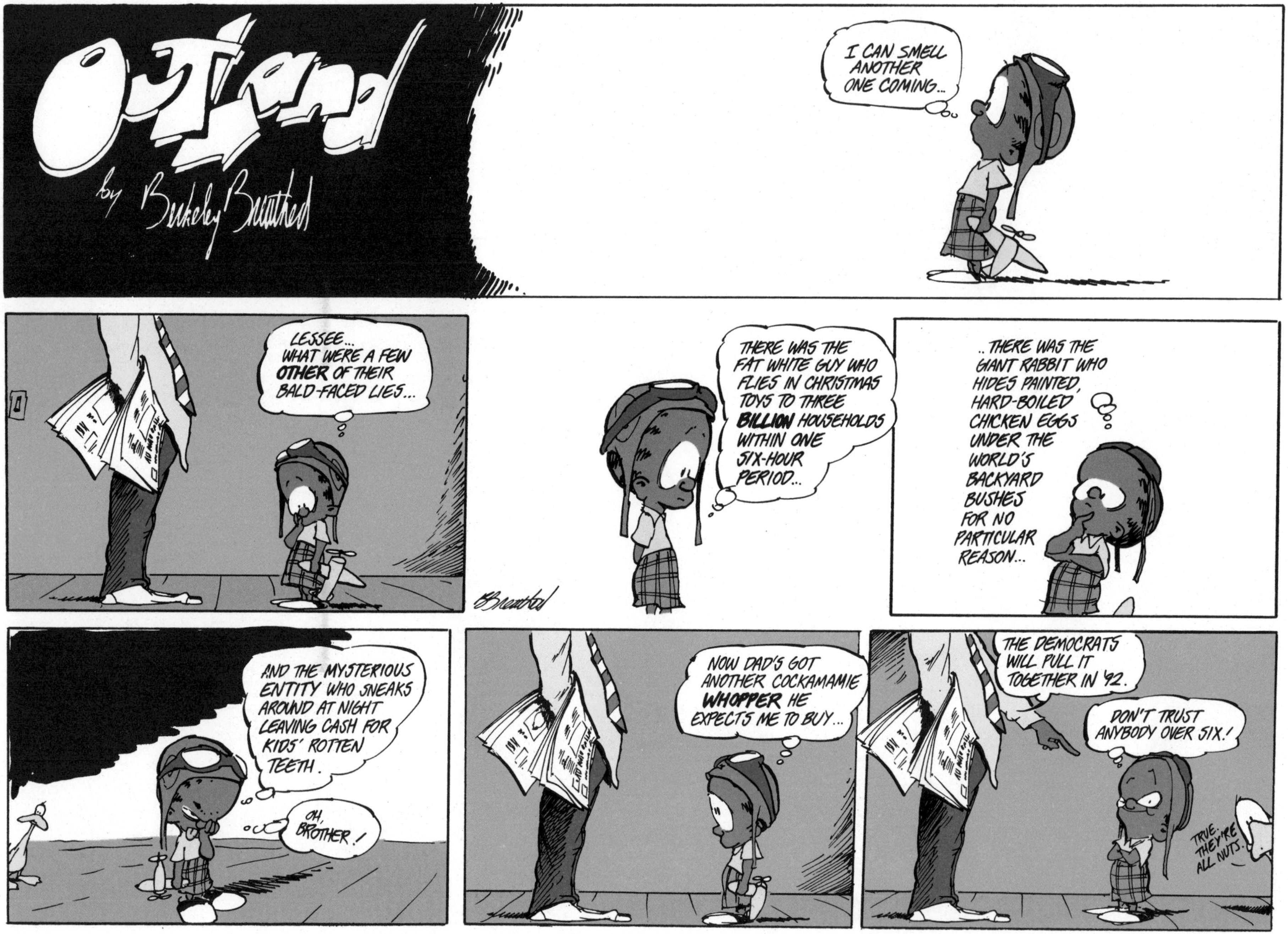
Outland
by Berkeley Breathed
I CAN SMELL ANOTHER ONE COMING...
LESSEE... WHAT WERE A FEW OTHER OF THEIR BALD-FACED LIES...
THERE WAS THE FAT WHITE GUY WHO FLIES IN CHRISTMAS TOYS TO THREE BILLION HOUSEHOLDS WITHIN ONE SIX-HOUR PERIOD...
...THERE WAS THE GIANT RABBIT WHO HIDES PAINTED, HARD-BOILED CHICKEN EGGS UNDER THE WORLD'S BACKYARD BUSHES FOR NO PARTICULAR REASON...
AND THE MYSTERIOUS ENTITY WHO SNEAKS AROUND AT NIGHT LEAVING CASH FOR KIDS' ROTTEN TEETH.
OH, BROTHER!
NOW DAD'S GOT ANOTHER COCKAMAMIE WHOPPER HE EXPECTS ME TO BUY...
THE DEMOCRATS WILL PULL IT TOGETHER IN '92.
DON'T TRUST ANYBODY OVER SIX.!
TRUE. THEY'RE ALL NUTS.

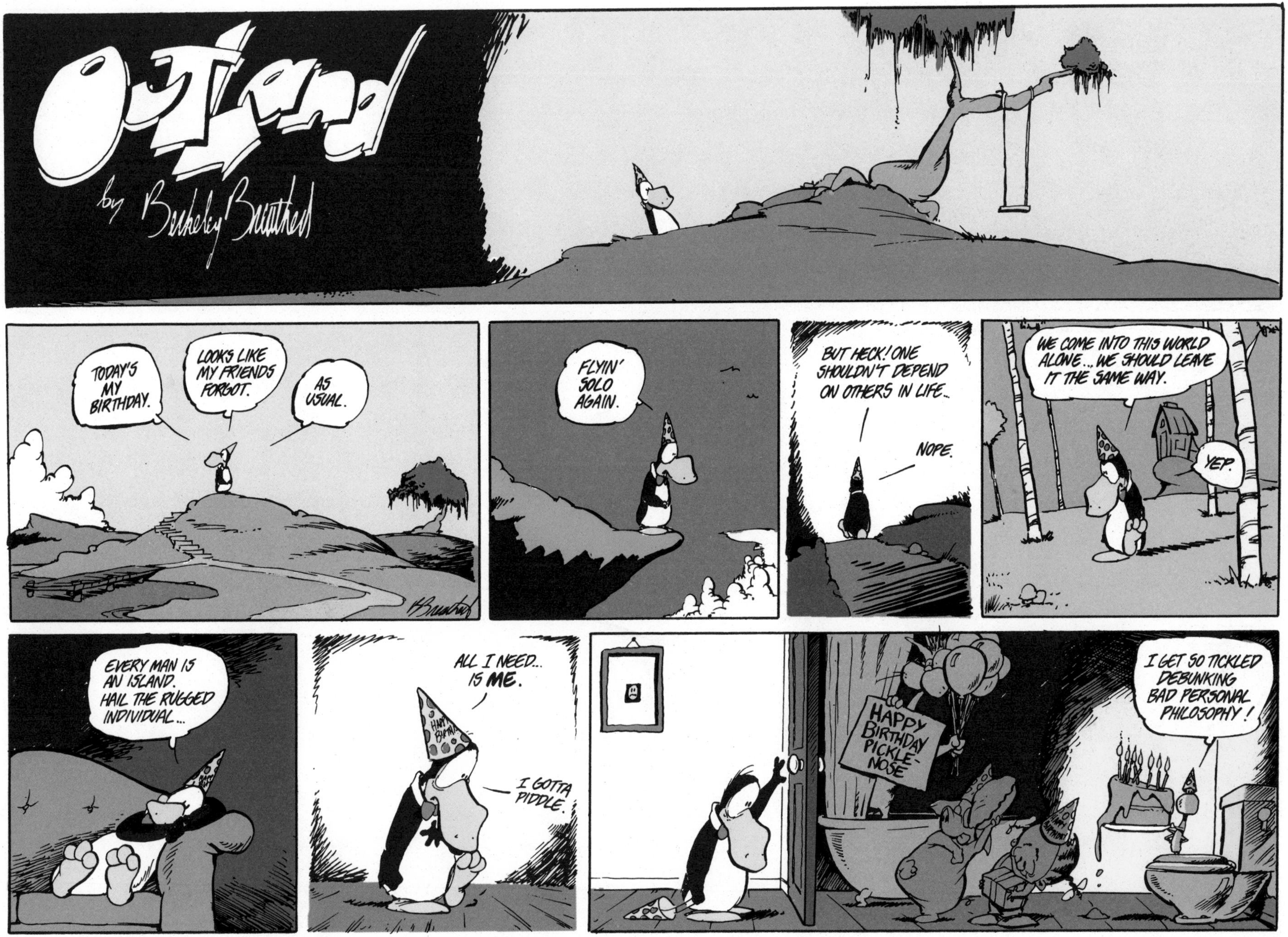

Outland
by Berkeley Breathed
TODAY'S MY BIRTHDAY.
LOOKS LIKE MY FRIENDS FORGOT.
AS USUAL.
FLYIN' SOLO AGAIN.
BUT HECK! ONE SHOULDN'T DEPEND ON OTHERS IN LIFE..
NOPE.
WE COME INTO THIS WORLD ALONE... WE SHOULD LEAVE IT THE SAME WAY.
YEP.
EVERY MAN IS AN ISLAND. HAIL THE RUGGED INDIVIDUAL...
ALL I NEED... IS ME.
I GOTTA PIDDLE.
HAPPY BIRTHDAY PICKLE-NOSE
I GET SO TICKLED DEBUNKING BAD PERSONAL PHILOSOPHY!

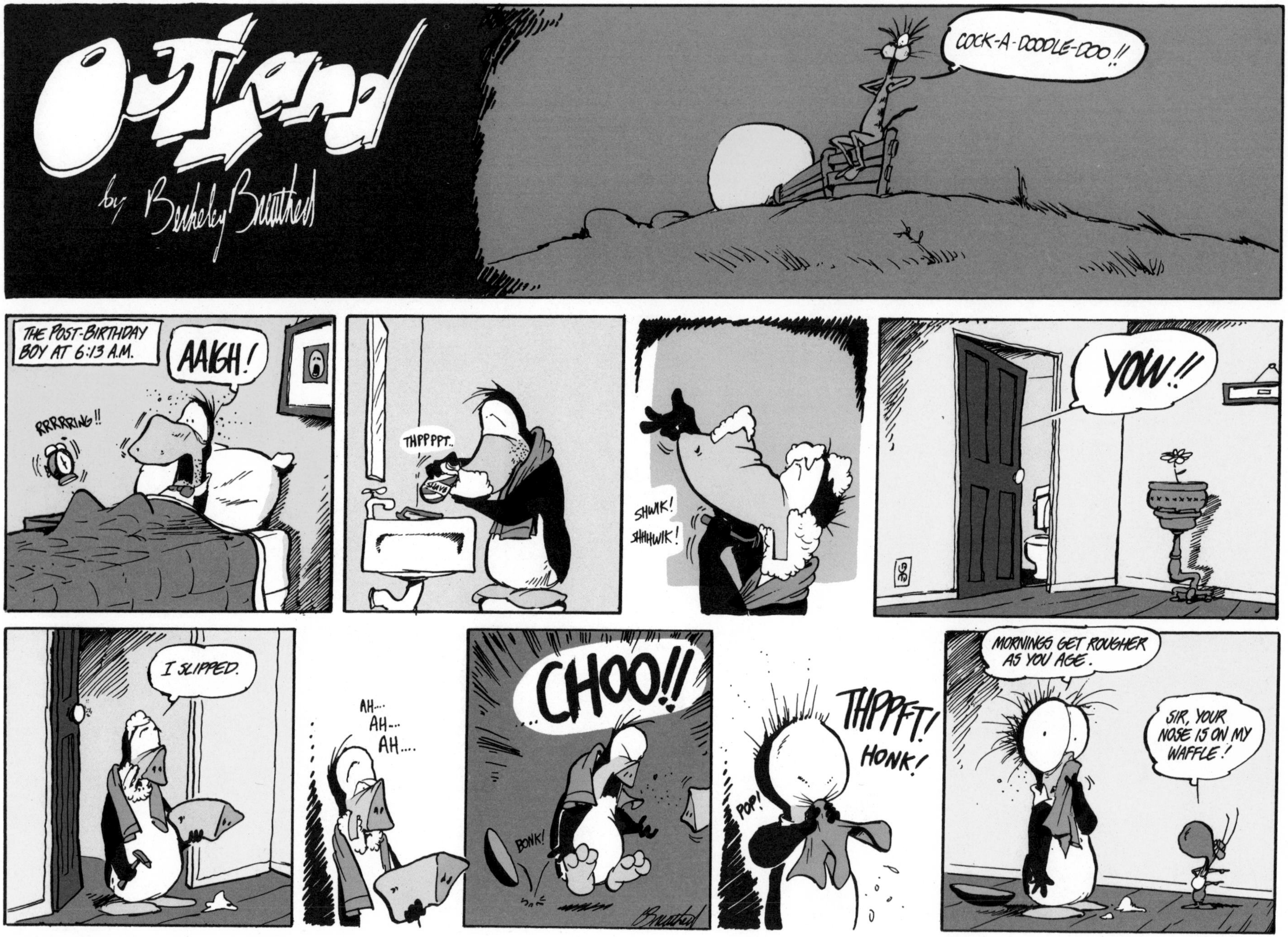
Outland
by Berkeley Breathed
COCK-A-DOODLE-DOO!!
THE POST-BIRTHDAY BOY AT 6:13 A.M.
AAIGH!
RRRRRING!!
THPPPPT..
SHAVE
SHWIK! SHHHWIK!
YOW!!
I SLIPPED.
AH... AH... AH....
...CHOO!!
BONK!
THPPFT!
HONK!
POP!
MORNINGS GET ROUGHER AS YOU AGE.
SIR, YOUR NOSE IS ON MY WAFFLE!
Breathed

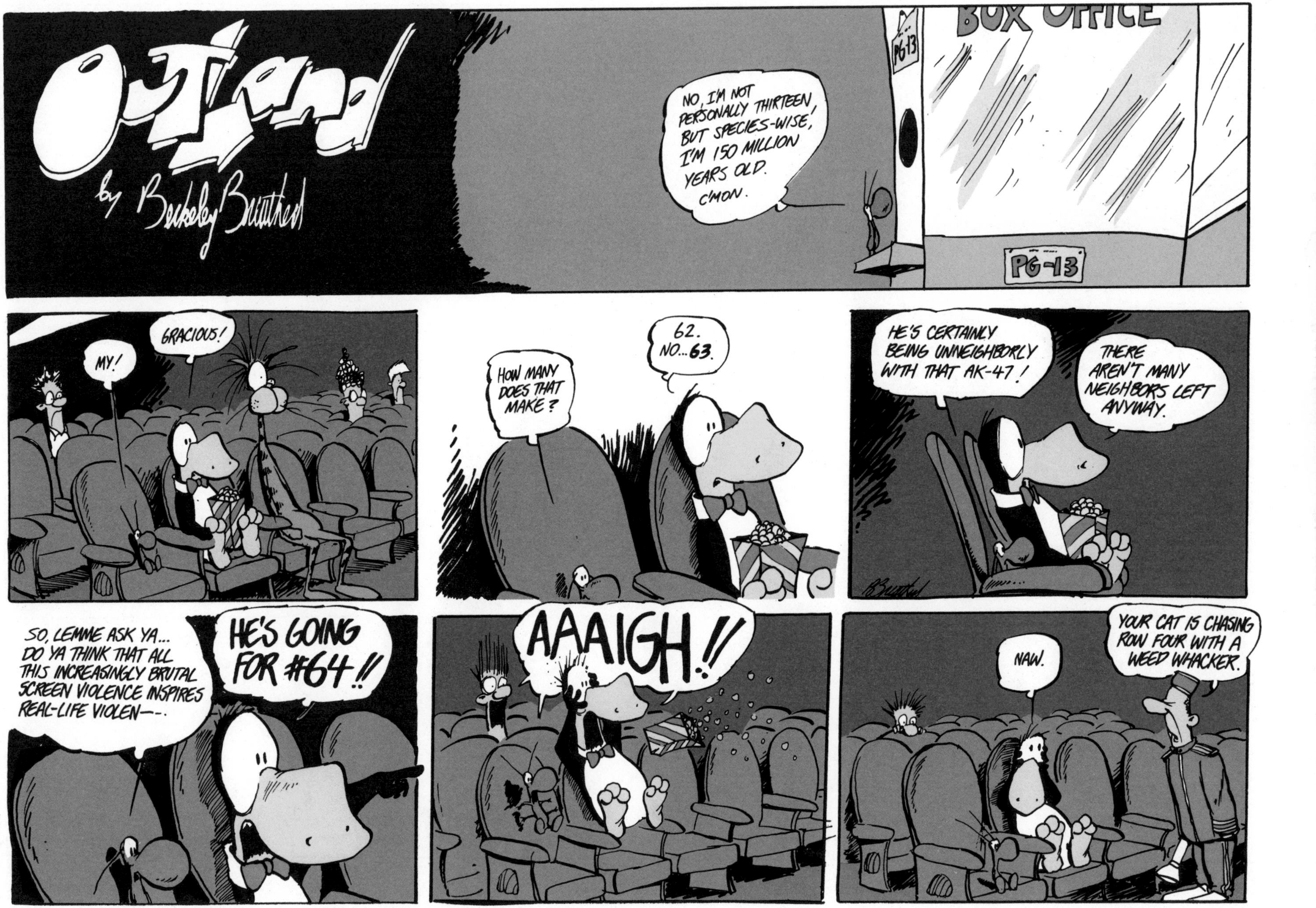

Outland
by Berkeley Breathed
NO, I'M NOT PERSONALLY THIRTEEN, BUT SPECIES-WISE, I'M 150 MILLION YEARS OLD. C'MON.
BOX OFFICE
PG-13
PG-13
MY!
GRACIOUS!
HOW MANY DOES THAT MAKE?
62. NO... 63.
HE'S CERTAINLY BEING UNNEIGHBORLY WITH THAT AK-47!
THERE AREN'T MANY NEIGHBORS LEFT ANYWAY.
SO, LEMME ASK YA... DO YA THINK THAT ALL THIS INCREASINGLY BRUTAL SCREEN VIOLENCE INSPIRES REAL-LIFE VIOLEN—.
HE'S GOING FOR #64!!
AAAIGH!!
NAW.
YOUR CAT IS CHASING ROW FOUR WITH A WEED WHACKER.

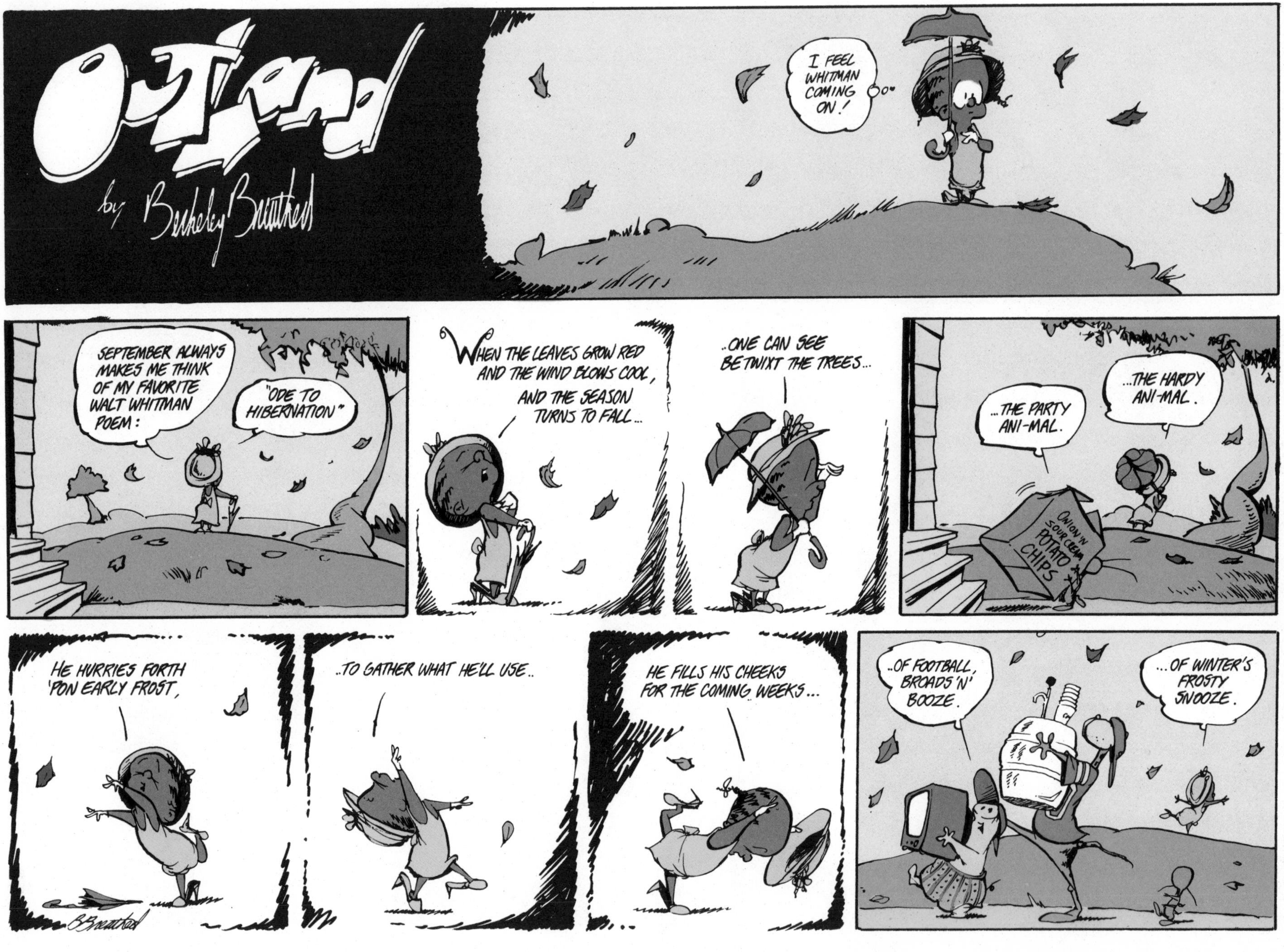
Outland
by Berkeley Breathed
I FEEL WHITMAN COMING ON!
SEPTEMBER ALWAYS MAKES ME THINK OF MY FAVORITE WALT WHITMAN POEM:
"ODE TO HIBERNATION"
WHEN THE LEAVES GROW RED AND THE WIND BLOWS COOL,
AND THE SEASON TURNS TO FALL...
..ONE CAN SEE BETWIXT THE TREES...
...THE PARTY ANI-MAL.
...THE HARDY ANI-MAL.
ONION 'N SOUR CREAM POTATO CHIPS
HE HURRIES FORTH 'PON EARLY FROST,
..TO GATHER WHAT HE'LL USE..
HE FILLS HIS CHEEKS FOR THE COMING WEEKS...
..OF FOOTBALL, BROADS 'N' BOOZE.
...OF WINTER'S FROSTY SNOOZE.
B Breathed

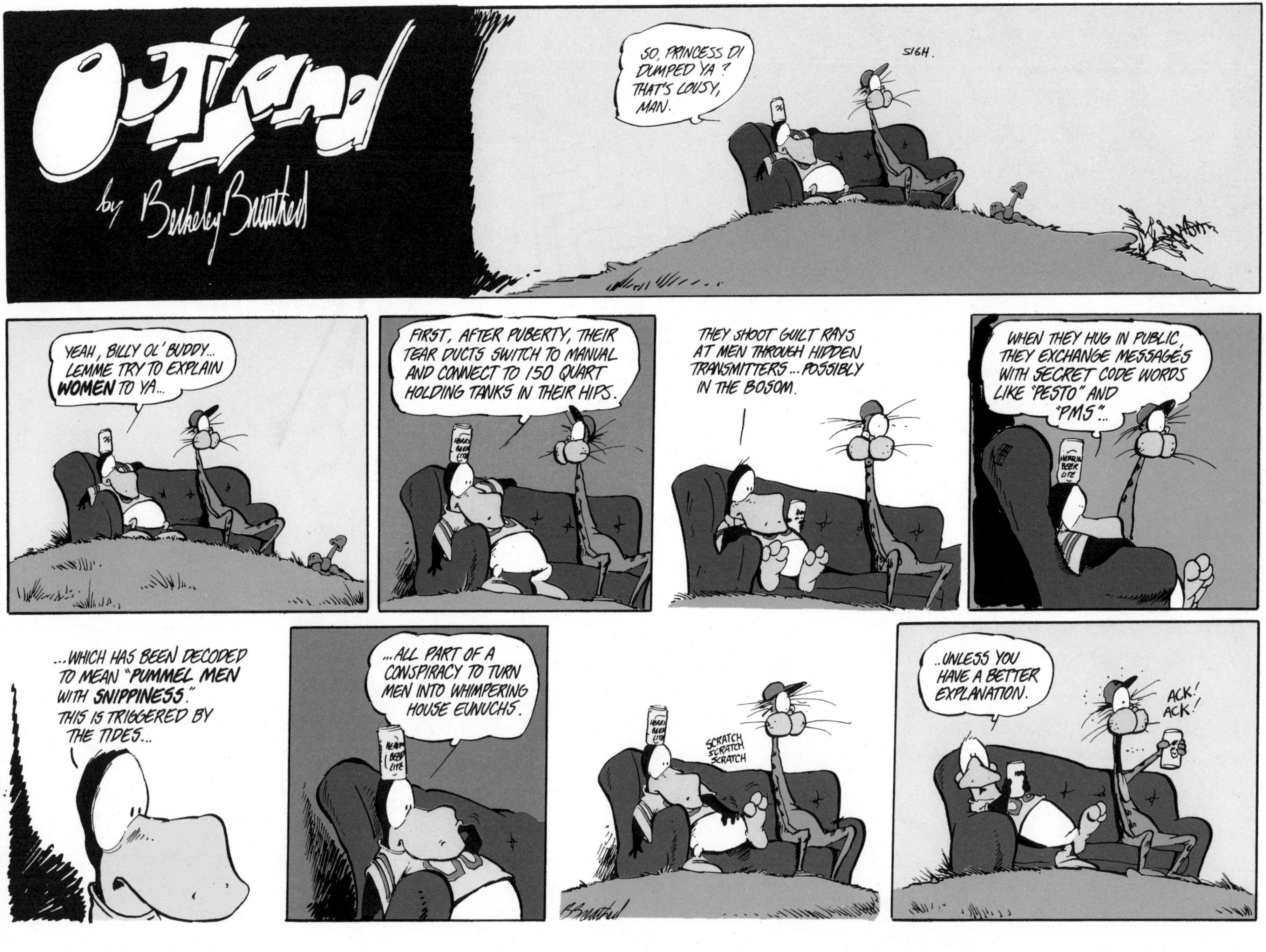
Outland
by Berkeley Breathed
SO, PRINCESS DI DUMPED YA? THAT'S LOUSY, MAN.
SIGH.
YEAH, BILLY OL' BUDDY... LEMME TRY TO EXPLAIN WOMEN TO YA...
FIRST, AFTER PUBERTY, THEIR TEAR DUCTS SWITCH TO MANUAL AND CONNECT TO 150 QUART HOLDING TANKS IN THEIR HIPS.
THEY SHOOT GUILT RAYS AT MEN THROUGH HIDDEN TRANSMITTERS... POSSIBLY IN THE BOSOM.
WHEN THEY HUG IN PUBLIC, THEY EXCHANGE MESSAGES WITH SECRET CODE WORDS LIKE "PESTO" AND "PMS"...
...WHICH HAS BEEN DECODED TO MEAN "PUMMEL MEN WITH SNIPPINESS." THIS IS TRIGGERED BY THE TIDES...
...ALL PART OF A CONSPIRACY TO TURN MEN INTO WHIMPERING HOUSE EUNUCHS.
SCRATCH SCRATCH SCRATCH
...UNLESS YOU HAVE A BETTER EXPLANATION.
ACK! ACK!

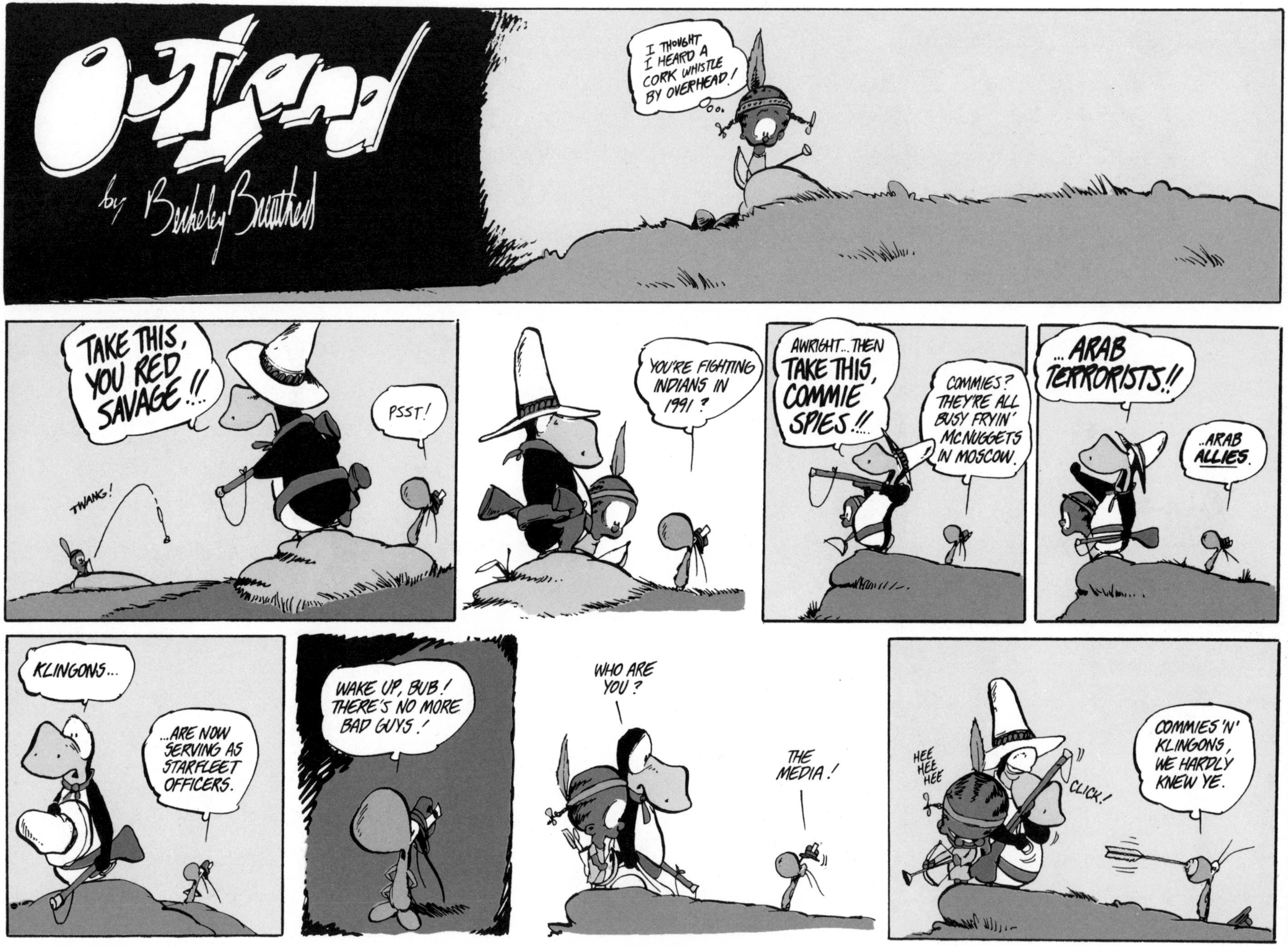

Outland
by Berkeley Breathed
I THOUGHT I HEARD A CORK WHISTLE BY OVERHEAD!
TAKE THIS, YOU RED SAVAGE!!...
TWANG!
PSST!
YOU'RE FIGHTING INDIANS IN 1991?
AWRIGHT... THEN TAKE THIS, COMMIE SPIES!!...
COMMIES? THEY'RE ALL BUSY FRYIN' McNUGGETS IN MOSCOW.
...ARAB TERRORISTS!!
...ARAB ALLIES.
KLINGONS...
...ARE NOW SERVING AS STARFLEET OFFICERS.
WAKE UP, BUB! THERE'S NO MORE BAD GUYS!
WHO ARE YOU?
THE MEDIA!
HEE HEE HEE
CLICK!
COMMIES 'N' KLINGONS, WE HARDLY KNEW YE.

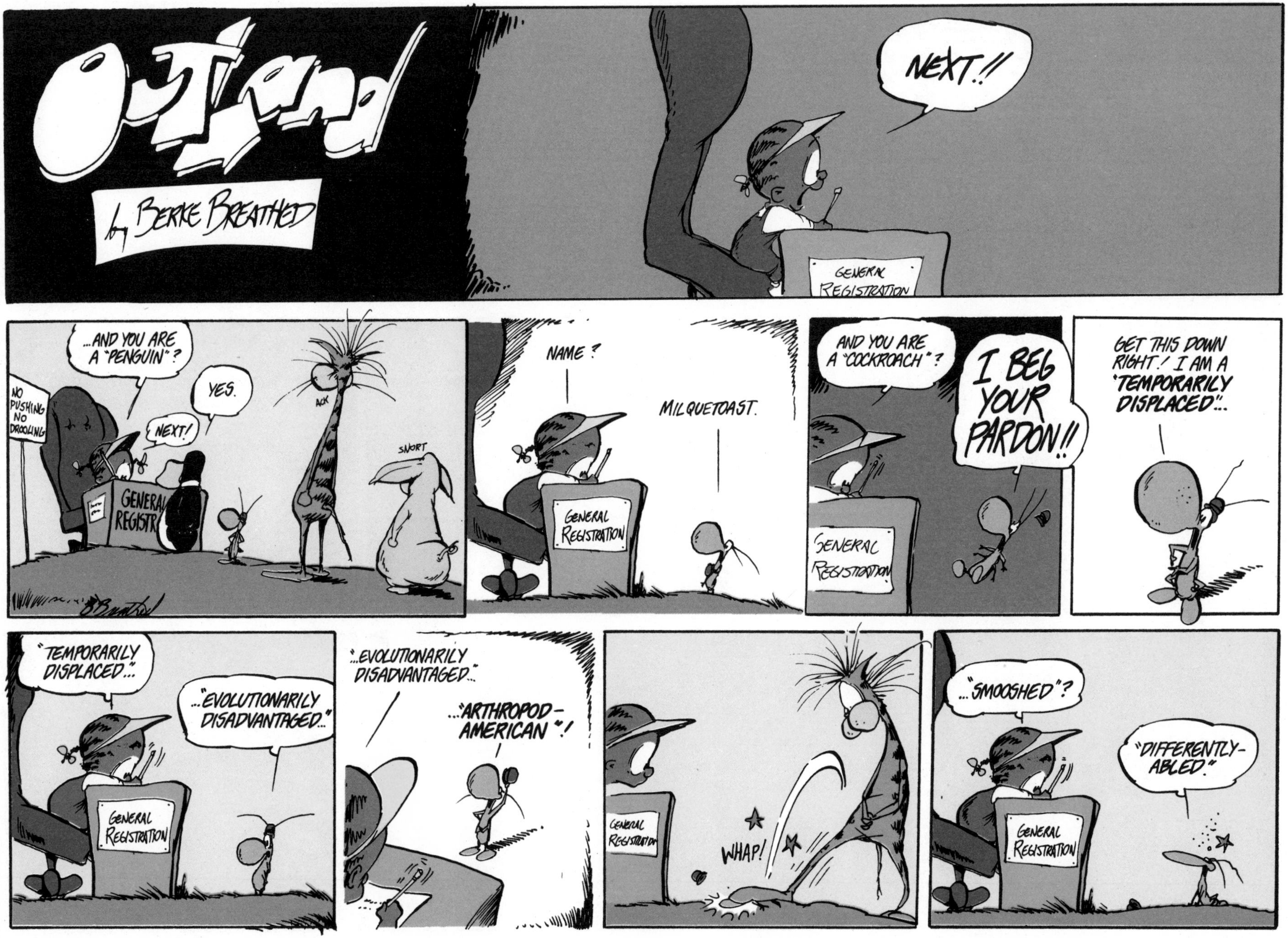
Outland
by Berke Breathed
NEXT.!!
GENERAL REGISTRATION
...AND YOU ARE A "PENGUIN"?
NO PUSHING NO DROOLING
NEXT!
YES.
ACK
SNORT
GENERAL REGISTR
NAME?
MILQUETOAST.
GENERAL REGISTRATION
AND YOU ARE A "COCKROACH"?
I BEG YOUR PARDON!!
GENERAL REGISTRATION
GET THIS DOWN RIGHT! I AM A "TEMPORARILY DISPLACED"...
"TEMPORARILY DISPLACED"...
..."EVOLUTIONARILY DISADVANTAGED"...
GENERAL REGISTRATION
..."EVOLUTIONARILY DISADVANTAGED"...
..."ARTHROPOD-AMERICAN"!
GENERAL REGISTRATION
WHAP!
..."SMOOSHED"?
"DIFFERENTLY-ABLED."
GENERAL REGISTRATION

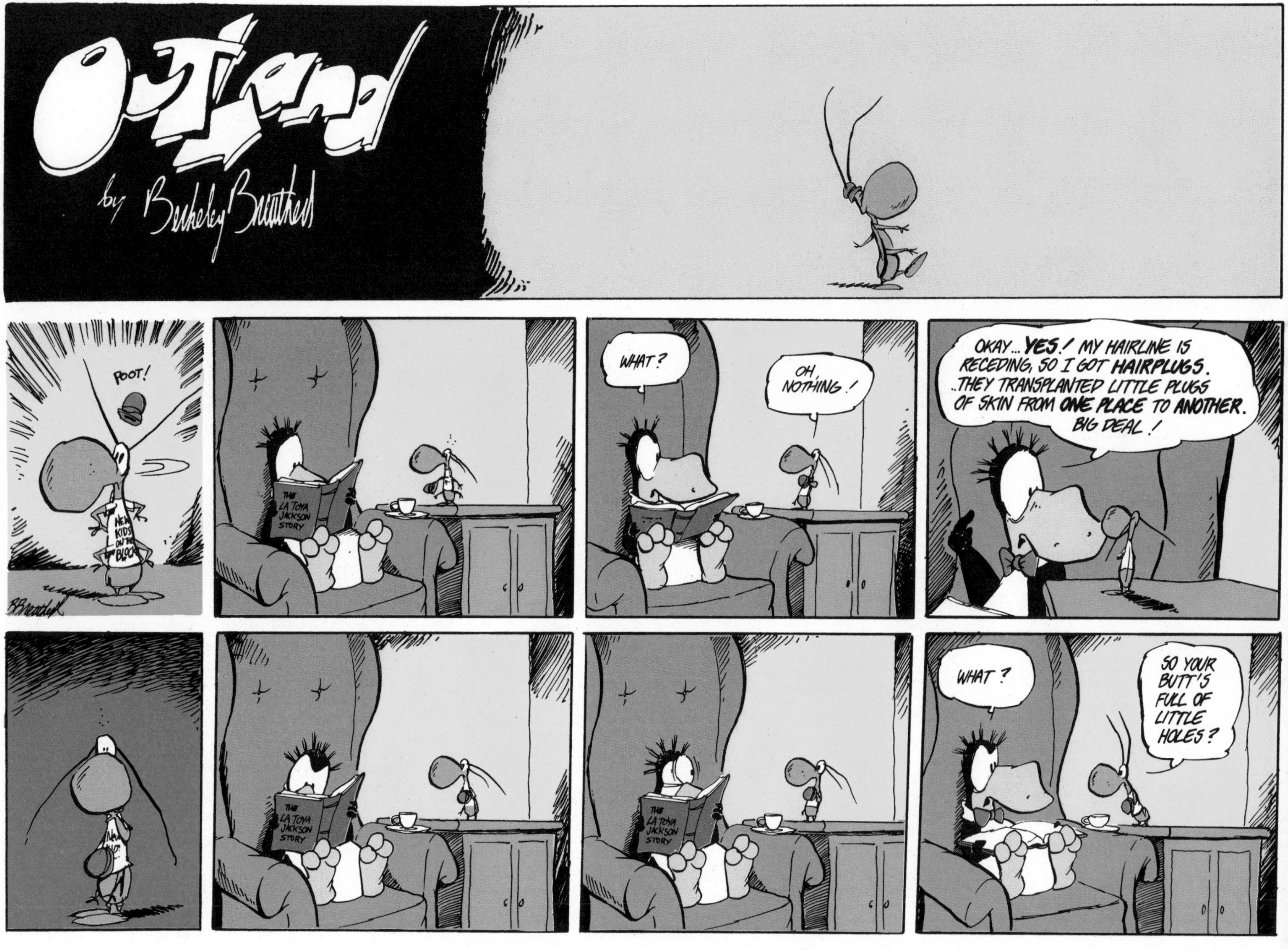
Outland
by Berkeley Breathed
POOT!
NEW KIDS ON THE BLOCK
THE LA TOYA JACKSON STORY
WHAT?
OH NOTHING!
OKAY... YES! MY HAIRLINE IS RECEDING, SO I GOT HAIRPLUGS. ..THEY TRANSPLANTED LITTLE PLUGS OF SKIN FROM ONE PLACE TO ANOTHER. BIG DEAL!
THE LA TOYA JACKSON STORY
THE LA TOYA JACKSON STORY
WHAT?
SO YOUR BUTT'S FULL OF LITTLE HOLES?

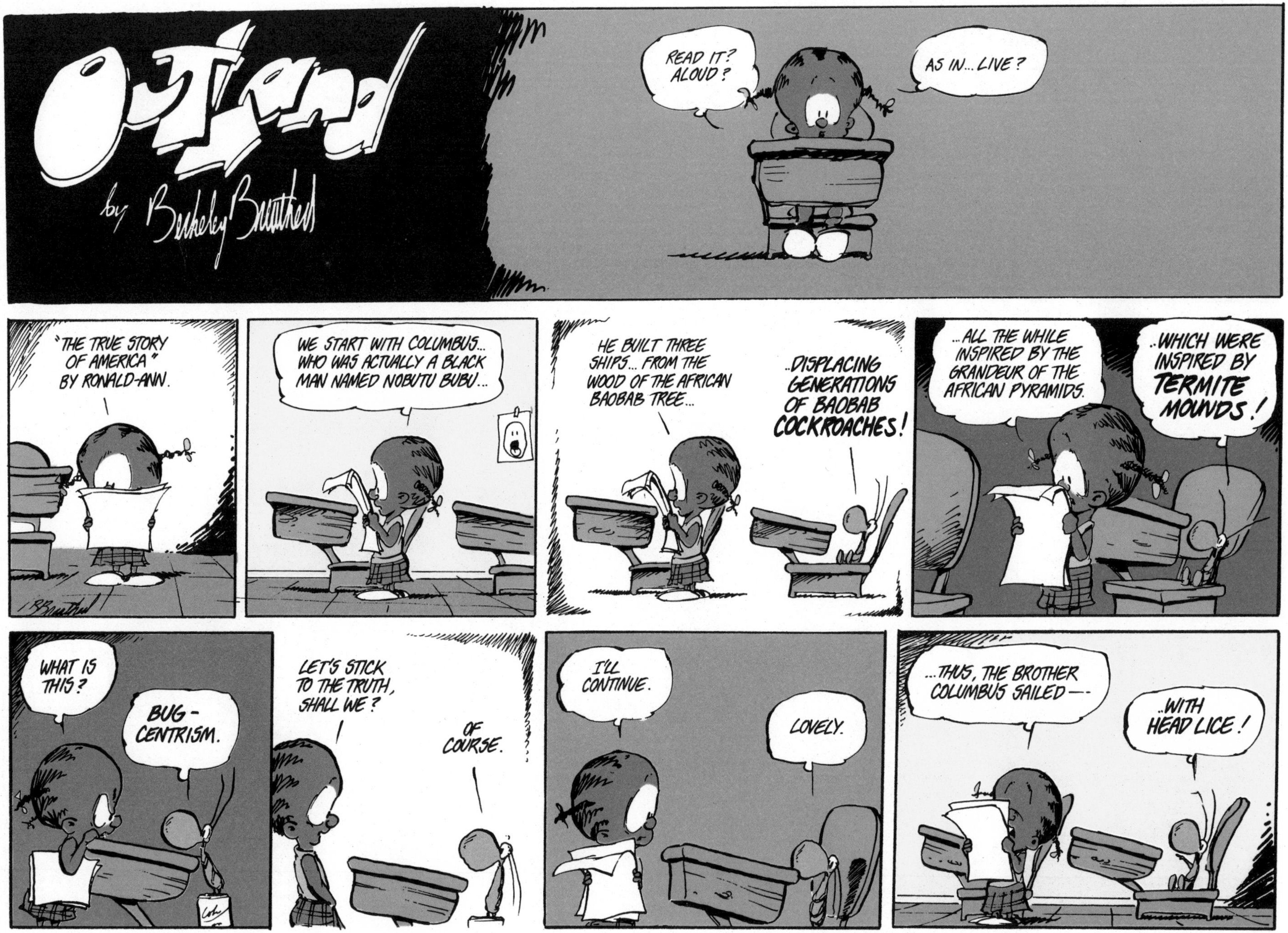
Outland
by Berkeley Breathed
READ IT? ALOUD?
AS IN... LIVE?
"THE TRUE STORY OF AMERICA" BY RONALD-ANN.
WE START WITH COLUMBUS... WHO WAS ACTUALLY A BLACK MAN NAMED NOBUTU BUBU...
HE BUILT THREE SHIPS... FROM THE WOOD OF THE AFRICAN BAOBAB TREE...
..DISPLACING GENERATIONS OF BAOBAB COCKROACHES!
...ALL THE WHILE INSPIRED BY THE GRANDEUR OF THE AFRICAN PYRAMIDS.
..WHICH WERE INSPIRED BY TERMITE MOUNDS!
WHAT IS THIS?
BUG-CENTRISM.
LET'S STICK TO THE TRUTH, SHALL WE?
OF COURSE.
I'LL CONTINUE.
LOVELY.
...THUS, THE BROTHER COLUMBUS SAILED—
..WITH HEAD LICE!

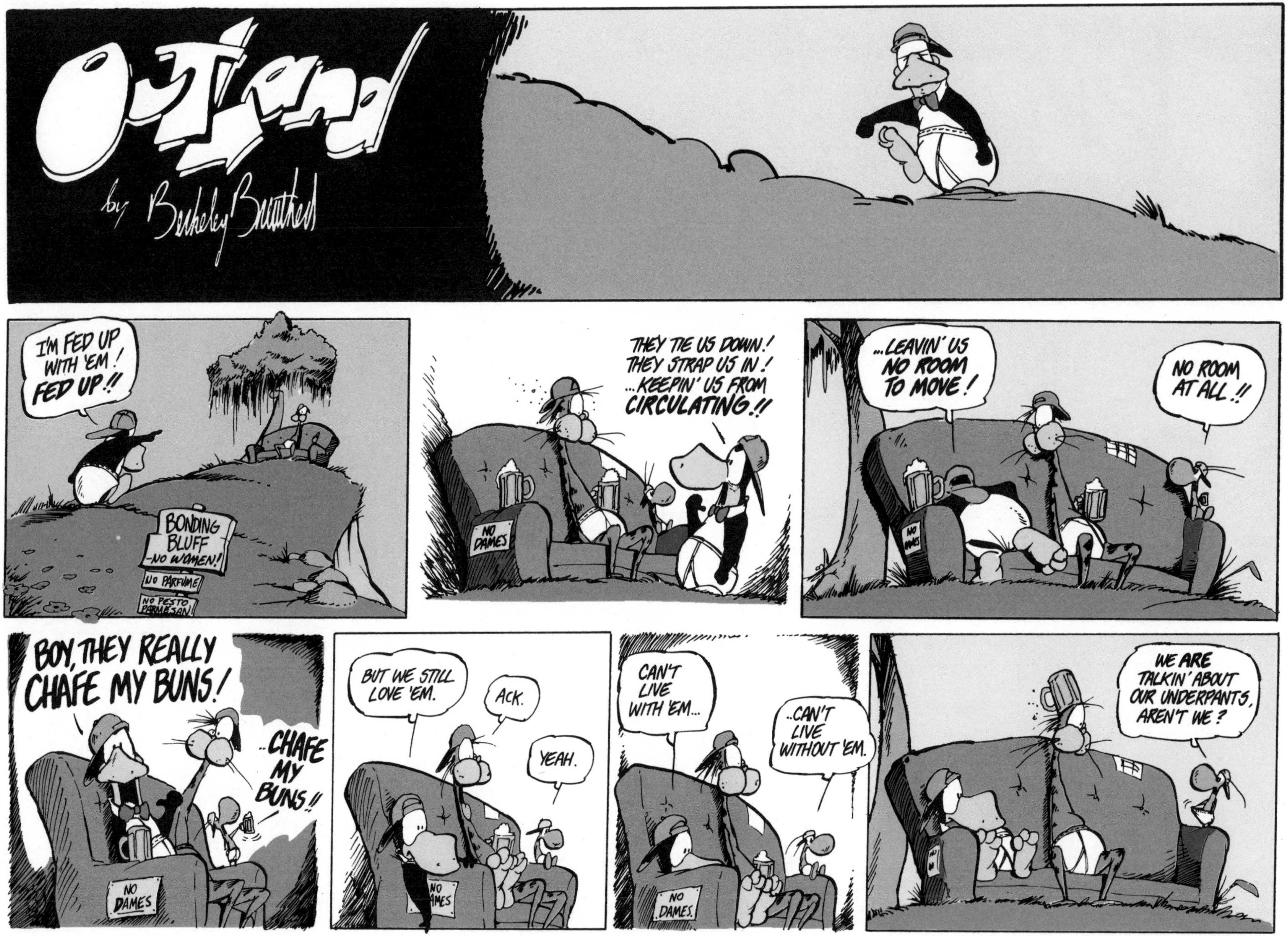
Outland
by Berkeley Breathed
I'M FED UP WITH 'EM! FED UP!!
BONDING BLUFF -NO WOMEN!
NO PARFUME!
NO PESTO PARMESAN!
THEY TIE US DOWN! THEY STRAP US IN! ...KEEPIN' US FROM CIRCULATING!!
NO DAMES
...LEAVIN' US NO ROOM TO MOVE!
NO ROOM AT ALL!!
NO DAMES
BOY, THEY REALLY CHAFE MY BUNS!
..CHAFE MY BUNS!!
NO DAMES
BUT WE STILL LOVE 'EM.
ACK.
YEAH.
CAN'T LIVE WITH 'EM...
..CAN'T LIVE WITHOUT 'EM.
NO DAMES.
WE ARE TALKIN' ABOUT OUR UNDERPANTS, AREN'T WE?

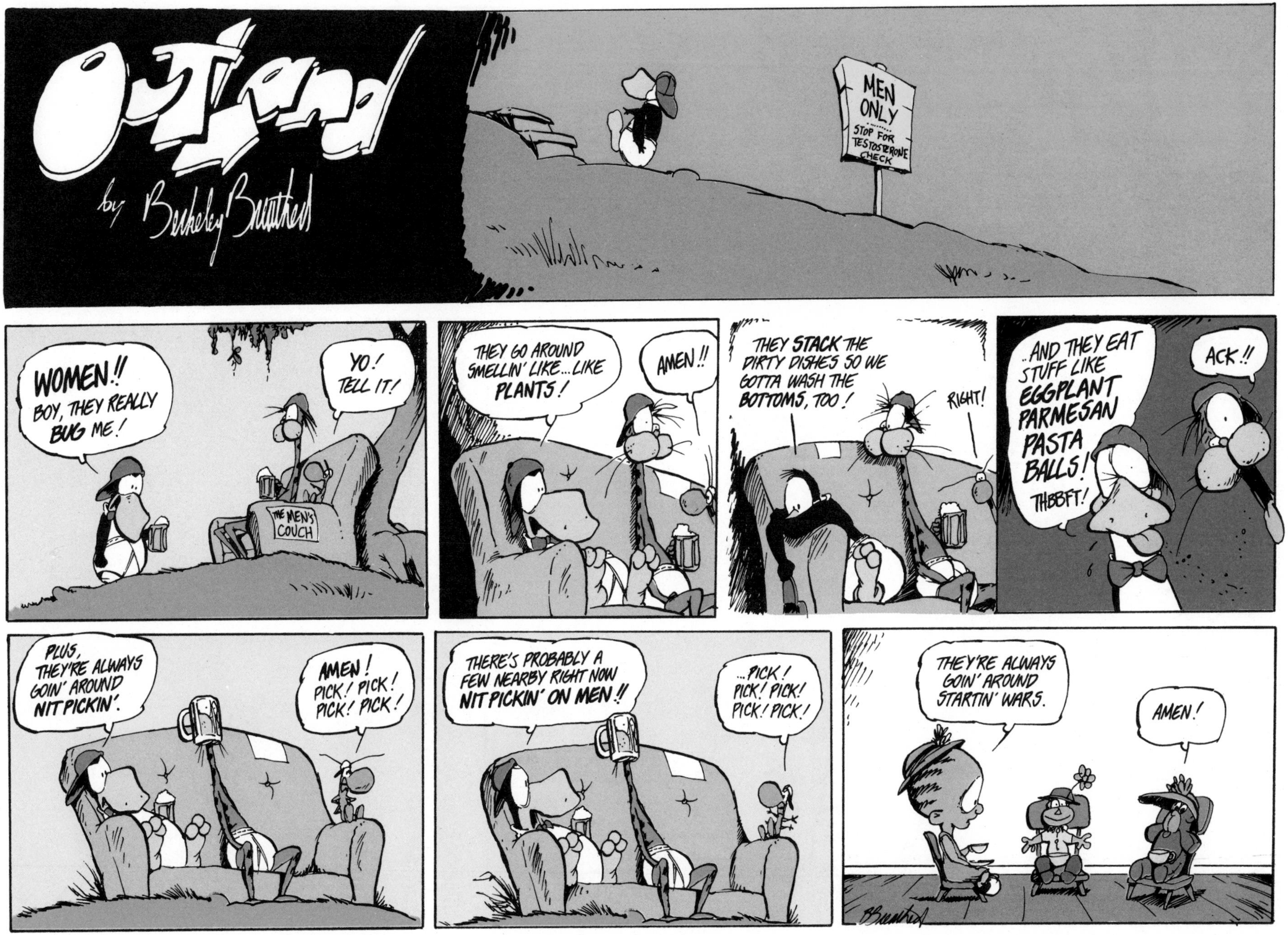

Outland
by Berkeley Breathed
MEN ONLY
STOP FOR TESTOSTERONE CHECK
WOMEN!! BOY, THEY REALLY BUG ME!
YO! TELL IT!
THE MEN'S COUCH
THEY GO AROUND SMELLIN' LIKE... LIKE PLANTS!
AMEN!!
THEY STACK THE DIRTY DISHES SO WE GOTTA WASH THE BOTTOMS, TOO!
RIGHT!
..AND THEY EAT STUFF LIKE EGGPLANT PARMESAN PASTA BALLS! THBBFT!
ACK!!
PLUS, THEY'RE ALWAYS GOIN' AROUND NIT PICKIN'.
AMEN! PICK! PICK! PICK! PICK! PICK!
THERE'S PROBABLY A FEW NEARBY RIGHT NOW NIT PICKIN' ON MEN!!
...PICK! PICK! PICK! PICK! PICK!
THEY'RE ALWAYS GOIN' AROUND STARTIN' WARS.
AMEN!

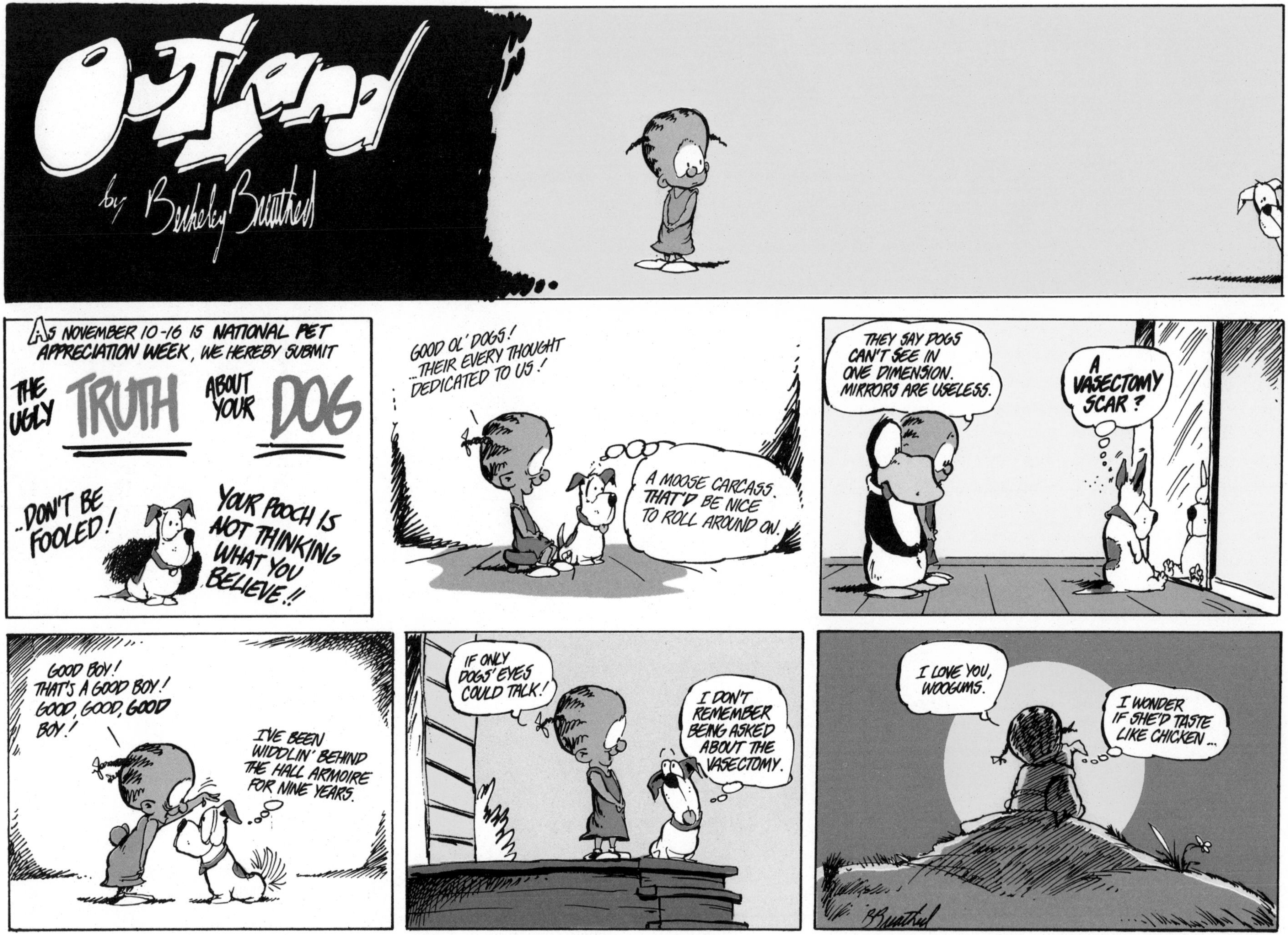
Outland
by Berkeley Breathed
As November 10-16 is National Pet Appreciation Week, we hereby submit
The ugly TRUTH about your DOG
...Don't be fooled!
Your pooch is not thinking what you believe!!
Good ol' dogs! ...Their every thought dedicated to us!
A moose carcass. That'd be nice to roll around on.
They say dogs can't see in one dimension. Mirrors are useless.
A vasectomy scar?
Good boy! That's a good boy! Good, good, good boy!
I've been widdlin' behind the hall armoire for nine years.
If only dogs' eyes could talk!
I don't remember being asked about the vasectomy.
I love you, Woogums.
I wonder if she'd taste like chicken...
B Breathed

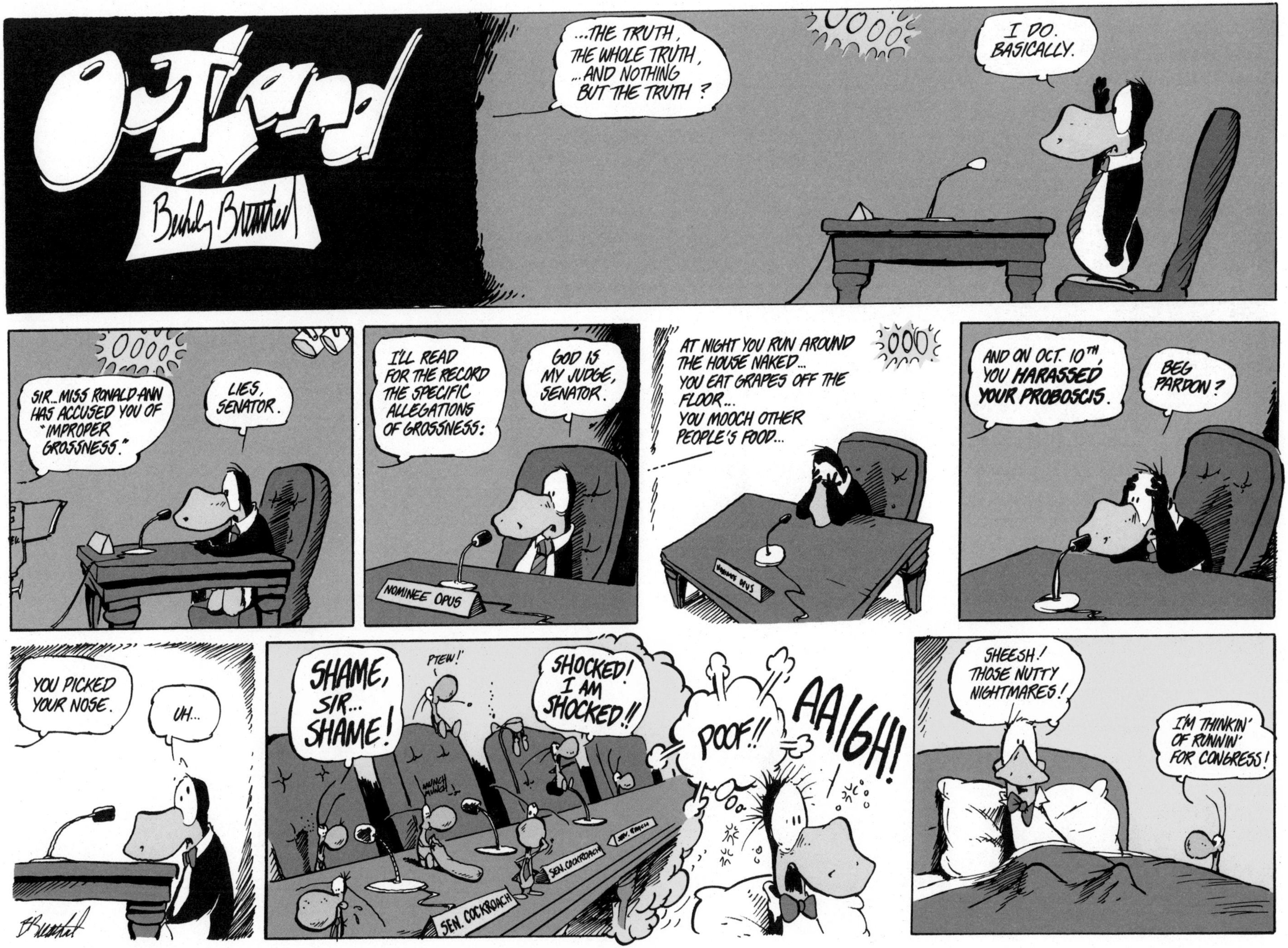

Outland
Berkeley Breathed
...THE TRUTH, THE WHOLE TRUTH, ...AND NOTHING BUT THE TRUTH ?
OOOO
I DO. BASICALLY.
OOOO
SIR...MISS RONALD-ANN HAS ACCUSED YOU OF "IMPROPER GROSSNESS."
LIES, SENATOR.
I'LL READ FOR THE RECORD THE SPECIFIC ALLEGATIONS OF GROSSNESS:
GOD IS MY JUDGE, SENATOR.
NOMINEE OPUS
AT NIGHT YOU RUN AROUND THE HOUSE NAKED... YOU EAT GRAPES OFF THE FLOOR... YOU MOOCH OTHER PEOPLE'S FOOD...
OOO
AND ON OCT. 10TH, YOU HARASSED YOUR PROBOSCIS.
BEG PARDON ?
YOU PICKED YOUR NOSE.
UH...
SHAME, SIR... SHAME!
PTEW!
SHOCKED! I AM SHOCKED!!
MUNCH MUNCH
SEN. COCKROACH
SEN. COCKROACH
POOF!!
AAIGH!
SHEESH! THOSE NUTTY NIGHTMARES!
I'M THINKIN' OF RUNNIN' FOR CONGRESS!

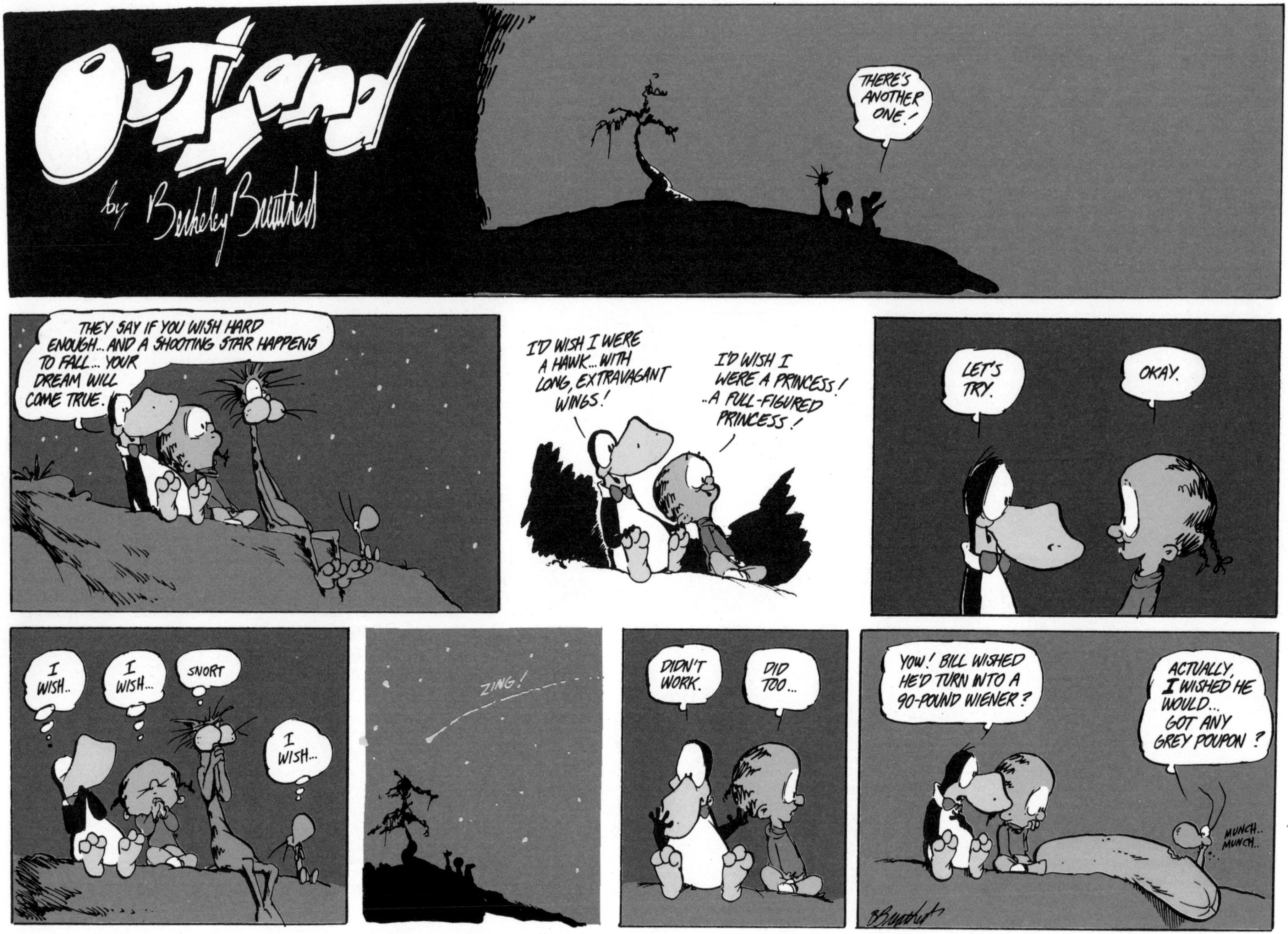
Outland
by Berkeley Breathed
THERE'S ANOTHER ONE!
THEY SAY IF YOU WISH HARD ENOUGH... AND A SHOOTING STAR HAPPENS TO FALL... YOUR DREAM WILL COME TRUE.
I'D WISH I WERE A HAWK... WITH LONG, EXTRAVAGANT WINGS!
I'D WISH I WERE A PRINCESS! ..A FULL-FIGURED PRINCESS!
LET'S TRY.
OKAY.
I WISH..
I WISH...
SNORT
I WISH...
ZING!
DIDN'T WORK.
DID TOO...
YOW! BILL WISHED HE'D TURN INTO A 90-POUND WIENER?
ACTUALLY, I WISHED HE WOULD... GOT ANY GREY POUPON?
MUNCH.. MUNCH..

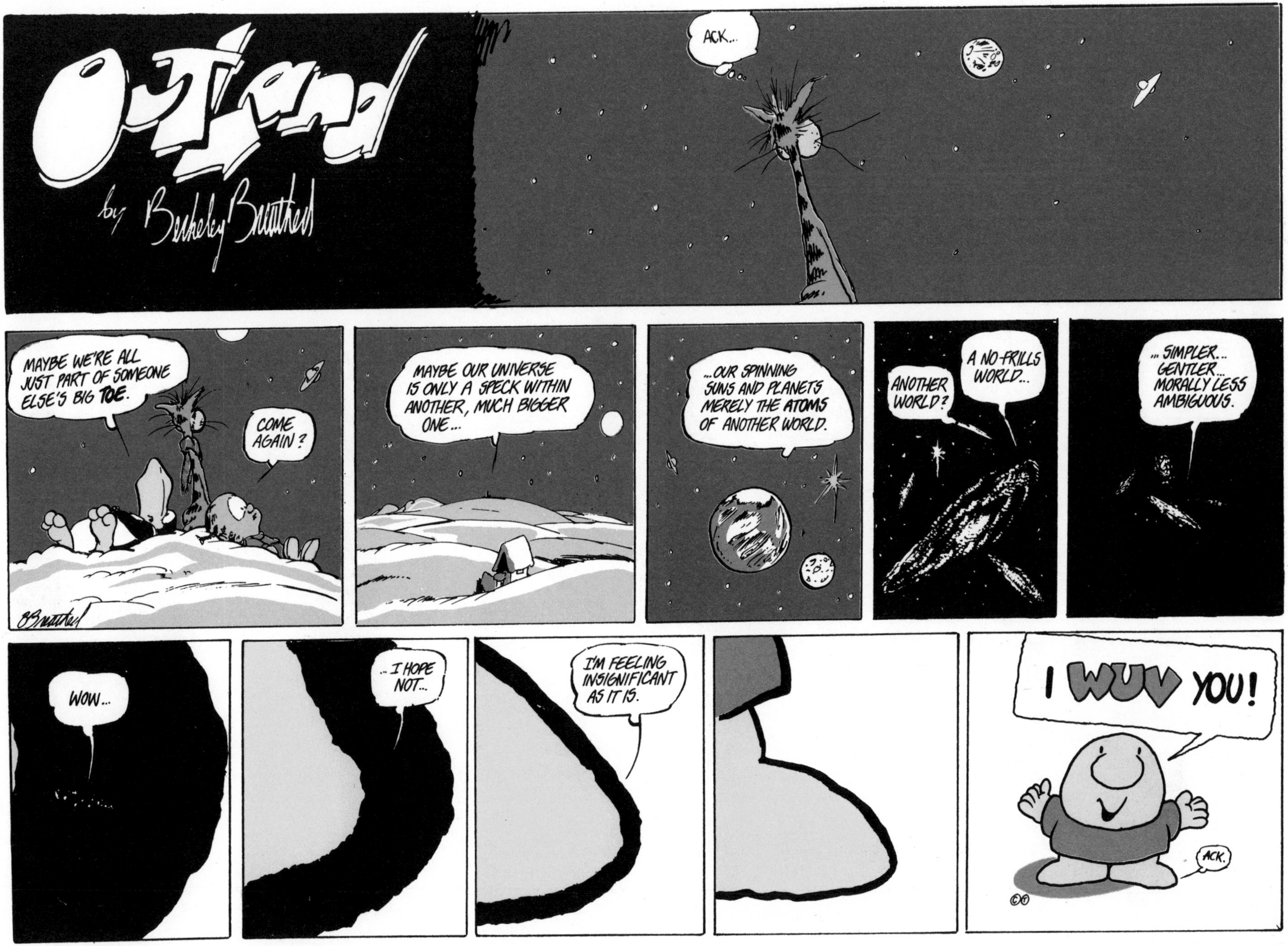
Outland
by Berkeley Breathed
ACK...
MAYBE WE'RE ALL JUST PART OF SOMEONE ELSE'S BIG **TOE**.
COME AGAIN?
MAYBE OUR UNIVERSE IS ONLY A SPECK WITHIN ANOTHER, MUCH BIGGER ONE...
...OUR SPINNING SUNS AND PLANETS MERELY THE **ATOMS** OF ANOTHER WORLD.
ANOTHER WORLD?
A NO-FRILLS WORLD...
...SIMPLER... GENTLER... MORALLY LESS AMBIGUOUS.
WOW...
...I HOPE NOT...
I'M FEELING INSIGNIFICANT AS IT IS.
I WUV YOU!
ACK.

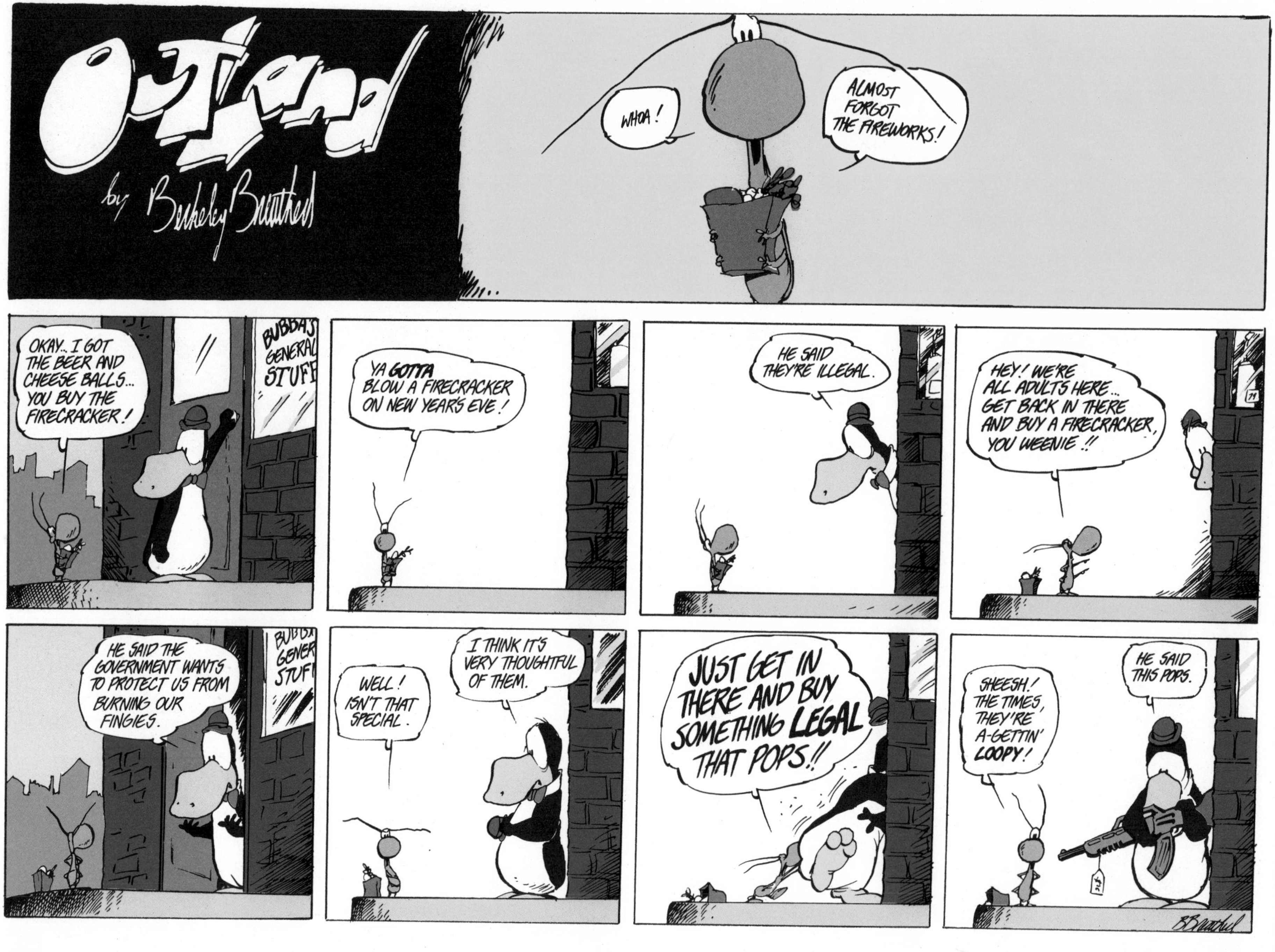
Outland
by Berkeley Breathed
WHOA!
ALMOST FORGOT THE FIREWORKS!
OKAY.. I GOT THE BEER AND CHEESE BALLS... YOU BUY THE FIRECRACKER!
BUBBA'S GENERAL STUFF
YA **GOTTA** BLOW A FIRECRACKER ON NEW YEAR'S EVE!
HE SAID THEY'RE ILLEGAL.
HEY! WE'RE ALL ADULTS HERE... GET BACK IN THERE AND BUY A FIRECRACKER, YOU WEENIE!!
HE SAID THE GOVERNMENT WANTS TO PROTECT US FROM BURNING OUR FINGIES.
WELL! ISN'T THAT SPECIAL.
I THINK IT'S VERY THOUGHTFUL OF THEM.
JUST GET IN THERE AND BUY SOMETHING **LEGAL** THAT POPS!!
HE SAID THIS POPS.
SHEESH! THE TIMES, THEY'RE A-GETTIN' **LOOPY**!
B Breathed

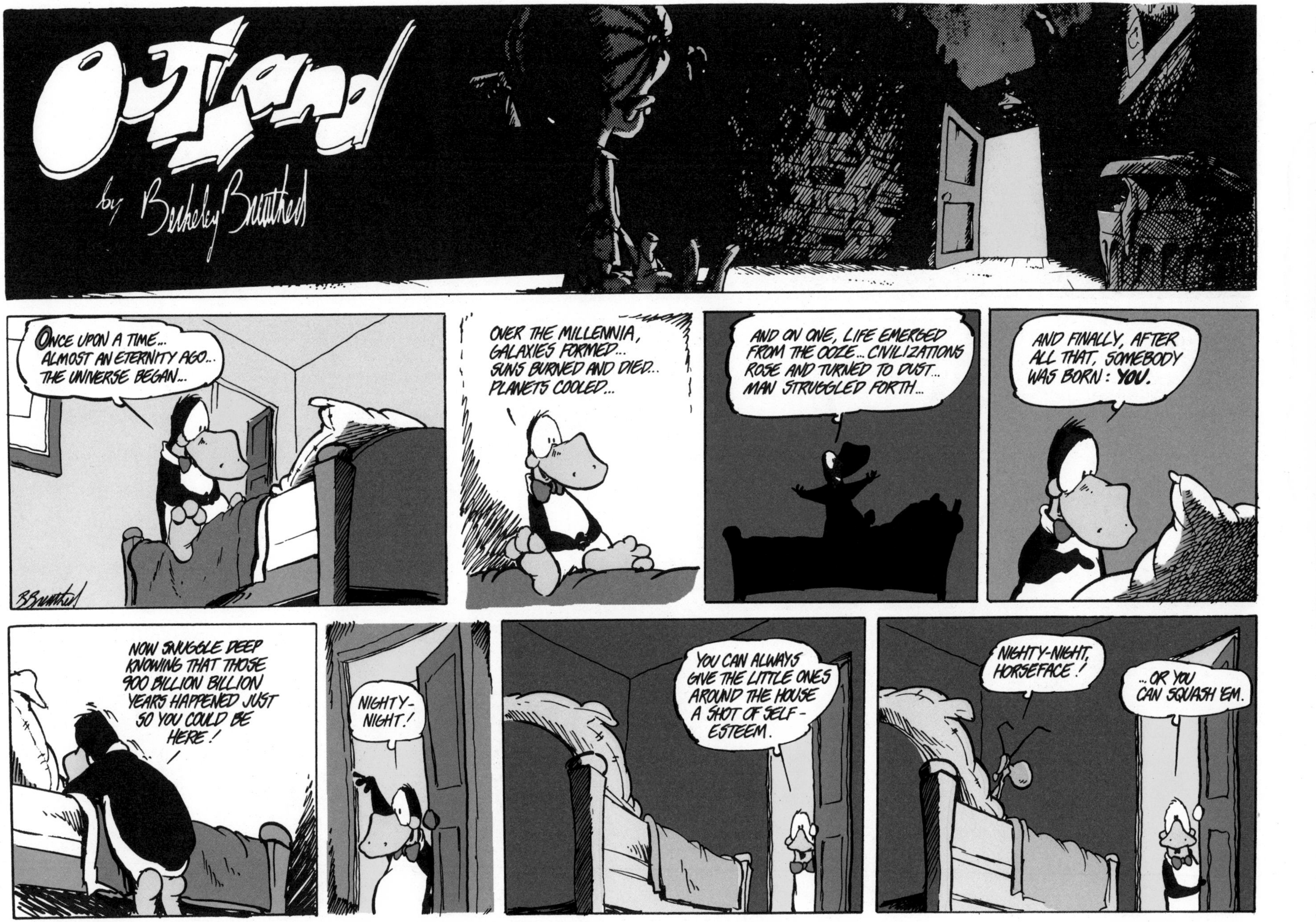

Outland
by Berkeley Breathed
ONCE UPON A TIME... ALMOST AN ETERNITY AGO... THE UNIVERSE BEGAN...
OVER THE MILLENNIA, GALAXIES FORMED... SUNS BURNED AND DIED... PLANETS COOLED...
AND ON ONE, LIFE EMERGED FROM THE OOZE... CIVILIZATIONS ROSE AND TURNED TO DUST... MAN STRUGGLED FORTH...
AND FINALLY, AFTER ALL THAT, SOMEBODY WAS BORN: YOU.
NOW SNUGGLE DEEP KNOWING THAT THOSE 900 BILLION BILLION YEARS HAPPENED JUST SO YOU COULD BE HERE!
NIGHTY-NIGHT!
YOU CAN ALWAYS GIVE THE LITTLE ONES AROUND THE HOUSE A SHOT OF SELF-ESTEEM.
NIGHTY-NIGHT, HORSEFACE!
...OR YOU CAN SQUASH 'EM.

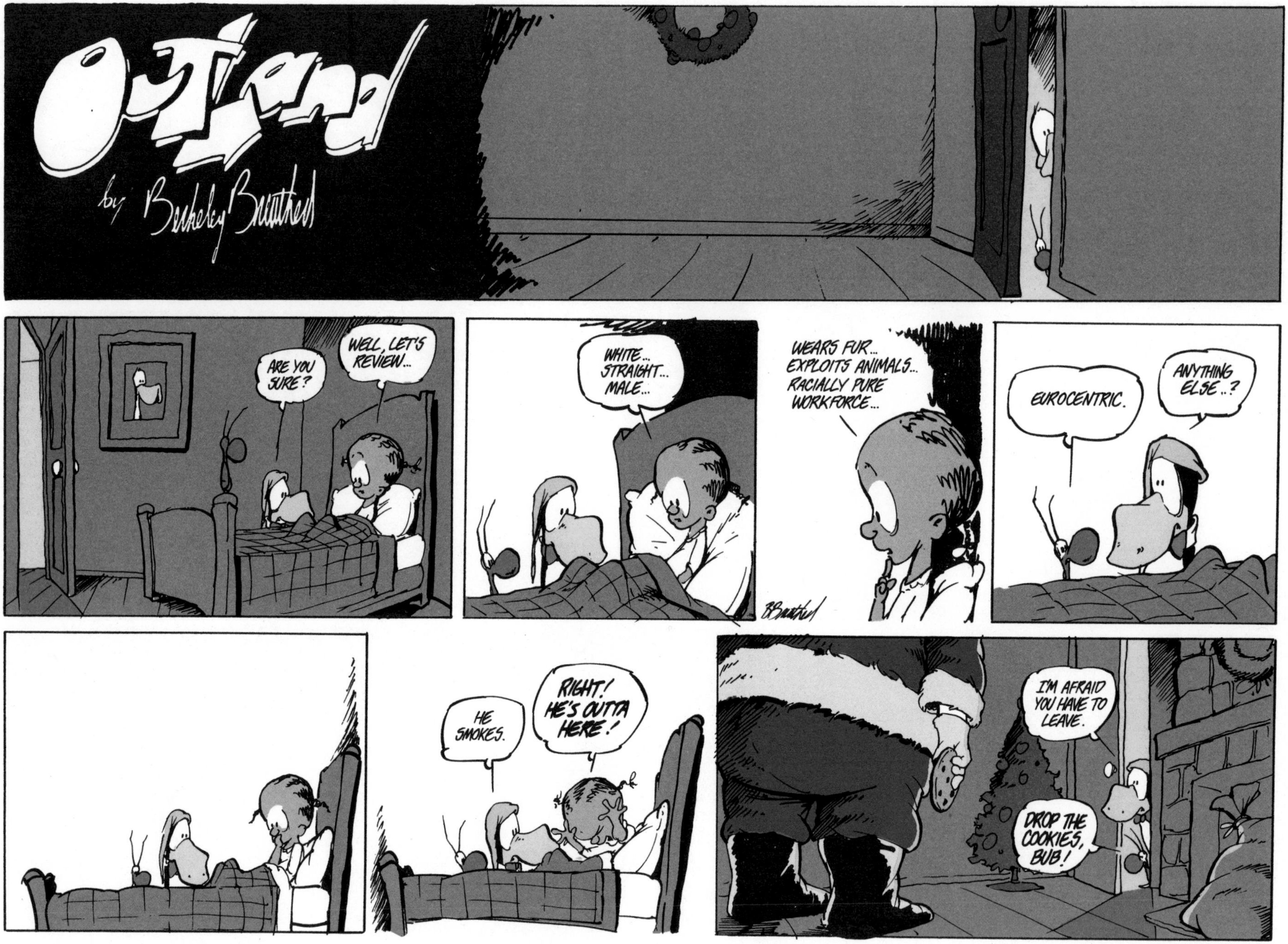
Outland
by Berkeley Breathed
ARE YOU SURE?
WELL, LET'S REVIEW...
WHITE... STRAIGHT... MALE...
WEARS FUR... EXPLOITS ANIMALS... RACIALLY PURE WORKFORCE...
B. Breathed
EUROCENTRIC.
ANYTHING ELSE..?
HE SMOKES.
RIGHT! HE'S OUTTA HERE!
I'M AFRAID YOU HAVE TO LEAVE.
DROP THE COOKIES, BUB!

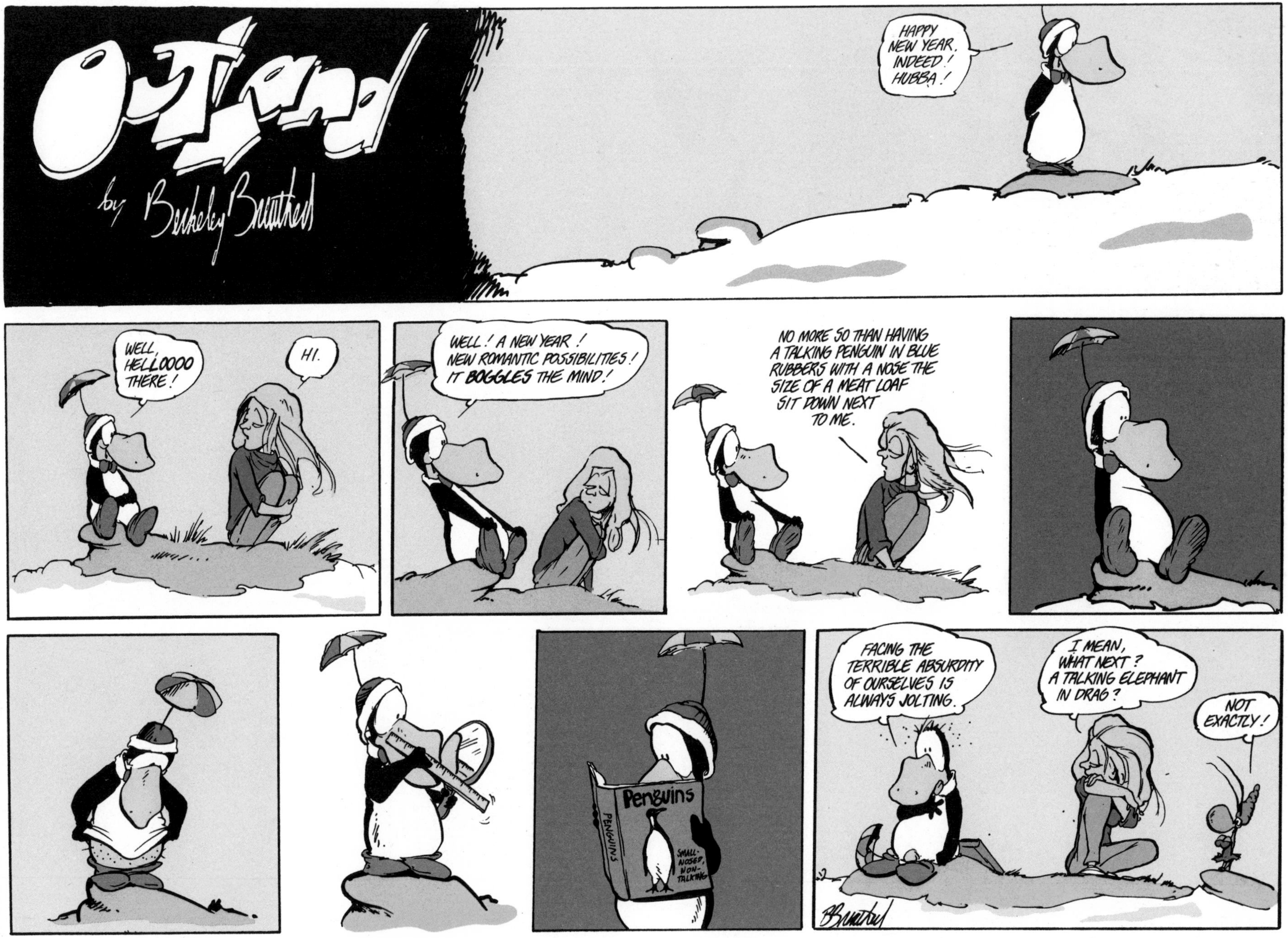
Outland
by Berkeley Breathed
HAPPY NEW YEAR, INDEED! HUBBA!
WELL, HELLOOOO THERE!
HI.
WELL! A NEW YEAR! NEW ROMANTIC POSSIBILITIES! IT BOGGLES THE MIND!
NO MORE SO THAN HAVING A TALKING PENGUIN IN BLUE RUBBERS WITH A NOSE THE SIZE OF A MEAT LOAF SIT DOWN NEXT TO ME.
Penguins
PENGUINS
SMALL-NOSED, NON-TALKING
FACING THE TERRIBLE ABSURDITY OF OURSELVES IS ALWAYS JOLTING.
I MEAN, WHAT NEXT? A TALKING ELEPHANT IN DRAG?
NOT EXACTLY!
BBreathed

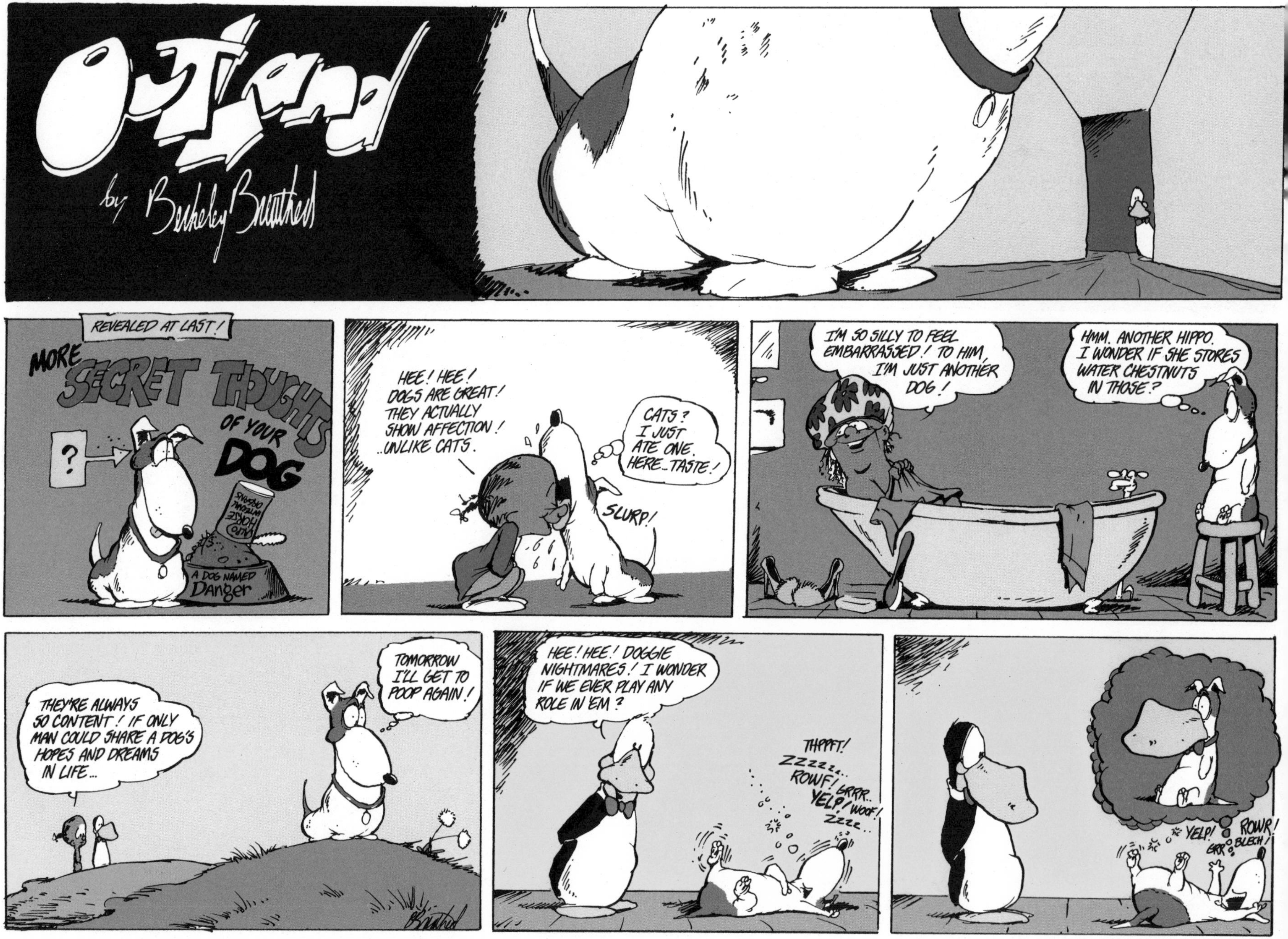
Outland
by Berkeley Breathed
REVEALED AT LAST!
MORE SECRET THOUGHTS OF YOUR DOG
?
A DOG NAMED Danger
HEE! HEE! DOGS ARE GREAT! THEY ACTUALLY SHOW AFFECTION! ..UNLIKE CATS.
CATS? I JUST ATE ONE. HERE...TASTE!
SLURP!
I'M SO SILLY TO FEEL EMBARRASSED! TO HIM, I'M JUST ANOTHER DOG!
HMM. ANOTHER HIPPO. I WONDER IF SHE STORES WATER CHESTNUTS IN THOSE?
THEY'RE ALWAYS SO CONTENT! IF ONLY MAN COULD SHARE A DOG'S HOPES AND DREAMS IN LIFE...
TOMORROW I'LL GET TO POOP AGAIN!
HEE! HEE! DOGGIE NIGHTMARES! I WONDER IF WE EVER PLAY ANY ROLE IN 'EM?
THPPFT! ZZzzz.. ROWF! GRRR.. YELP! WOOF! ZZZZ..
YELP! GRR ROWR! BLECH!
Breathed

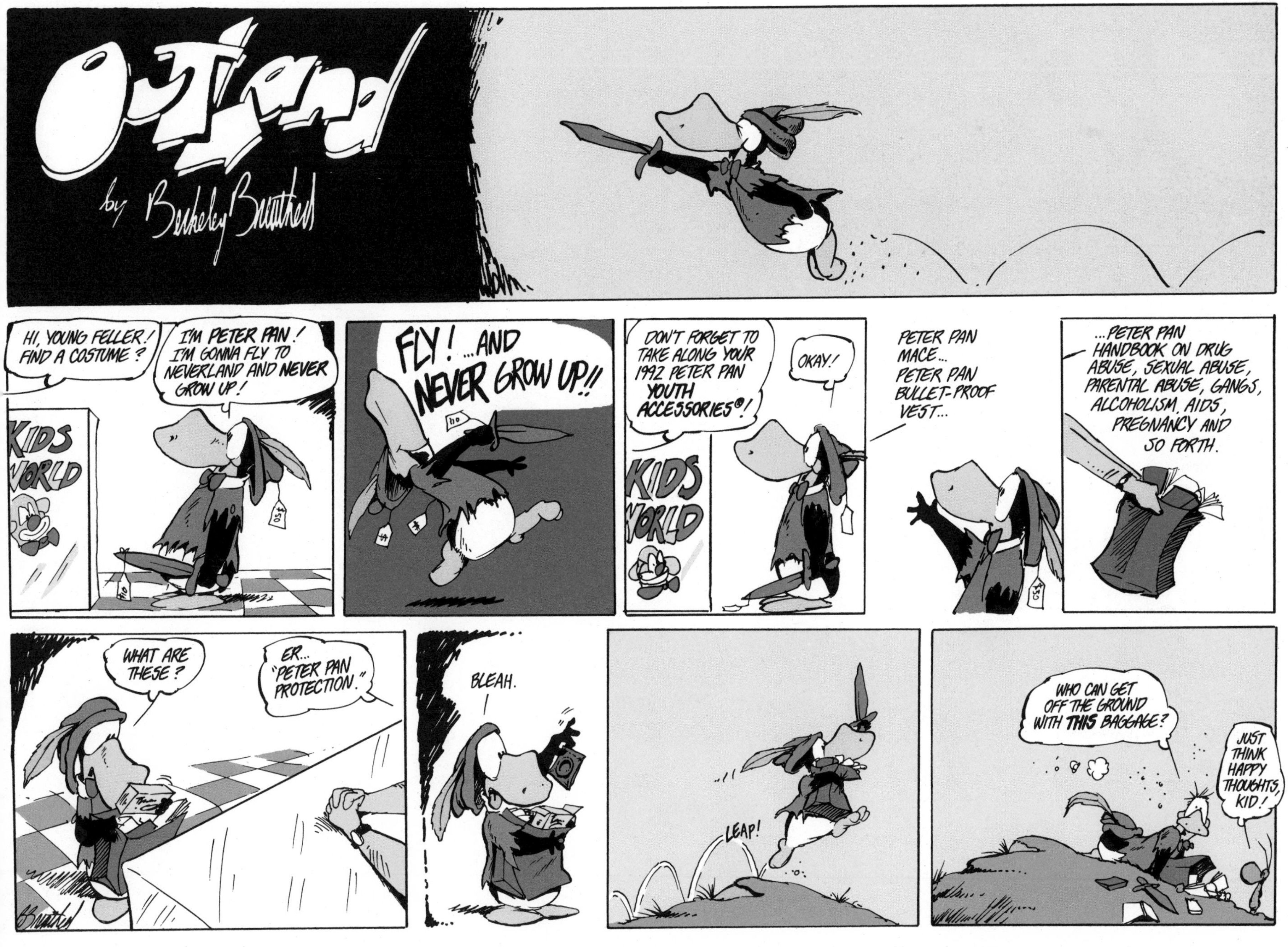
Outland
by Berkeley Breathed
HI, YOUNG FELLER! FIND A COSTUME?
I'M PETER PAN! I'M GONNA FLY TO NEVERLAND AND NEVER GROW UP!
KIDS WORLD
FLY! ...AND NEVER GROW UP!!
DON'T FORGET TO TAKE ALONG YOUR 1992 PETER PAN YOUTH ACCESSORIES®!
OKAY!
KIDS WORLD
PETER PAN MACE... PETER PAN BULLET-PROOF VEST...
...PETER PAN HANDBOOK ON DRUG ABUSE, SEXUAL ABUSE, PARENTAL ABUSE, GANGS, ALCOHOLISM, AIDS, PREGNANCY AND SO FORTH.
WHAT ARE THESE?
ER... "PETER PAN PROTECTION."
BLEAH.
LEAP!
WHO CAN GET OFF THE GROUND WITH THIS BAGGAGE?
JUST THINK HAPPY THOUGHTS, KID!

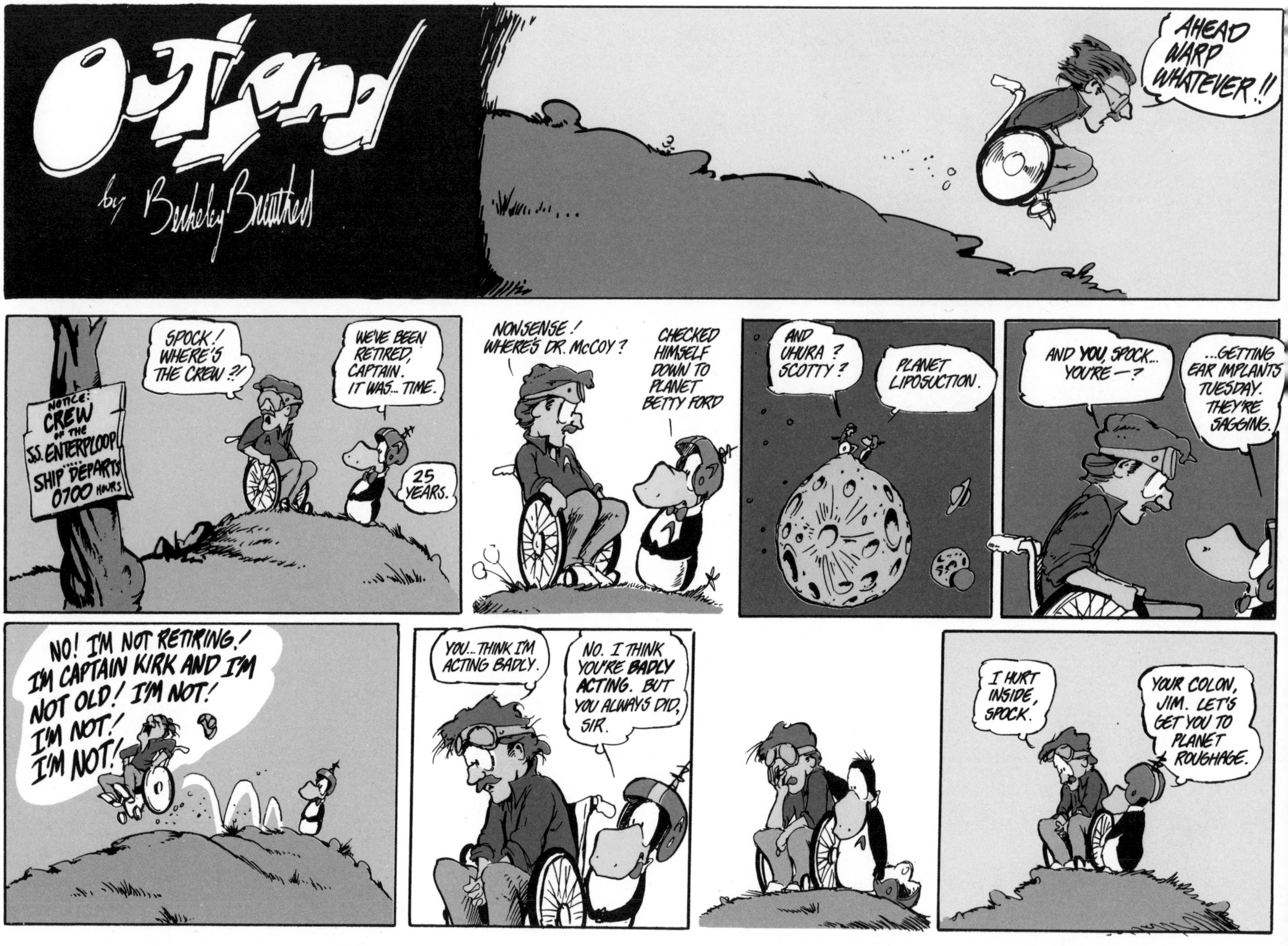
Outland
by Berkeley Breathed
AHEAD WARP WHATEVER!!
SPOCK! WHERE'S THE CREW ?!
WE'VE BEEN RETIRED, CAPTAIN. IT WAS... TIME.
NOTICE: CREW OF THE S.S. ENTERPLOOP ..... SHIP DEPARTS 0700 HOURS
25 YEARS.
NONSENSE! WHERE'S DR. McCOY?
CHECKED HIMSELF DOWN TO PLANET BETTY FORD
AND UHURA? SCOTTY?
PLANET LIPOSUCTION.
AND YOU, SPOCK... YOU'RE —?
...GETTING EAR IMPLANTS TUESDAY. THEY'RE SAGGING.
NO! I'M NOT RETIRING! I'M CAPTAIN KIRK AND I'M NOT OLD! I'M NOT! I'M NOT! I'M NOT!
YOU... THINK I'M ACTING BADLY.
NO. I THINK YOU'RE BADLY ACTING. BUT YOU ALWAYS DID, SIR.
I HURT INSIDE, SPOCK.
YOUR COLON, JIM. LET'S GET YOU TO PLANET ROUGHAGE.

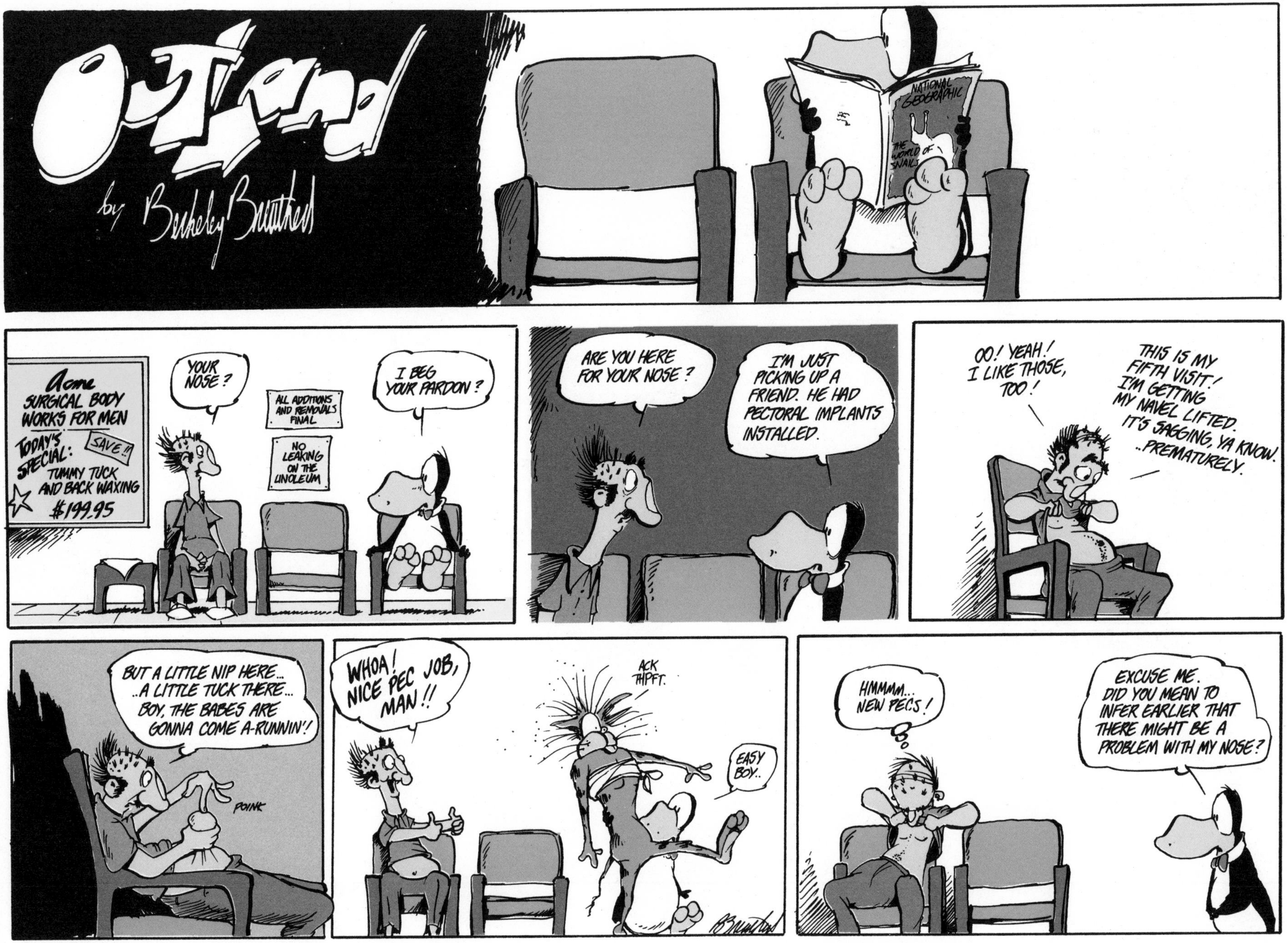
Outland
by Berkeley Breathed
NATIONAL GEOGRAPHIC
THE WORLD OF SNAILS
Acme SURGICAL BODY WORKS FOR MEN
TODAY'S SPECIAL: TUMMY TUCK AND BACK WAXING $199.95
SAVE!!
ALL ADDITIONS AND REMOVALS FINAL
NO LEAKING ON THE LINOLEUM
YOUR NOSE?
I BEG YOUR PARDON?
ARE YOU HERE FOR YOUR NOSE?
I'M JUST PICKING UP A FRIEND. HE HAD PECTORAL IMPLANTS INSTALLED.
OO! YEAH! I LIKE THOSE, TOO!
THIS IS MY FIFTH VISIT! I'M GETTING MY NAVEL LIFTED. IT'S SAGGING, YA KNOW. ..PREMATURELY.
BUT A LITTLE NIP HERE... ..A LITTLE TUCK THERE... BOY, THE BABES ARE GONNA COME A-RUNNIN'!
POINK
WHOA! NICE PEC JOB, MAN!!
ACK THPFT.
EASY BOY..
HMMMM... NEW PECS!
EXCUSE ME. DID YOU MEAN TO INFER EARLIER THAT THERE MIGHT BE A PROBLEM WITH MY NOSE?

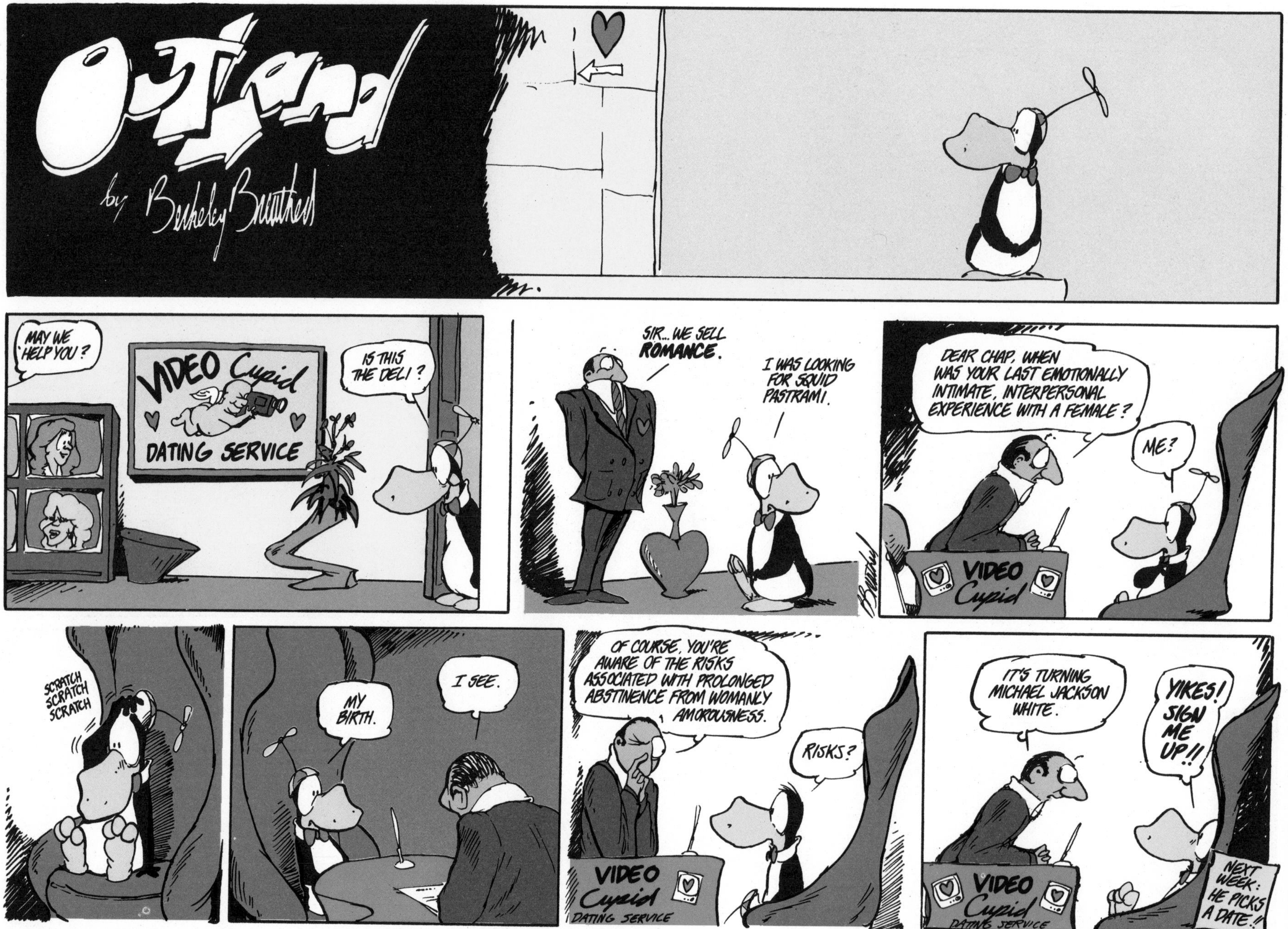
Outland
by Berkeley Breathed
MAY WE HELP YOU?
VIDEO Cupid
DATING SERVICE
IS THIS THE DELI?
SIR... WE SELL ROMANCE.
I WAS LOOKING FOR SQUID PASTRAMI.
DEAR CHAP, WHEN WAS YOUR LAST EMOTIONALLY INTIMATE, INTERPERSONAL EXPERIENCE WITH A FEMALE?
ME?
VIDEO Cupid
SCRATCH SCRATCH SCRATCH
MY BIRTH.
I SEE.
OF COURSE, YOU'RE AWARE OF THE RISKS ASSOCIATED WITH PROLONGED ABSTINENCE FROM WOMANLY AMOROUSNESS.
RISKS?
VIDEO Cupid
DATING SERVICE
IT'S TURNING MICHAEL JACKSON WHITE.
YIKES! SIGN ME UP!!
VIDEO Cupid
DATING SERVICE
NEXT WEEK: HE PICKS A DATE!!

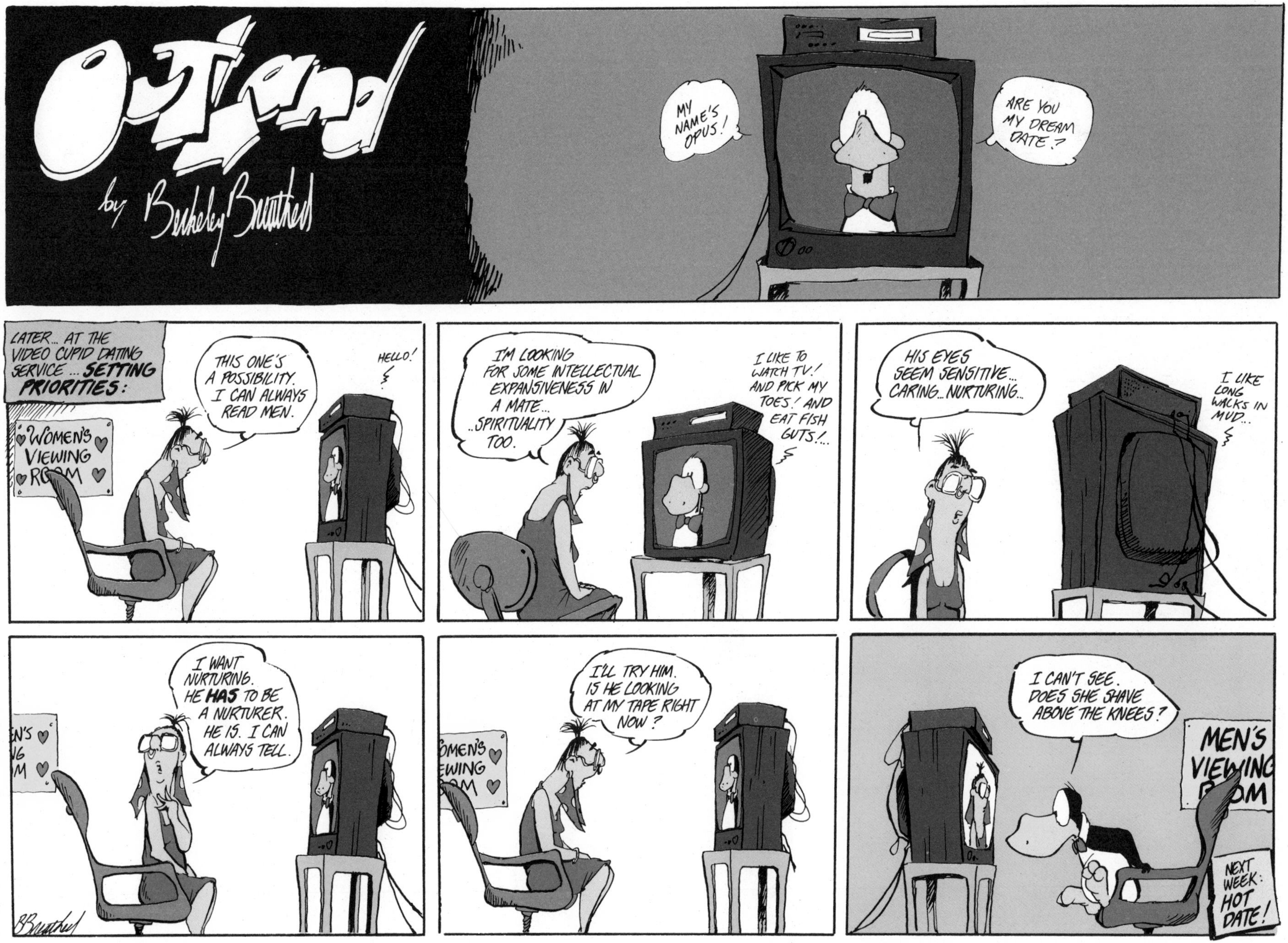
Outland
by Berkeley Breathed
MY NAME'S OPUS!
ARE YOU MY DREAM DATE?
LATER... AT THE VIDEO CUPID DATING SERVICE ... SETTING PRIORITIES:
WOMEN'S VIEWING ROOM
THIS ONE'S A POSSIBILITY. I CAN ALWAYS READ MEN.
HELLO!
I'M LOOKING FOR SOME INTELLECTUAL EXPANSIVENESS IN A MATE... ..SPIRITUALITY TOO.
I LIKE TO WATCH TV! AND PICK MY TOES! AND EAT FISH GUTS!...
HIS EYES SEEM SENSITIVE... CARING... NURTURING...
I LIKE LONG WALKS IN MUD...
I WANT NURTURING. HE HAS TO BE A NURTURER. HE IS. I CAN ALWAYS TELL.
I'LL TRY HIM. IS HE LOOKING AT MY TAPE RIGHT NOW?
I CAN'T SEE. DOES SHE SHAVE ABOVE THE KNEES?
MEN'S VIEWING ROOM
NEXT WEEK: HOT DATE!
B Breathed

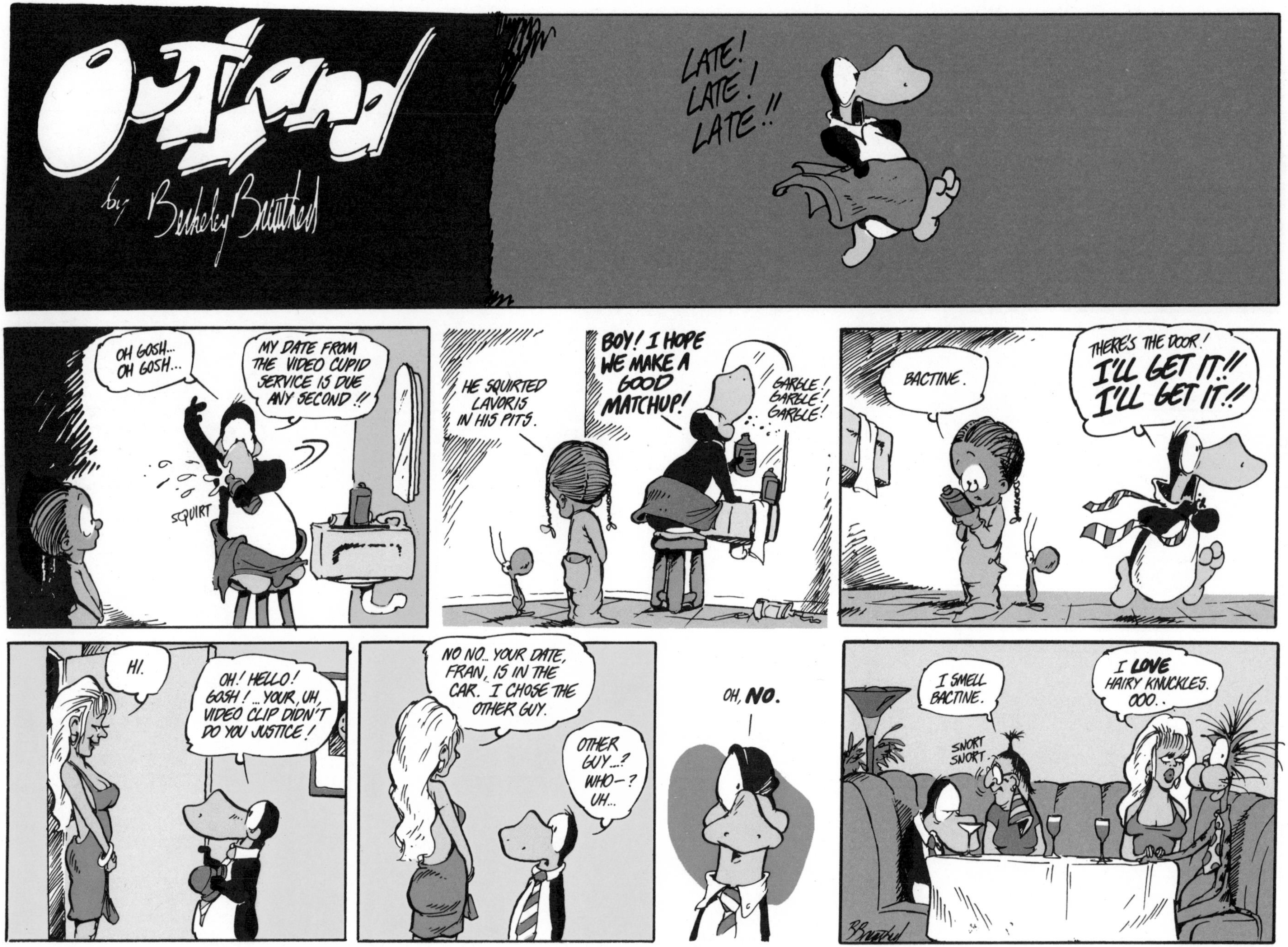
Outland
by Berkeley Breathed
LATE! LATE! LATE!!
OH GOSH... OH GOSH...
MY DATE FROM THE VIDEO CUPID SERVICE IS DUE ANY SECOND!!
SQUIRT
HE SQUIRTED LAVORIS IN HIS PITS.
BOY! I HOPE WE MAKE A GOOD MATCHUP!
GARGLE! GARGLE! GARGLE!
BACTINE.
THERE'S THE DOOR! I'LL GET IT!! I'LL GET IT!!
HI.
OH! HELLO! GOSH! ...YOUR, UH, VIDEO CLIP DIDN'T DO YOU JUSTICE!
NO NO... YOUR DATE, FRAN, IS IN THE CAR. I CHOSE THE OTHER GUY.
OTHER GUY...? WHO--? UH...
OH, NO.
I SMELL BACTINE.
SNORT SNORT.
I LOVE HAIRY KNUCKLES. OOO..

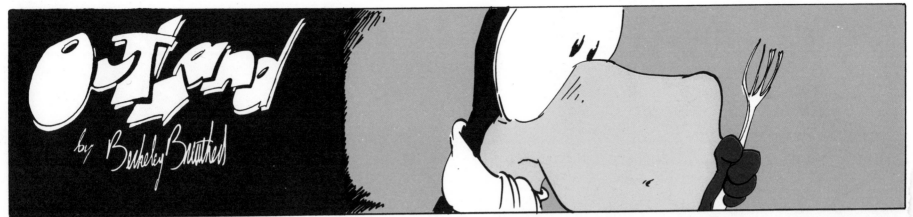

**Outland** by Berkeley Breathed

*The DATE: TWO ADULTS SEARCHING FOR THAT ELUSIVE COMMON GROUND IN WHICH LOVE TAKES ROOT...*

NICE FORK.

YEAH.

SNORT   THPFFT!

READY TO LEAVE, MISS BRAN?

YES. PLEASE CALL ME FRAN.

SNIFF..

DID YOU ENJOY YOUR TOFU AND LAWN CLIPPINGS?

YES. DID YOU ENJOY YOUR COW BUTTOCK?

YES. SO, NOW WHAT SHOULD WE DO FOR FUN?

LOOK. THAT WOMAN'S WEARING A FUR.

INDEED, SHE IS WEARING A FUR.

I'LL BE RIGHT BACK.

I SUPPOSE WE COULD GO BOWLING... OR TAKE A WALK...

RUN!!

RUN? TOGETHER? LIKE, GO JOGGING? BLECH..

I BELIEVE YOUR DATE POURED CATSUP ON MY OL' LADY.

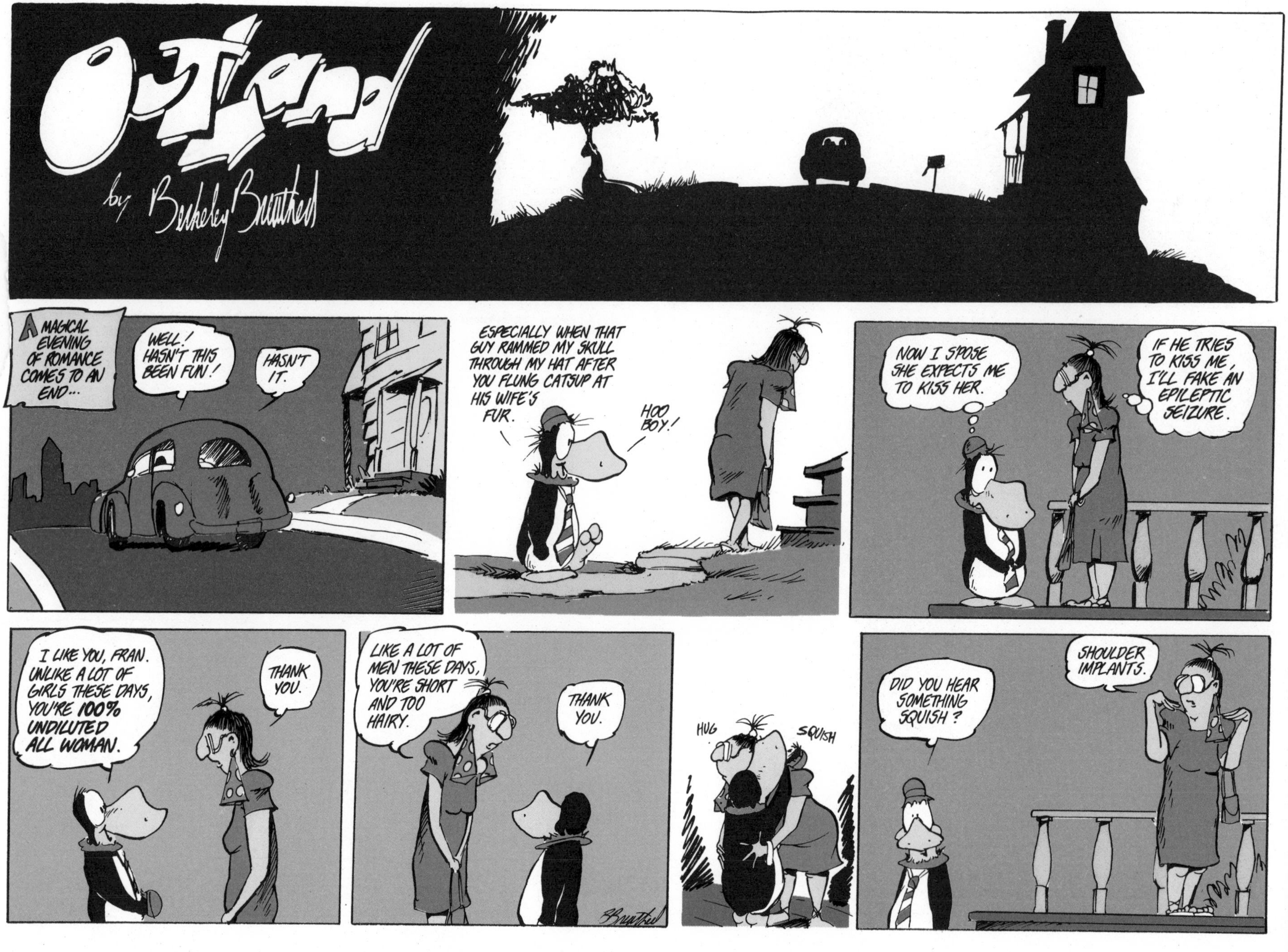
Outland
by Berkeley Breathed
A MAGICAL EVENING OF ROMANCE COMES TO AN END...
WELL! HASN'T THIS BEEN FUN!
HASN'T IT.
ESPECIALLY WHEN THAT GUY RAMMED MY SKULL THROUGH MY HAT AFTER YOU FLUNG CATSUP AT HIS WIFE'S FUR.
HOO BOY!
NOW I S'POSE SHE EXPECTS ME TO KISS HER.
IF HE TRIES TO KISS ME, I'LL FAKE AN EPILEPTIC SEIZURE.
I LIKE YOU, FRAN. UNLIKE A LOT OF GIRLS THESE DAYS, YOU'RE 100% UNDILUTED ALL WOMAN.
THANK YOU.
LIKE A LOT OF MEN THESE DAYS, YOU'RE SHORT AND TOO HAIRY.
THANK YOU.
HUG
SQUISH
DID YOU HEAR SOMETHING SQUISH?
SHOULDER IMPLANTS.

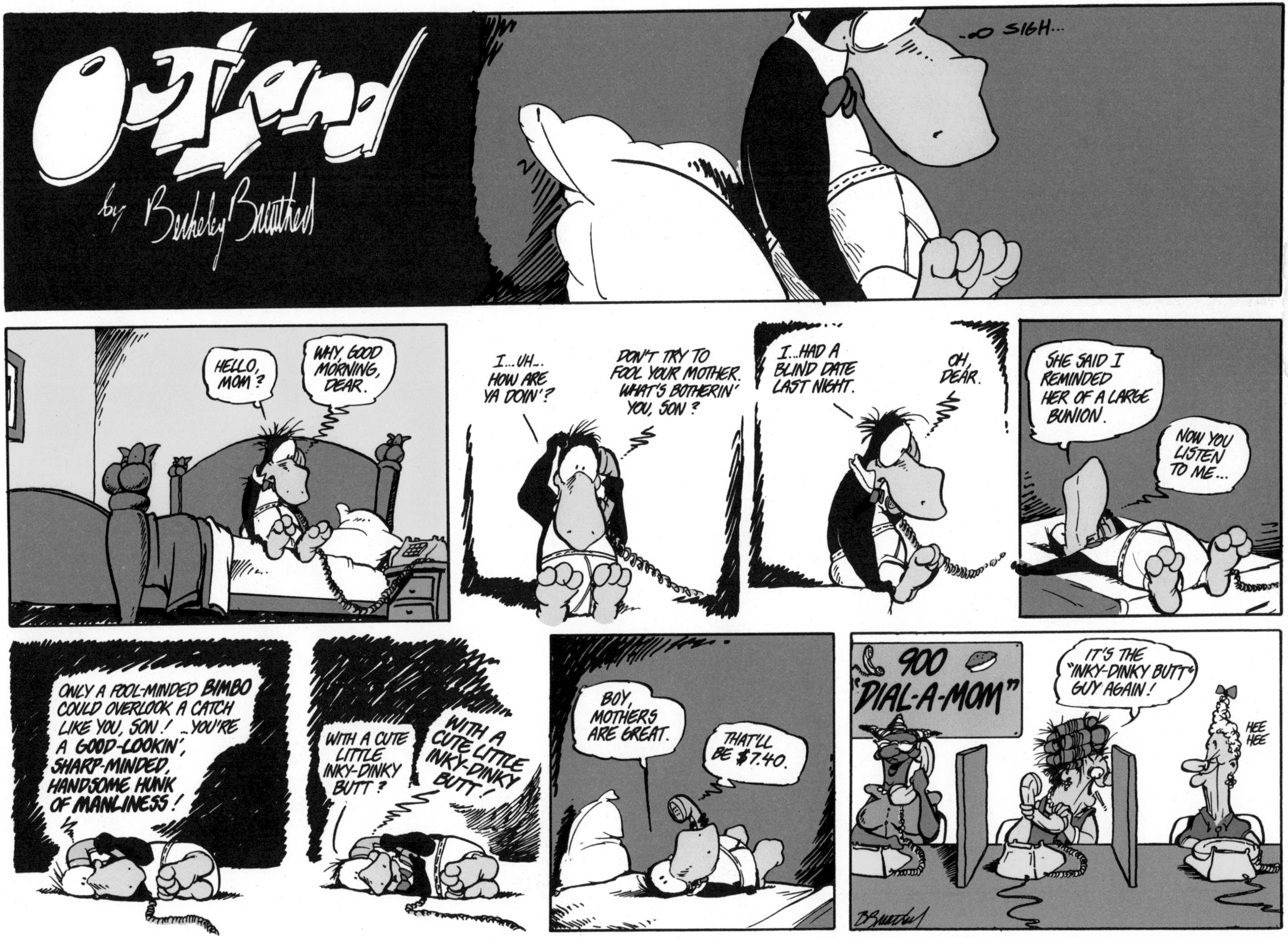
Outland
by Berkeley Breathed
...O SIGH...
HELLO, MOM?
WHY, GOOD MORNING, DEAR.
I...UH... HOW ARE YA DOIN'?
DON'T TRY TO FOOL YOUR MOTHER. WHAT'S BOTHERIN' YOU, SON?
I...HAD A BLIND DATE LAST NIGHT.
OH, DEAR.
SHE SAID I REMINDED HER OF A LARGE BUNION.
NOW YOU LISTEN TO ME...
ONLY A FOOL-MINDED BIMBO COULD OVERLOOK A CATCH LIKE YOU, SON! ...YOU'RE A GOOD-LOOKIN', SHARP-MINDED, HANDSOME HUNK OF MANLINESS!
WITH A CUTE LITTLE INKY-DINKY BUTT?
WITH A CUTE LITTLE INKY-DINKY BUTT!
BOY, MOTHERS ARE GREAT.
THAT'LL BE $7.40.
900 "DIAL-A-MOM"
IT'S THE "INKY-DINKY BUTT" GUY AGAIN!
HEE HEE
B Breathed